The Natural Law Foundations of Modern Social Theory

After several decades in which it became a prime target for critique, universalism remains one of the most important issues in social and political thought. Daniel Chernilo reassesses the universalistic orientation of social theory and explains its origins in natural law theory, using an impressive array of classical and contemporary sources that include, among others, Jürgen Habermas, Karl Löwith, Leo Strauss, Weber, Marx, Hegel, Rousseau and Hobbes. *The Natural Law Foundations of Modern Social Theory* challenges previous accounts of the rise of social theory, recovers a strong idea of humanity and revisits conventional arguments on sociology's relationship to modernity, the Enlightenment and natural law. It reconnects social theory to its scientific and philosophical roots, its descriptive and normative tasks and its historical and systematic planes. Chernilo's defence of universalism for contemporary social theory will surely engage students of sociology, political theory and moral philosophy alike.

DANIEL CHERNILO is a Senior Lecturer in Sociology at Loughborough University.

The Natural Law Foundations of Modern Social Theory

A Quest for Universalism

Daniel Chernilo

CAMBRIDGE
UNIVERSITY PRESS

CAMBRIDGE UNIVERSITY PRESS
Cambridge, New York, Melbourne, Madrid, Cape Town,
Singapore, São Paulo, Delhi, Mexico City

Cambridge University Press
The Edinburgh Building, Cambridge CB2 8RU, UK

Published in the United States of America by
Cambridge University Press, New York

www.cambridge.org
Information on this title: www.cambridge.org/9781107009806

First published 2013

Printed and bound in the United Kingdom by the MPG Books Group

A catalogue record for this publication is available from the British Library

Library of Congress Cataloguing in Publication data

Chernilo, Daniel.
The natural law foundations of modern social theory : a quest for universalism / Daniel Chernilo.
p. cm.
Includes bibliographical references.
ISBN 978-1-107-00980-6 (Hardback)
1. Natural Law–Social aspects. 2. Sociological jurisprudence–Philosophy.
I. Title.
K460.C55 2013
300.1–dc23

2012027742

ISBN 978-1-107-00980-6 Hardback

Contents

Acknowledgements

I would not have been able to complete this book without Robert Fine and Aldo Mascareño's support and friendship. They read and reread innumerable versions of the materials that now make up this book, offered advice on most aspects of it and encouraged me to keep going at key moments of doubt. My personal and intellectual gratitude to them is immense.

My thanks to Sabina Mihelj who carefully commented on various chapters at different stages of this project and to the Press's anonymous reviewers whose suggestions were most helpful in sharpening up my original ideas. I have also benefited a great deal from conversations, discussions with several friends and colleagues, and from their suggestions and objections: Omar Aguilar, Rafael Alvear, Margaret Archer, Luis Campos, Rodrigo Cordero, Sérgio Costa, José Maurício Domingues, George Lawson, William Outhwaite, Csaba Szaló, Chris Thornhill and Bryan Turner. Material support during the early part of this project was provided by a research Grant from the Chilean Council for Science and Technology (1080213). The usual disclaimer of sole responsibility for all errors contained here applies in full.

Paula has once again generously shared the satisfactions and tribulations of the past few years of our life together. My daughter Leonor has been the main inspiration throughout this project and it is a wonderful coincidence that a printed copy of this book may reach her hands just at a time when she is beginning to put words together. She will be able to read by herself that I dedicated it to her: *Leonor, aquí está tu libro.*

Introduction

> Without universality, there would be no mankind other than the aggregate of members of a biological species; there would be no more a history of mankind than there is a history of catkind or horsekind.
>
> (Eric Voegelin 2000b: 377)

'Metaphysics', 'mythical and religious thought', 'old European thinking', 'foundationalism', 'rationalism', 'Platonism' are all terms that have been used over the past two centuries or so to mark the kind of intellectual sources, traditions and ways of thinking that modern social theory, and the social sciences at large, have been systematically trying to overcome and leave behind. This book reassesses the historical, philosophical and normative foundations of *modern social theory* by reconsidering its interrelationships with the tradition of *natural law.*

I understand 'natural law' as a long-standing intellectual tradition whose intellectual core lies in the problem of universalism, and I use it as an umbrella term to capture some commonalities that are implied in the opening terms of the first paragraph. Natural law asserts that a universalistic orientation is needed in order to understand human life, society and justice; it is a tradition that seeks to advance, and rationally justify, transcultural and transhistorical propositions. While below I will distinguish between traditional and modern natural law and elaborate on their differences, I shall remain mostly interested in the substantive problem of universalism as the core component of the natural law tradition as a whole.

For its part social theory is here conceived as the modern intellectual programme that, over the past two hundred or so years, has sought to understand the rise and main features of a number of socio-historical trends that still very much configure the world we live in: capitalism, democracy, the international system of states and the (functional) differentiation of different spheres of social life. The radically enhanced experiences of historical transformation, socio-cultural variety and normative disagreements to be found in modernity have made apparent the difficulties that are involved in keeping a universalistic orientation alive. But a main contention of this book is that the very idea of social theory depends on the ways in which it is able to refine and recast, rather than to abandon and 'definitively overcome', a universalistic orientation. Intellectual developments in social theory come from, and enter into dialogue with, different intellectual traditions; so although I will work with a 'conventionally sociological' understanding of social theory (from Marx and Weber to Habermas), it will soon become apparent that the idea of social theory I have sought to reconstruct and would like to promote is not particularly troubled by disciplinary boundaries. I will draw insights equally from political and moral philosophy, the history of ideas, political theory and indeed natural law theory itself. While below I will use the terms 'sociology', 'social science' and 'social theory' depending on the context and nature of the argument, my commitment to the last term is justified, I hope, because a wider (and admittedly somewhat loose) use of social theory allows it to be connected with general intellectual trends and debates. We need philosophically inclined, historically grounded and normatively conscious social science, and that is precisely the reason why I think the case must be made for *more and better social theory*.

The interrelationships between the two traditions will be pursued below through the working hypothesis that social theory constantly tries to overcome, but in so doing also systematically reintroduces, the universalistic orientation that is at the centre of natural law. Social theory's development can then be reconstructed as the *Aufhebung* – the sublation, the simultaneous transcendence and the conservation, suspension and carrying forward – of the claim to universalism that it inherited from natural law. In order to fully understand all the religious, ethnic and socio-cultural variation to be found in modernity, social theory is pushed to find ever better justifications for universalistic propositions on the ultimate unity of the human species and fundamental equality of all human beings. To that extent social theory keeps reverting, although by different means, to some key themes of the tradition of natural law: How do individual and social factors come to define our shared humanity? Where does morality come from and what makes it binding? Is there a way to rationally criticise different forms of socio-political arrangement? Are we the masters of our lives or are they rather being determined by forces which lie beyond our control?

As we shall see below, social theorists have been consistently dissatisfied with the ways in which previous 'universalistic' propositions uncritically reflected undue generalisations of particular instances. Social theory has, on the whole, been critical of natural law even though its claims to have definitively succeeded in breaking free from it are somewhat exaggerated (this is the first, negative side of the *Aufhebung*). At the same time, we need to explore why classical social theory emerged and developed *as a critique* of essentialist or particularistic chauvinism. Classical social theory sought to preserve some kind of universalistic orientation precisely to face up to the dramatically enhanced awareness of sociocultural diversity that modernity brought about (this constitutes the second, positive side of the *Aufhebung*). The key thesis that I am interested in constructing is that, at its best, social theory has systematically tried to comprehend the heterogeneity of modern forms of life in terms of a single humanity that encompasses the whole globe: all human beings were thought of as able to make and remake social relations. Differently put, the challenges of relativism and particularism are built into the ways in which social theory's claim to universalism seeks to conceptualise the heterogeneity of the modern world, which consists of one and the same human species.

Modern social theory is not the most recent incarnation of natural law. The language and modes of addressing social life have altered fundamentally, of course, and yet the social sciences can be seen as one particularly modern form of posing questions that are not altogether different from those the natural law tradition has long been raising. To be sure, in their everyday practices neither social scientists nor (most) social theorists would consider themselves as heirs of the natural law tradition while pursuing their scientific and intellectual work – and surely they are not mistaken. Yet the deeper we all go in our research the more we are actually pressed to go beyond 'normal' scientific stances, and the more fundamental are the questions that present themselves about the human conditions. If social theory has a contribution to make to the description as well as the normative assessment of the world we live in, it is my contention that a universalistic orientation remains central to it. Social theory emerged in modernity, and it has developed a particularly acute sense of the key features and challenges of modern social life. But in looking at its connections to natural law, this question of the cult of 'the new', 'the post' and the 'beyond' has taken hold in much of contemporary social theory. Taking universalism seriously means that, as social theory tries to comprehend our modern living conditions, it becomes more successful when it is able to reflect on general questions about the human condition as such – what is it that makes us all human beings in modernity.[1]

[1] The relationship between social theory and natural law was raised as an explicit concern in the opening conference of the German Sociological Society in 1910 (Tönnies 2005, Troeltsch 2005). It has since figured intermittently in the literature from various points of

Universalism

I understand universalism as the belief in the fundamental unity of the human species, the proposition that all individuals belong to the same species of living being. Universalism presupposes that all human beings are equally equipped biologically, but seeks to justify this unity of the species beyond its physiological constitution. It is a way of imagining, indeed creating, a view about what the inalienable features of our common humanity are. Of course, many different ideas have been offered about what the fundamental 'human' element of our common humanity is: we are social beings, moral/rational beings, cooperative and compassionate beings, selfish and hedonistic beings, labouring beings. Yet as a way of thinking universalism is itself universal: it is found across different historical times and cultural contexts.

Universalism always comes with problems and difficulties but remains a condition of possibility of trying to conceptualise and normatively reflect on human affairs. Universalism is not a one-size-fits-all conception of humanity. It does not presuppose that all human beings have to think or behave in the same manner, it requires no teleological projection of perpetual peace, and it entails no ultimate substantive conception of the good life to which all our actions will necessarily accommodate. Universalism emerges rather out of the recognition that peoples change over time, do things differently and, quite crucially, value things differently. It is because human beings live their lives differently, and thus imagine what they share with and what separates them from other human beings, that universalism is always and necessarily expressed *through* rather than *against* our socio-cultural, historical and normative differences. A universalistic orientation argues that it is possible to assess certain practices, institutions and values as preferable to others. We reflect on the normative basis of our life in common and ask: Is this (un)fair? Is it (un)just? Is it 'natural'? How can it be transformed? Universalism is possibly best seen *as a quest*.

Universalism lies at the centre of our real ability to think of ourselves beyond ourselves and as members of a single human species. It takes seriously, rather than merely rejecting, the relationships between

view: Christian natural law (Messner 1964), mainstream sociology (Selznick 1961), Marx and critical theory (Habermas 1974, Fine 2002, Wellmer 1998), political theory (Strauss 1974), Greek classical philosophy (Gouldner 1965, Inglis and Robertson 2004, McCarthy 2003), modern science (Toulmin 1990) and postmodern critique (Bauman 2009). See also the articles by Robert Fine (2013), Chris Thornhill (2013) and Bryan Turner (2013) in a special issue on social theory and natural law in the *Journal of Classical Sociology* that I edited with Robert Fine.

people's particular motivations and their sense of duty. It offers and seeks to foster a sense of equality and justice in which human beings are to treat one another as bearers of an inalienable dignity that is to be upheld irrespective of their particular affiliations. To be sure, social life does not always promote this type of universalistic orientation but, as argued in the opening epigraph, the assessments we make about our life in common as *human* life depend upon our ability to construct a universalistic sense of belonging.

Universalism is not inseparable from the tradition of natural law, but natural law has remained systematically committed to advancing a universalistic orientation. Universalism is not conventionally considered as a defining feature of social theory but it is my contention that, in the terms I have just defined it, universalism is central to the actual functioning of social theory. While natural law has come up with explicit ideas of human nature, which are also substantive, social theory has mostly operated with implicit notions of human nature but explicit concepts of the social. This may also explain why procedural formulations of universalism, from Hobbes and Rousseau, via Kant, to Habermas, have become increasingly important in modernity. Modern proceduralism has the crucial advantage that it explicitly offers meta-norms with the help of which we can assess specific practices, values, institutions and indeed norms themselves. As it becomes more inclusive in terms of participants, more reflective in terms of justifications, and increasingly open ended in terms of its final decisions, proceduralism creates a sense of impartiality that constitutes one of modernity's most crucial innovations, normatively as well as institutionally. Yet we shall see that modern proceduralism is dependent upon substantive ideas of our shared humanity that remain at least partly transcendental. Differently put, although procedural universalism has proved to be the best way to decide on normative conflicts, we need to accept that the justification of its key presupposition on our shared humanity remains problematic. Theorising the location of the normative in modernity involves a tension between immanent justifications that make arguments rationally acceptable and transcendental grounds that make them binding. Thanks to its procedural turn, modern universalism can be seen as a regulative ideal, as *a claim to universalism*.

Expressed in the tension between description and normativity, social theory takes up the traditional philosophical challenge of the mediation between theory and praxis. My own commitment to social theory in this book also involves both dimensions. Descriptively, modern social theory requires a universalistic orientation in explicating the social as an autonomous and emergent ontological domain. Normatively, the future of social theory depends upon its remaining committed to universalism by seeking to refine it and make it more reflective. The best tradition of social theory is the one that carefully, deliberately and explicitly engages with the question of universalism as it seeks to promote more inclusive, open and just forms of life.

The decline of the normative in contemporary social theory

Universalism does not have the greatest of reputations in contemporary social theory. A strong 'anti-foundationalist' thrust, which puts at its centre the aporias of all kinds of universalistic arguments, has been prevalent over the past three or four decades. Indeed, from Foucault's genealogy to Derrida's deconstruction, from Lyotard's postmodern condition to Rorty's criticisms of the 'Plato–Kant' consensus, from Luhmann's thoroughgoing critique of 'old European thinking' to Latour's blurred distinction between the human and the non-human, from Bourdieu's struggles for capital and resources to the postcolonial unfathomable 'other'– in all cases we find a similar underlying motif: a canonical version of philosophical and social scientific traditions that have outlived themselves and are now blocking our ability to grapple with contemporary epistemological, social and normative issues. All their differences notwithstanding, these views agree on the need for a reinvention of how we practise socio-political enquiry that, quite crucially, involves transcending the limitations of universalism and its unwarranted natural law baggage.

Somewhat paradoxically, the status of 'the normative' in our post-positivistic age goes beyond positivism's wildest dreams. For positivism normative challenges were essentially alien to the tasks of social scientific research, but the argument nowadays is that there is no space for serious normative considerations because social life itself has been emptied of its normative dimension: we are witnessing the *ontological amplification of positivism*. The empirical diagnoses of modern society's increasing complexity and pluralisation have led to the idea that normativity plays no role in the real world; normativity is no longer necessary to comprehend social life. Careful consideration of what is normatively at stake in society, and why it is important for actors themselves, is being replaced by the empirical question of the actor's bargaining position *vis-à-vis* others. It seems to me that the resistance against universalism in contemporary social theory no longer lies in its past mistakes but in this restrictive understanding of social life as one with no normativity: universalism not as a way of imagining and creating a sense of common belonging but as a mere strategy actors deploy to promote whatever it is they are after because that is all actors do in the social world. As events in the social world are exclusively conceptualised in terms of promoting our interests and securing our identities, that is in effect all that matters in the social world. As a variation of the foundational Weberian problem of value-neutral social sciences, a main difference is that whereas for Weber the challenge was that our disciplines did not save us from having to decide what ought to be done because the social world was populated by too many value orientations, the contemporary argument is that there is no single value left in social reality.

Yet neither social actors nor human beings consider themselves purely as strategic beings; there is more to social life than ontologies of power, strategic bargaining and essentialist identities. Human beings also need and actively search for normative justifications, so I should like to challenge this representation of the social world as a place where there is no place for the normative. The substantive problem to be addressed by reassessing the relationship between social theory and natural law is precisely trying to explicate what the normative is and how it works in the social world. We need to think about human normativity in terms of a duality of immanence and transcendence; human normativity as (immanent), human-made principles that, however, place inviolable (quasi-transcendental) limits on what is acceptable in social life.

Under the conditions of current global modernity, locating the normative in social life requires us to re-engage with the universalistic thrust that effectively underpins such ideas and ideals as democracy, autonomy, freedom or human dignity. Several challenges follow from this, of course – not least, whether this can be done without resorting to the unwarranted generalisations that led to the rise of the anti-foundationalist, postmodern and globalist critiques in the first place. But these are issues that can only be seriously discussed if we are prepared to reflect on the strong universalistic orientations that are built into our conceptualisations of social life.

This book engages only partly with contemporary debates but has of course been written in their context. I am not at all interested in any uncritical revival of natural law but rather in understanding and reassessing those elements of the natural law tradition that have become part of social theory and may contribute to it in the future. This book is partly an attempt to address this idea that our disciplines have become increasingly ill equipped to understand the normative in social life. It is an intervention in contemporary social theory debates whose potential contribution lies in *looking underneath* some of their philosophical and normative foundations by *going back* in the history of social and political thought.

Plan of the book

This book is divided into three parts. Part I sets the general tone of the enquiry by spelling out the various interconnections between social theory and natural law in recent social theory. Chapter 1 concentrates on Jürgen Habermas as the contemporary social theorist who has arguably offered the most detailed account of the interconnections between the two traditions. Habermas acknowledges a certain family resemblance between his own work and natural law, but his interest in natural law results from his attempt to reinvigorate social theory. The differentiation between republican and liberal natural law, the rise of sociology, universalism and the status of the postmetaphysical are all themes that figure centrally in Habermas's work and that also help me frame much of what will follow in the rest of this book. Chapter 2 goes back to the middle of the twentieth century and inverts Habermas's standpoint, as it focuses on a natural law critique of modern social theory. Writing in the relatively immediate aftermath of the Holocaust, Karl Löwith, Leo Strauss and Eric Voegelin were all dramatically aware of the weaknesses and unfulfilled promises of modern institutions and values. By concentrating on the questions of secularisation, immanent knowledge and the critique of Gnosticism, these three writers allow us to reflect on the limitations of modern social theory when it refuses to engage seriously with natural law. I read them against the grain, however, as I will not be endorsing their eventual dismissal of social theory. Yet their works offer valuable insights for thinking about the location of the normative in social life as a tension between immanence and transcendence.

Part II concentrates explicitly on the tradition of natural law. Chapter 3 focuses on the connections between universalism and natural law, elaborates further on how universalism engages with questions of historical change, socio-cultural diversity and normative disagreement, and by introducing the idea of the early Enlightenment in the second part of the seventeenth century it distinguishes between traditional and modern natural law. Chapter 4 takes up the notion of the early Enlightenment and offers a combined reading of Hobbes and Rousseau as central to the rise of modern natural law. I revisit the universalistic underpinnings of their arguments on the state of nature, the civil condition, natural law and natural rights, explicate how their universalism was advanced on fully immanent terms and discuss their incipient proceduralism. Above all, I show how Hobbes and Rousseau equally argue that the key aspects of asocial human nature are cancelled precisely at the moment when individuals leave the state of nature. This new 'social nature' is a sublation of a human being's natural qualities: they make social life possible but are radically transformed through social life itself. Chapter 5 turns its attention to how Kant and Hegel engage with previous natural law and uses the strengths and weaknesses of their arguments to start delineating the more reflective universalistic orientation I am interested in developing. Kant criticised Hobbes's and Rousseau's anthropological attempts at founding human morality on the state of nature; more importantly, his categorical imperative is discussed as the most radical innovation in the emergence of modern proceduralism. Hegel builds on Kant's critique of state of nature theories but forcefully criticises the formalism and individualism of Kant's moral theory. The problem of mediating between the 'crude dichotomies' of modern natural law becomes central to Hegel: how to grasp the movement between the universal and the particular, the ideal and the real, immanence and transcendence, the individual and the state.[2]

Part III turns to social theory and revisits its rise and main features *vis-à-vis* the reconstruction of natural law in Part II. Chapter 6 concentrates on how Marx, Tönnies and Durkheim engaged with the tradition of natural law on various planes: their ideas of universalism, their explicit reading of modern natural law theorists and the substantive connections that become apparent in such themes as alienation, the state of nature and the relationships between scientific and philosophical knowledge. I pay special attention to whether classical social theory's foundational dichotomy between *Gemeinschaft* and *Gesellschaft* needs to be interpreted as the modern rendition of natural law's key theorem on the transition from the state of nature to the civil condition. Chapter 7 devotes attention to how Simmel and Weber handle the question of universalism as a problem as much as a key dimension of any serious intellectual enquiry. They were as critical of natural law as of the mainstream historicism of their day and yet found proceduralism a fundamental development of modern society in general. Simmel's concern with the 'democratic structure of sociality' and Weber's equation of natural law with 'legal reasonableness' make apparent the importance they gave to a serious engagement with the tradition of natural law. Chapter 8, finally, discusses several accounts of the rise of social theory with a view to reassessing the role of natural law in its emergence. It addresses the novelty of social theory as a modern intellectual genre and reflects on the problems of

2 The four major writers on whom I concentrate here are surely not the only ones who deserve attention. Because I see it as a tradition, my general argument on the relationships between social theory and natural law should work also for those other writers who share the features I have described and who saw themselves as part of modern natural law theory: for instance Montesquieu, Adam Smith, Adam Ferguson and John Locke.

universalism, modernity and 'the social' as an emergent ontological domain. It offers an argument on the role of social theory in terms of its ability to recast universalistic normative concerns in ways that are acceptable to our modern forms of life. Social theory is thus seen as the natural law of an artificial realm: social relations.

The general narrative of this book is therefore partly historical and partly analytical. By starting with a discussion of Habermas's social theory, plus three twentieth-century natural law critiques of modern social and political thought, Part I highlights the current importance of looking at the interrelationships between the two traditions. It is only after that contemporary case has been made that I start reconstructing their connections historically. A strictly chronological reading of the book is of course also possible: commencing in Chapter 3, the book moves forward from early ideas of universalism in traditional natural law, to modern natural law in Hobbes, Rousseau, Kant and Hegel and then to the rise of social theory in Marx, Tönnies, Durkheim, Simmel and Weber. In this case Chapters 1, 2 and 8 function as a reflection on the current implications that can be derived from this historical reconstruction. They try to elucidate what is at stake in the present when social theory and natural law are being jointly reinterpreted.

Ten theses on the relationships between natural law and modern social theory

I should like to close this introduction by spelling out some of the implications that follow from systematically exploring the relationships between natural law and social theory. I present them in the form of theses.

Thesis 1: Universalism. Both traditions are united in their commitment to universalism. Yet they differ in that while natural law has taken up the problem of universalism explicitly and deductively, modern social theory has done so mostly in a more implicit manner and through a differentiated articulation in the conceptual, methodological and normative planes.

Thesis 2: *Aufhebung*. Social theory emerged as a critique of natural law's unwarranted metaphysics and yet it adopts several of its key concepts and intuitions. Social theory's development can then be reconstructed as the sublation of the claim to universalism that it inherited from natural law.

Thesis 3: The Enlightenment. The transition between traditional and modern natural law theory took place in the context of the early Enlightenment. As modern social theory emerged as one critical heir of the

Enlightenment, historically as well as intellectually, it thus remains fundamentally immersed in the tradition of natural law.

Thesis 4: Rationality. Both traditions assume the ultimate cognoscibility of human affairs as they presuppose that human beings understand each other in what they do. Procedural formulations, a key outcome of modern natural law, create through their emphasis on rational argumentation a sense of impartiality that constitutes one of modern society's major resources, normatively as well as institutionally.

Thesis 5: Immanence and transcendence. Both traditions have recourse to immanent and transcendental claims in their accounts of social life. But while for natural law the transcendental resides outside immanence, in social theory our shared humanity is the transcendental that resides inside social relations.

Thesis 6: Description and normativity. The centrality of normative challenges makes both traditions accept that the study of social life includes a tensional handling of descriptive and normative planes. But they do so differently because while natural law has tended to emphasise more the normative side, social theory tends to favour its descriptive dimension.

Thesis 7: Critical and conservative. In modernity, universalistic normative statements are those that can rationally appeal to transhistorical and transcultural validity while simultaneously carrying the subjective approval of individuals themselves. As they try to grapple with always difficult normative challenges, neither tradition is critical or conservative *per se*.

Thesis 8: Community and society. Social theory's key dichotomy between community and society is a modern rendition of natural law's key distinction between the state of nature and the civil condition.

Thesis 9: Social theory as the natural law of an artificial realm. While natural law has sought to grasp the ultimate status of 'the human', social theory offers analogous arguments about 'the social'. Modern social theory can thus be understood as the natural law of social relations as an emergent and artificial realm.

Thesis 10: Reconstructing the relationships between social theory and natural law. Instead of arguing that social theory must 'definitively' break free from natural law, social theory may need to learn how to handle the universalistic legacy it inherited from natural law: what makes human life human under modern conditions.

Corollary: Towards a philosophical sociology. The task of a philosophical sociology can be defined as the attempt to understand the implicit ideas of human nature that underpin sociology's explicit conceptions of social relations. It is no substitute for conventional sociological enquiry and nor does it attempt to uncover an intrinsic sociological normativity that is waiting to be discovered. It rather seeks to redefine, though in the language and following the requirements of modern intellectual enquiry, a universalistic orientation that allows us to think about the location of the normative in society.

Part I

On the relationships between social theory and natural law

1 Contemporary social theory and natural law: Jürgen Habermas

Jürgen Habermas's fifty-year engagement with the philosophical, sociological and normative foundations of modern social and political thought is arguably the most accomplished of his generation. It is then of particular interest that Habermas has explicitly argued that the tradition of natural law remains of crucial importance when trying to come to terms with modern intellectual challenges. To be sure, Habermas's reassessment of natural law is attempted from the point of view of modern social theory: we ought to embrace modernity's scientific developments fully although without surrendering to positivistic restrictions, and learn to handle the tension between the descriptive and normative tasks that are inscribed in the understanding of social life. We will only be able to renovate a universalistic orientation if we avoid resorting to first philosophies or traditional ideas of the good life. Habermas's long-term intellectual project can be observed from the point of view of the relationships between social theory and natural law – indeed, it still *needs* to be reassessed in relation to its only partially acknowledged debt to the natural law tradition (Fine 2001: 21).

But, as we shall see, Habermas acknowledges a debt and at times even a family resemblance between social theory and *rational* or *modern* natural law; what makes his work particularly important is that it addresses the interrelationships between both traditions without obsessively seeking to sever all possible connections to natural law. As we shall see in Chapters 4, 5 and 6, a claim to this kind of rupture and originality is constitutive of modern natural law and has been passed on to social theory. Because Habermas is not interested in a claim to novelty for its own sake, his more sober engagement with natural law is better equipped to offer the critique of natural law than that of more vocal approaches which obsessively deny all possible connections, exaggerate their own novelty and in my view fail to deliver the rupture they are after (Foucault 2001, Latour 1993, Luhmann 1995, Rorty 1989). While below I will not be offering a conventionally Habermasian argument about communicative action and communicative rationality, my work in what follows is deeply indebted to Habermas's outlook on the development of modern social and political thought.

The decline of natural law in modernity can be seen as the integrated result of three different challenges for which the tradition of natural law has found no answers: teleological approaches to history lose empirical plausibility; the pluralism of complex societies makes substantive ideas of human nature and the uncritical recourse to our own intellectual or cultural traditions highly problematic; the gap between facts and norms becomes wider and deeper. This socio-historical constellation creates the intellectual conditions within which natural law arguments have lost a great deal of their previous normative plausibility and justificatory legitimacy. In modernity, because of the absence of institutions whose legitimisation can be unproblematically taken for granted, individuals cannot *ultimately* delegate the responsibility for their normative decisions. But this is of course only one side of the story, because the view that normative reflections are neither meaningful nor eventually possible in modernity – as advocated by positivism and postmodernism alike – poses in Habermas's view as great an intellectual threat as old-fashioned or even conservative natural law (Specter 2010: 166). One way of characterising Habermas's position may then be to argue that while natural law is not directly relevant in the explanation of the structural developments of modernity, it remains a crucial normative resource at the level of the intellectual foundations of many of modernity's institutional foundations: equality before the law, the distinction between private and public autonomy, scientific rationality, the constitutional justification of modern democracies and even humanitarian military interventions (Habermas 1992a, 1996, 1999, 2003a).

We might then start with Habermas's own acknowledgements of the interconnections between his work, and modern social theory more generally, and natural law. Indeed, as we shall explore in some detail below, this engagement is a constant of his intellectual career: right from *The Structural Transformation of the Public Sphere* (Habermas 1989 [1968]) and *Theory and Practice* (Habermas 1974 [1963]) through *Between Facts and Norms* (Habermas 1996 [1992]) to his work of the past decade on cosmopolitanism, human rights, religion and 'human nature' (Habermas 2001a, 2003c, 2006, 2008). In the late 1980s, for instance, Habermas explicated the interconnections between the traditions as he tried to describe the foundational problem of modern philosophy as follows:

[i]n terms of its genealogy, it is better to speak, for the sake of clarity, of metaphysical *and* religious questions. Thus, I do not believe that we, as Europeans, can seriously understand concepts like morality and ethical life,

person and individuality, or freedom and emancipation, without appropriating the substance of the Judeo-Christian understanding of history in terms of salvation. (Habermas 1992a: 15)

He argued similarly in the opening pages of *Between Facts and Norms*. As Habermas seeks to reconstruct and reassess the normative foundations of modern democratic and legal theory, the role of the tradition of natural law is stated in even stronger terms:

In connection with questions raised by modern natural law, I attempt to show how the old promise of a self-organizing community of free and equal citizens can be reconceived under the conditions of complex societies ... Recasting the basic concepts of 'practical reason' in terms of a 'communicative rationality' has the advantage of *not cutting social theory off from the issues and answers developed in practical philosophy from Aristotle to Hegel*. In fact, it is far from clear that the price we have to pay for the premises of postmetaphysical thinking must be an indifference to such questions, which in any case continue to be felt within the lifeworld. (Habermas 1996: 7–9, my italics)

And in his more recent *Between Naturalism and Religion*, the argument is taken one step further as natural law now plays a role in both the self-description of his philosophical journey and the positive characterisation of its ultimate normative orientation:

I understand political liberalism (which I defend in the specific form of Kantian republicanism) as a nonreligious, post-metaphysical justification of the normative foundations of constitutional democracy. *This theory is situated in the tradition of rational natural law that eschews the strong cosmological or soteriological assumptions of classical and religious natural law* ... The post-Kantian justification of liberal constitutional principles in the twentieth century had less trouble with the remnants of objective natural law (and the material ethics of values) than with historicist and empiricist forms of criticism. (Habermas 2008: 102–3, my italics)

In spite of these and similar comments elsewhere to be discussed below, we still do not have a full account of the connections between Habermas's social theory and the tradition of natural law.[1] My goal in this chapter is twofold. I should first like to explicate what Habermas understands by natural law in order to account for its wider relevance as a key intellectual resource in modern social theory. By so doing, this chapter creates a framework for the book as a whole. Secondly, I will unpack the natural law elements that still reside in Habermas's thinking and assess them in their own terms and thus try to offer a general interpretation of

[1] A partial assessment of the natural law elements in Habermas's legal theory can be found in a special issue of *Ratio Juris* (vol. 12(4), 1999) devoted to the discussion of *Between Facts and Norms*.

his intellectual project. In terms of structure, I start by revisiting Habermas's definition of natural law and the role of natural law in modernity's claim to normative self-foundation. The chapter then explicates the role that Habermas attributes to sociology as the discipline that never loses sight of the problems of society as a whole. Being simultaneously a scientific approach and a normative theory of modern society, the sociological tradition is thus reconstructed in connection with rather than in opposition to natural law. I conclude this chapter by looking at his attempt to found an explicitly universalistic programme and assess it as a sublation of natural law: I read Habermas's social theory as *postmetaphysical natural law.*

Modernity and natural law

Natural law is a long-standing philosophical tradition in the West that of course needs to be traced back to before the rise of modernity (see Chapter 3). Habermas describes it as highly heterogeneous and consisting of a fundamental split between traditional natural law (in its Greek, Roman and Christian variants) and modern or rational natural law, which he sees as having evolved from Hobbes to Hegel via Rousseau, Kant and the Scottish Enlightenment (Habermas 1974, 1996). He follows here the somewhat standard view in the literature: while traditional natural law grounded its normative core on cosmological or transcendental propositions, modern natural law offers a more decidedly immanent approach to human affairs. In the context of a recent discussion about the idea of human dignity, for instance, Habermas elaborates on this distinction by arguing that traditional natural law had a strong sense of the universality of the human species but missed the idea of the individual as an inviolable moral agent. Classical and religious natural law:

> [d]eveloped well a *collective* notion of *dignitas humana*, but it was explained in terms of a distinguished ontological status of human beings in the cosmos … The superior value of the species might have justified some kind of species protection but not the inviolability of the dignity of the human person as a source of normative claims … the relative superiority of humanity and its members must be replaced by the absolute worth of any person. The issue is the *unique worth* of each person. (Habermas 2010: 473–4)

The importance of individuality in modern social theory is something that Habermas inherited from modern natural law (see Chapters 4 and 5). If we take individual human beings seriously, self-legislation becomes central to a sense of rational acceptability that is ultimately undelegable: only affected parties themselves can give approval for those decisions that directly touch on their courses of action, on the one hand, and the reasons they give cannot be only an expression of subjective preferences but must be able to carry potential universal agreement, on the other. Normative claims in modernity are pulled in these two different and often also conflicting directions, both of which are a result of their universalistic orientation. Norms must be considered valid 'objectively' or 'externally' because they refer to human beings in general. But they must also and simultaneously be found acceptable by individuals themselves, as moral accord is ultimately dependent on 'subjective' approval by persons themselves in particular socio-cultural lifeworlds. Traditional natural law has had a tendency to emphasise the former – hence its conservative bias – while social theory is more geared towards the latter – hence its relativistic thrust. This is the tension Habermas seeks to address.

Arguably his most explicit account of the role of the modern natural law in the rise of political modernity is found in the early text 'Natural Law and Revolution' from 1963 (Habermas 1974: 82–119). This essay is an enquiry into the role of natural law in modernity's foundational act of normative constitution in which Habermas connects the tradition of natural law with such 'inaugural' events as the American and French revolutions. Based as it is on the idea of the individual, the immanentist orientation of rational natural law lent itself to the kind of transformative politics that inaugurate modernity. Its appeal as an intellectual tradition was that its normative content could somehow remain and yet be turned upside down, so that what was previously used to defend the old status quo could now promote social change. We witness a dramatic change in the way in which natural law arguments started to be used: '[t]he appeal to *classical* Natural Law [*Naturrecht*] was not as revolutionary as the appeal to *modern* Natural Law has come to be' (83, my italics). At the onset of political modernity both the American and French revolutionary movements resorted to natural law as they sought to give centrality to an idea of fundamental rights: 'the act by which the positivization of Natural Rights [*Naturrecht*] was initiated, in America as well as in France, was a declaration of fundamental rights' (85).[2] The importance of these declarations of fundamental rights can hardly be exaggerated, but in this early piece Habermas is more interested in contrasting the ways in which both declarations were differently

[2] Although in the English translation the terms 'natural law' and 'natural rights' are used interchangeably, in the original German edition Habermas (1978: 89–127) only uses *Naturrecht*. I have inserted the term in these first two quotations, but will not continue to do so below.

construed and justified.[3] The comparison between the American and French cases makes apparent a fundamental ambivalence in the role of natural law arguments in modernity's normative self-conceptions because, although in 'both cases a *constitution* is set up which remains within the framework of the declared fundamental rights', the two cases are in the pursuit of different political goals: '[w]ith their recourse to the Rights of Man, the American colonists want to legitimize their independence from the British Empire; the French to legitimize the overthrow of the ancient regime' (87). Their different purposes are expressed further by the position they occupy in their respective foundational texts: while the declaration of rights precedes 'the French Constitution as a preamble' it is 'merely attached to the American Constitution as *amendments*'; as the American Bill of Rights provides '*another basis of legitimation for the traditional substance of rights*; the French declaration, in contrast, is intended to *assert positively for the first time* a fundamentally new system of rights' (87, my italics).

Habermas argues that the American rendition of the natural law tradition was couched in fundamentally naturalistic terms, as it sought to restore a sense of natural justice that now appeared under threat because of the violation of traditional values, practices and institutions. The principles to which the American Revolution appealed were the original rights of man – that is, anthropologically grounded ideas of human nature such as the need for self-defence and private property. For the founding figures of the American Revolution, 'the rights of man coincide with the principles of society under the common name of Laws of Nature' and therefore the 'positivization of Natural Law is not a matter of revolution' (Habermas 1974: 95). This Habermas calls the liberal understanding of natural law because it is based on the idea of negative freedom – the state's main function is to prevent individuals from infringing on each other's autonomous spheres of action such as in economic exchange, religious beliefs and family life: '[n]atural rights will find their reliable counterpart in the laws of trade and commerce, but these laws are obeyed by private persons because this is immediately in their interest and not because the state imposes formal laws under the threat of punishment' (95).

Appeals to natural law during the French Revolution were of a radically different kind because there 'right was the *result* of a contract and

[3] Habermas's own later interest in the role of constitutional texts, and their key position in the moral as well as political self-understanding of modern political communities, systematically refers to the foundational principles upon which modern constitutions are established (Habermas 2001b).

not a *principle* from which true statements could be deduced' (Habermas 1974: 96, my italics). Crucially, Habermas claims that these creative and participatory features are key to accounting for the political role of natural law arguments in eighteenth-century France:

> Freedom and equality, and in consequence also life, security and happiness, these citizens do not owe to the automatism, secured by private law, of either natural rights or social intercourse based on nature. Rather, that these principles of freedom and equality cannot be violated is based solely on the structure of the *volonté générale*, although this will as the *pouvoir souverain* is free to enact whatever laws it likes – as long as they are laws. (Habermas 1974: 98)

In this formulation, the definition and later implementation of newly established fundamental rights is essentially political, and eventually democratic, via the twin principles of the *general will* and *popular sovereignty*. There is then a clear contrast between this 'social' natural law put forward during the French Revolution and its 'natural' version in the American case. We shall see below that as an account of modern natural law this contraposition is problematic: from Hobbes to Hegel via Kant and Rousseau, all conceptions of natural law have tried to deal with the dual, natural as well social, foundation of our shared humanity as the basis on which to reflect on how social order is possible. At the same time, however, a major tension of modern political thought has now been made apparent: the radically democratic principle that rejects all external limitations on the results of free political deliberations can only begin to be implemented if and when individuals are predefined as bearers of fundamental and inviolable rights whose origin is in fact prepolitical – and hence cannot be discretionarily modified by acts of self-legislation.

This early reconstruction of natural law in the 1960s became the basis of Habermas's legal theory as developed in *Between Facts and Norms* in the early 1990s, where Habermas elaborates further on these two different strands of modern natural law. The first 'liberal' understanding of natural law emphasises the intrinsic and prepolitical qualities of certain natural rights that all individual human beings possess *qua* individual human beings. Human rights lie at its centre and the main role of the state in this tradition becomes that of securing basic human rights. The second 'republican' version centres on the idea of 'the people' as a politically constituted community through an imaginary yet voluntary contract. Its key notion is popular sovereignty and the state is now in charge of actively promoting social cohesion on the basis of equality before the law. However far the process of detraditionalisation of modern societies has moved on, Habermas claims that it is still the case that these two fundamental principles of normative self-understanding in modernity remain deeply embedded in modern natural law:

[h]uman rights and the principle of popular sovereignty still constitute *the sole ideas that can justify modern law.* These two ideas represent the precipitate left behind, so to speak, once the normative substance of an ethos embedded in religious and metaphysical traditions has been forced through the filter of posttraditional justification. (Habermas 1996: 99, my italics)

The importance of both strands of natural law for his discourse theory of law and democracy becomes apparent in Habermas's attempt to justify the *co-originality* of 'human rights' and 'popular sovereignty' as central to modernity's normative self-understanding. Their co-originality in modernity is in one sense historical, as their articulation is dated roughly at the same time during the American and French revolutions of the eighteenth century. But they are also conceptually and normatively co-dependent because the organisation of modern political communities equally presupposes ideas of human rights and of popular sovereignty – not least because modern conceptions of the individual require that we theorise private and public autonomy as coterminous: neither form of autonomy should act as a model for or be subordinated to the other (Habermas 1996: 104).[4]

Yet after having ascertained their co-originality and co-dependence, problems remain in fully accounting for this strong thesis.[5] According strictly equal status to human rights and to popular sovereignty creates the difficulty of how to account for the socio-historical origins of human rights or, differently put, where the normative validity of human rights ultimately comes from. As Habermas rejects the purely objectivistic mode of argumentation of traditional natural law, which would allow for a 'firm' justification for human rights only at the price of their being introduced externally, the legitimacy of human rights can only be secured internally – i.e. by individuals mutually granting themselves these rights communicatively in an open and non-coercive manner. In *Between Facts and Norms*, this argument is introduced thus:

The scope of citizens' public autonomy is not restricted by natural or moral rights just waiting to be put into effect, nor is the individual's private autonomy merely instrumentalized for the purposes of popular sovereignty. Nothing is

[4] It is worthy of mention that Habermas's (1996: 84) critique of Kant's *legal* theory centres on the fact that while Kant accepts the historical co-originality of public and private autonomy, he models the former on the latter (although arguably in his moral theory Kant moves in the opposite direction from private to public autonomy). Durkheim criticised Rousseau on similar grounds; see Chapter 6.

[5] Thus Matthew Specter's (2010: 178–9) recent argument that '[t]reating human rights *as a foundational a priori, beyond reflection*, reifies in a manner Habermas finds unacceptable. Popular sovereignty, not human rights, is Habermas's ultimate priority'. As an interpretation of Habermas's intentions this seems to be the case, but we still need to explicate the intellectual challenges that are actually involved in conceptualising popular sovereignty and human rights as actually co-dependent.

> given prior to the citizen's practice of self-determination *other than the discourse principle*, which is built into the conditions of communicative association in general, and the legal medium as such. (Habermas 1996: 127–8, my italics)[6]

We shall leave until the final section of this chapter the discussion of what is entailed in this need for a discourse principle in terms of the 'quasi-transcendental' status of some of Habermas's philosophical presuppositions. But now we can none the less address the consequences of this argument as we return to his recent discussion of the notion of human dignity. Its dense normative content makes the idea of human dignity adequate as the substantive normative core of modern human rights, argues Habermas. But also in this case human dignity must remain grounded on the principle of popular sovereignty because ideas of human dignity are never independent of what citizens make of it:

> As a modern *legal* concept, human dignity is associated with the status that citizens assume in the *self-created* political order. As addressees, citizens can come to enjoy the rights that protect their human dignity only by first uniting as authors of the democratic undertaking of establishing and maintaining a political order based on human rights. (Habermas 2010: 473)

The challenge is now apparent: according strictly equal weight to both human rights and popular sovereignty, to private and public autonomy, is the ideal solution and yet it always proves problematic. Universal human rights (or human dignity) can only be justified as the act of popular sovereignty of a democratically organised political community, but that community is formed by human beings who are bearers of a universal dignity and who recognise each other as possessors of essential attributes that the democratic legislator cannot alter at will. Human rights are either independent from popular sovereignty, in which case their normative justification can be deemed problematic in the case of potentially falling below the threshold of democratic (and postmetaphysical) justifications or, conversely, human rights are truly a creation of popular sovereignty, in which case we need to remain open to at least the possibility of public deliberation transforming and indeed downgrading their normative status. More than internal consistency in relation to Habermas's co-originality thesis is at stake here, as this touches on the key issue that we expect our normative conceptions to be objectively valid as well as subjectively acceptable. We are facing a

[6] See la Torre (2006) for a distinction between *exclusive* and *inclusive* natural law theories on these grounds. While the exclusive natural law has to have recourse to substantive universalistic *statements* (i.e. human nature consists of X), inclusive versions obtain from a more procedural operation, that is, the substantive outcome of the individual application of the metanorm that secures the correctness of the moral action.

question that will accompany us throughout: understanding the location of the normative in modernity involves a tension between immanent justifications that make arguments rationally acceptable and transcendental grounds that make them binding. Universalism is a condition of possibility for modern normative thinking but this duality, which has itself been inherited from natural law, creates its own difficult challenges.

Sociology, modernity and the problem of the normative

Habermas's intellectual project defies single disciplinary or thematic identifications, so the decision to focus on any particular discipline, sociology in my case, may be criticised for mistakenly taking as central the disciplinary tradition one just happens to know best. While sociology is *not* the axis around which Habermas's intellectual project ultimately coheres, I should like to contend that it is central to his understanding of both natural law and the problem of universalism.

Indeed, it is well known that in *Theory of Communicative Action* Habermas turns explicitly to sociology as the social science that offers the most systematic attempt to combine empirical description, theoretical explanation and normative critique of modern social life. This is somewhat of a rupture from what he had done before, however. Philosophy and jurisprudence, rather than sociology, were Habermas's 'original' disciplinary background and apart from one important early article to be discussed below, up to the publication of *Theory of Communicative Action* in 1981 his engagement with sociology was relatively marginal.[7] Modelled on Parsons's early (1968) *The Structure of Social Action*, *Theory of Communicative Action* is surely a book in the history of sociological theory which, at the same time, seeks to offer a general theory of modern society with a critical intent. Understanding modernity requires us to simultaneously address descriptive and normative tasks and in Habermas's view that makes sociology unique among the modern disciplines devoted to the study of social life: 'alone among the disciplines of social science, sociology has retained its relations to the problems of society as a whole. Whatever else it has become, it has always remained a theory of society as well' (Habermas 1984a: 5). Structured in two volumes, one dedicated to the lifeworld (Habermas 1984a), and the other to rational systems (Habermas 1987), *Theory of Communicative*

[7] See, however, a short and somewhat naïve piece on Parsons (Habermas 1988: 45–52). Paradigmatic in this context is the debate with Niklas Luhmann that effectively triggered Habermas's interest in contemporary functionalism (Habermas and Luhmann 1971).

Action builds on the long-lasting sociological tradition of thinking about modern society in terms of a duality between communal and societal, expressive and instrumental, substantive and formal, social and systemic forms of social coordination. In Chapters 4 and 6 we shall extensively discuss the extent to which sociology's foundational distinction between *Gemeinschaft* and *Gesellschaft* is in fact a sublated version of natural law's foundational dichotomy between the state of nature and the civil condition: the relationships between individual human nature and social life, first, and between forms of social life that either contribute to or impede the full development of our human potentials, second. Descriptively, system and lifeworld are equally real and equally fundamental in modern society but normative legitimacy can only be derived from and renewed in the lifeworld. In this section I should like to explain why the decision to concentrate on sociology depends on its potential to be both descriptive (or scientific) and normative (or philosophical). These planes need to be kept analytically apart so that they can talk to and learn from each other.

Writing in the late 1990s, Habermas opens the central article of his collection on *The Postnational Constellation* with the claim that 'sociology still has to come to terms with the disappointment over the impotence of the obligatory moment of natural law'. He partly explicates this by quoting approvingly from the work of German sociologist Siegfried Landshut, who in his *Kritik der Soziologie* of 1929 had argued that '"[s]ociety" is nothing more than the title meant to encompass the tensions, contradictions, and ambiguities, that arise from the realization of the ideals of freedom and equality' (Habermas 2001a: 59). On the basis of what we have discussed already this claim is hardly new: normative questions about human rights (equality) and popular sovereignty (freedom and autonomy) are central to the emergence of modern society. Indeed, in *Theory and Practice* Habermas had already argued that sociology's key theorem of the social as an emergent ontological domain had deep roots in natural law; society is the name for that 'which organizes the interrelationships of human life as a whole. It can neither be understood as a government which sanctions a legal order ... nor as that union of individuals themselves, which confronts the government as a contracting party' (Habermas 1974: 103). These connections between sociology and natural law are in fact the starting point of an early article on 'The critical and conservative tasks of sociology'.[8] Habermas begins his reconstruction with eighteenth-century Scottish moral philosophy

[8] Habermas's piece is not included in the English version of *Theory and Practice* from which I have been quoting so far (Habermas 1974). The following quotations are therefore my own translation from the German original (Habermas 1978).

and argues that the main task of nascent political economy was to connect society's current social issues with long-term historical trends that were still being conceived of as part of natural history. The challenge faced by this proto-sociology was to make political recommendations (both progressive and conservative) to address contemporary society's most pressing issues. Food shortages, poverty and decaying moral values were to be met by promoting the further advancement of modern technologies as well as by pushing for the reinvigoration of traditional values and institutions. Stated as an intractable conflict between 'authority and utility', the creative solution that in Habermas's view Adam Smith, Adam Ferguson and John Millar all offered was for sociology to take 'the party of natural history that society itself has discovered and conceptualised' (Habermas 1978: 292). In other words, while they supported the idea that the reorganisation of society was necessary (thus embracing sociology's critical tasks), the only grounds on which they found this was viable were reforms that could be justified through the pre-reflexive recourse to traditional authority (thus making sociology also a conservative project). Although Scottish moral philosophers understood that the solution to social problems required direct human intervention in human affairs, their underlying conception of human history as natural history curtailed their options for actual implementation. For the Scottish Enlightenment, then, nascent sociology was simultaneously critical and conservative.

In the post-revolutionary context of nineteenth-century France, sociology could still be regarded as simultaneously critical and conservative: 'sociology as a science of the crisis is then split from its inception. It has equally emerged from the spirit of the revolution as from that of the restoration; each camp of the civil war claimed it for itself' (Habermas 1978: 295). Owing to the explicitly political character of both the Revolution and the Napoleonic restoration, social affairs were no longer seen as part of natural history. Rather, from now on social life was increasingly regarded as the immanent result of social action itself. The challenge for the conservative position was to restore the legitimacy of a political regime which, although it saw itself as beyond the modern need for (democratic) legitimisation, was now being pushed to appeal for support to a reasoning public opinion. The difficulties for the progressive camp were equally vexing as, after the Terror, they needed to show that the reorganisation of society could be implemented peacefully, fairly and without resorting to natural or divine principles. As it remained useful to both camps of the civil war, sociology was normatively split at its core.[9]

[9] See Lepenies's (1988) and Heilbron's (1995) accounts of how Comte's sociology was being explicitly used in both progressive and conservative camps at the time.

By the second half of the twentieth century, we had surely grown definitively sceptical of the idea of a 'natural history of humanity that progresses towards its improvement that once had godfathered sociology' (Habermas 1978: 303–4). Key tendencies in contemporary sociology at the time such as positivism and technocratic decisionism shared the view that, in order to become fully modern and scientific, sociology ought to abandon all normative pretentions. But the price to be paid for this gain in scientific credentials and organisational potential is a net loss in sociology's ability to understand normative questions. While eighteenth- and nineteenth-century sociology could be both critical and conservative, twentieth-century sociology can, in good consciousness, be neither.[10]

Sociology is important to Habermas because it is the empirical social science that may be able to contribute to the intellectual tasks that philosophy can no longer pursue on its own. Given the history and philosophical background of its concepts, sociology is particularly well suited to become the empirical continuation of philosophical reflections about social life in general, not least in terms of the complicated relationships between description and normativity. And while the sense of intellectual continuity in this is undeniable, it is none the less worthy of mention that the issue of the tension between description and normativity has grown increasingly central in Habermas's work. This is how the question is stated in *Between Facts and Norms*:

> The theory of communicative action already absorbs the tension between facticity and validity into its fundamental concepts. With this risky decision it preserves the link with the classical conception of an internal connection, however mediated, between society and reason, and hence between the constraints and necessities under which the reproduction of social life is carried out, on the one hand, and the idea of a conscious conduct of life, on the other. (Habermas 1996: 8)[11]

Sociology's contribution to the empirical understanding and normative critique of modern society lies in how it re-engages with natural law:

[10] Habermas admits that this article ends with the rather self-defeating conclusion that contemporary sociology could only have recourse to its own tradition for the renovation of its normative energies: in order to be progressive, modern sociology needed to remain true to its old self (Habermas 1978: 304). It is only after he found an altogether different claim for the renovation of modern normative contents in the linguistic turn that sociology was offered the non-coercive normative power of linguistic interactions and communicative rationality as a firm normative standpoint.

[11] This tension is visible beyond sociology of course. It is constitutive of Habermas's early *The Structural Transformation of the Public Sphere*, whose goal was, on the descriptive side, to reconstruct historically the rise and main features of modern publicity and, on the normative side, to understand its decline with a view to the reinvigoration of its democratic potential (Habermas 1989, Habermas 1992b). Similarly, it is central to *Knowledge and Human Interest* in the late 1960s (Habermas 1972) and to his break with Marxism in the early 1970s (Habermas 1984b: 130–77).

Habermas wants to retain both dimensions and engage with both traditions without, however, eliding them. For instance, he favours Weber's and Parsons's approaches to modern law over Niklas Luhmann's purely descriptive and John Rawls's purely normative approaches. Although Weber and Parsons ultimately failed to conceptualise adequately the double normative and descriptive side of modern law, they at least saw clearly that both dimensions were equally important. Modern sociology is well equipped to capture this key aspect of modern law because of its systematic engagement with descriptive and normative questions:

> The ideas of a conscious organization and self-organization of the legal community – *initially framed in the language of modern natural law* – express an awareness of the ideal content of legal validity. To the extent that this awareness develops and the ideal content of law clashes with functional imperatives of the market economy and bureaucratic administration, *the normative self-understanding of law provokes an empirical critique.* (Habermas 1996: 42, my italics)[12]

Having established the link between sociology and natural law on the basis of their simultaneous engagement with descriptive and normative tasks, we now need to come back to the justification of universalism in Habermas's thought.

Universalism and the postmetaphysical

In this final section I turn explicitly to Habermas's arguments on the status of the postmetaphysical as the justificatory strategy for the universalistic orientation of his thinking. A methodological warning is needed before we proceed, however. A common feature of Habermas's reading of other writers consists in bringing them to task for resorting to arguments and presuppositions that they found unacceptable when criticising others.[13] It is one thing for an author to claim to have definitively moved beyond unwarranted 'metaphysics' and quite another for us to assess independently how successfully that task has actually been accomplished. Needless to say, this insight applies equally to Habermas himself. Reconstructing Habermas's arguments

[12] It is well documented that his understanding of modern law in *Between Facts and Norms* represents a major shift from Habermas's negative view of it in *Theory of Communicative Action* (McCarthy 1993, Chernilo 2002). For my purposes here, this reinforces the argument that the tension between description and normativity has become even more central in Habermas's work and that the connections between natural law and social theory are an essential resource in addressing this tension.

[13] Thus, for instance, he discusses Marx (Habermas 1972: 25–63), Foucault (Habermas 1990b: 238–65) and Rorty (Habermas 2002: 343–82).

on 'postmetaphysical thinking' will allow us to evaluate how he handles what remains of metaphysics in *post*metaphysics.

There is a first and arguably strong version of Habermas's argument on the postmetaphysical that centres on the paradigmatic shift from consciousness to language in twentieth-century philosophy. Best represented in the works of Kant (Habermas 1990a: 1–20, 2003b: 83–112) and Husserl (Habermas 2001c: 23–44), the *modern* metaphysical tradition centres on 'transcendental' arguments that now prove unwarranted because of their monological rather than intersubjective foundations. In addition to the question of intersubjectivity, at stake here is also the critique of philosophy's privileged cognitive status among competing cognitive strategies. It is philosophy's traditional role as the highest form of human knowledge that becomes fundamentally questioned: '[t]oday, the illumination of common sense by philosophy can only be carried out according to criteria of validity that are no longer at the disposition of philosophy itself. Philosophy must operate under conditions of rationality that it has not chosen' (Habermas 1992a: 18). Philosophy's claim to knowledge has lost its pride of place in relation not only to lay knowledge but also empirical science in general. In modernity, the old totalising concept of reason gives way to 'the procedural rationality of the scientific process that would decide whether or not a sentence has a truth-value in the first place ... philosophical thinking [has had to...] bow to the sciences' claim to exemplary status' (6). Philosophy provides neither the primary source from which new knowledge about human and natural affairs is now being produced nor controls the contexts within which knowledge claims are accepted as knowledge. In this strong version of the argument on the postmetaphysical, then, metaphysics is a way of referring to philosophical arguments that we no longer find adequate: '[m]etaphysics has emerged as the science of the universal, immutable, and necessary' whose only equivalent in modern philosophy 'was a theory of consciousness that states the necessary subjective conditions for the objectivity of universal synthetic judgements *a priori*' (13).

This is a strong argument because it effectively equates much of the modern philosophical tradition with unwarranted metaphysics, whereas the postmetaphysical becomes a thoroughgoing critique of modern philosophy at the level of substantive content as well as justificatory strategies. As transcendentalism becomes definitively untenable, it is now the *procedural* rationality of scientific knowledge that would allow us to insufflate new life into concepts that have become problematic. As we just saw above, however, Habermas has also argued that normatively meaningful discussions cannot sever all links to previous natural law.

And it is also the case that proceduralism itself is a philosophical product of previous 'metaphysical' thinking – most notably but not exclusively through Kant's categorical imperative (see Chapters 4 and 5 below). Proceduralism is of course central to Habermas's own communicative rationality as the way in which natural languages have a built-in orientation to understanding. His references to the scientific method above refer to the features it shares *as a procedure* with legal and moral arguments: '"Impartiality" in the sense of justice converges with "impartiality" in the sense of the discursive ascertainment of cognitive claims to validity' (Habermas 2003b: 105). The fact remains, then, that modern proceduralism is itself a philosophical and indeed transcendental discovery.

But there is also a softer version of the argument about our current postmetaphysical constellation in which 'the post' points to an increased reflexivity towards the philosophical underpinnings of our arguments. No intellectual tradition, no philosophical argument, can nowadays simply presuppose the adequacy of its foundations and justificatory strategies because the very standards of what constitute legitimate knowledge are themselves continuously open to debate. 'Under modern conditions', Habermas writes,

> [t]here can be no metaphysical thinking in the strict sense but at most the reworking of metaphysical problems ... In contrast one might insist ... upon *retaining* the expression 'metaphysics' for every manner of working through metaphysical questions, or those directed to the totality of (hu)man and world. (Habermas 1992a: 13, my italics)

Metaphysics still retains negative connotations in terms of unwarranted presuppositions, but now has also an affirmative role: there are enduring philosophical questions that are metaphysical because they are concerned with the human condition as a universal problem. As the sublation of metaphysics, postmetaphysics is a modern achievement in which metaphysics may still be seen as problematic but cannot be flatly rejected; it is no longer the most advanced way of justifying human knowledge and yet it still has a role to play in helping us reflect on who we are as human beings. And, of course, no one is fully exempt from surreptitiously reintroducing problematic presuppositions into their own arguments and ways of thinking.[14]

[14] This is also coherent with the way in which Habermas explicitly dealt with questions about globalisation in our *post*national constellation: in order to reflect on current globalisation processes we need to focus less on the past of national democracy and social solidarity and more on the fact that national frameworks cannot automatically or naturally be taken for granted for the purposes of reinvigorating democracy and social solidarity (Habermas 2001a, Chernilo 2007: 151–7).

The contemporary role of philosophy lies in its ability to translate traditional (i.e. metaphysical, religious) concerns into the kind of language and justifications that are acceptable under modern conditions. While philosophy's cognitive status has certainly diminished, metaphysics remains a crucial component of what the philosophical tradition can and ought to do for us in modernity:

Philosophy is supposed to make possible a life that is 'conscious' and 'controlled' in a nondisciplinary sense, through coming to a reflexive self-understanding. In this respect philosophy is still faced with the task of taking the answers of the tradition, i.e., the sacred knowledge of religions and the mundane knowledge of cosmologies developed in the high cultures, and appropriating them within the narrowed and sharpened spotlight of what can still convince the daughters and sons of modernity *with good reasons*. Behind the verbal dispute over whether 'metaphysics' is still possible after Kant, there is concealed a substantial disagreement about the existence and extent of those old truths that are capable of being critically appropriated, as well as disagreement about the character of the change of meaning to which old truths are subjected when they are critically appropriated. (Habermas 1992a: 14–15)

We will see throughout this book that the question of the empirical sciences carrying greater weight over against philosophical arguments figures centrally in modern natural law and classical social theory alike. It is also one of the early motifs that Habermas recovers from the programme that Horkheimer set out for critical social theory, whose successful development would need the best insights from modern sciences and the philosophical tradition (Habermas 1992a: 16). Habermas's own early critique of positivism is in fact inspired by this idea of wanting to recast the relationship between science and philosophy (instead of the former being hypostatised as first philosophy).[15] The danger we otherwise face is that in the absence of philosophical concepts that are able to retain some kind of control *vis-à-vis* our comprehension of normative challenges, we are left with no intellectual tools to address normative questions: '[t]he end of the cooperative division of labor between philosophy and social theory means uncoupling a critical self-understanding of modernity from an empirical observation and descriptive account of its tendencies to social crisis' (Habermas 2001a: 142).

Although I cannot reconstruct it in any great detail here, this insight is central to Habermas's first systematic project in *Knowledge and Human Interest* (Habermas 1972 [1968]). Two of the main arguments of that

[15] However different their works may be in other respects, it is the neglect of the normative as a central though never exclusive component of our intellectual tasks that is key to Habermas's critique of Comte (Habermas 1972: 71–90), Popper (Adorno 1976) and Luhmann (Habermas 1990b: 368–85).

book are, precisely, the relationships between empirical and philosophical knowledge, on the one hand, and the location of the normative, on the other. Habermas (1972: 4) thus opens with the claim that 'since Kant science has no longer been seriously comprehended by philosophy', so the task is to transcend the twin defects of philosophy's neglect of science and positivism's faith that the sciences have no further need of philosophy. Still within the mould of Marxian social theory, the claim is that the radical critique of knowledge in general is only possible inside a general theory of society. Not exempt from existential implications, Habermas's positive argument in *Knowledge and Human Interest* is that in modern society there are different ways of 'being in the world', all of which are equally human although they take place within their own institutional or structural domains. The problem with the modern reduction of human knowledge into scientific knowledge lies in its failure to acknowledge the complexity of human cognition beyond instrumental rationality: not all forms of knowledge can or need to become a productive force under capitalism. As known, Habermas then differentiates between three universal human interests in that book: a *control interest* that is the expression of our instrumental capabilities and has become institutionally anchored in the natural sciences; a *communicative interest* that expresses our innate sociability and whose cognitive manifestation lies in hermeneutics and the humanities; and a *critical or emancipatory interest* that has to do with our reflective ability to imagine alternative courses of action with a view to transforming them, as visible in psychoanalysis and ideology critique (308–17). The fact that Habermas later abandoned this model does not change three key results that proved long-lasting: (1) the natural sciences are not the only legitimate model from which to understand social life; (2) philosophy and the sciences can mutually learn from one another, and; (3) serious social scientific work comprises both explanatory and normative dimensions.

It is of course only with the linguistic turn during the 1970s, a process that culminates in the publication of *Theory of Communicative Action*, that Habermas found a new frame for addressing the problem of the relationships between philosophy and the empirical sciences. Abandoning the paradigm of consciousness and replacing it with a linguistic one based on the idea of intersubjectivity allowed Habermas to move from the transcendental conditions of experience of a knowing subject in general – a metaphysical formulation – to the study of the actual conditions within which linguistic interaction takes place – a postmetaphysical project. Above all, the linguistic turn makes it apparent that human language and communication are 'always already' particular and universal. All linguistic utterances are specific and context dependent while being simultaneously grounded on the universal conditions created by the possibility of redeeming problematic validity claims:

> [v]alidity claims are Janus-faced: as claims, they overshoot every context; at the same time, they must be both raised and accepted here and now if they are to support an agreement for effective coordination ... The universalistic meaning of the claimed validity exceeds all contexts, but only the local, binding act of acceptance enables validity claims to bear the burden of social context integration for a context-bound everyday practice. (Habermas 1996: 21)

Habermas construed his thesis of human language's orientation to understanding as an *empirical discovery* based on developments from such relevant disciplines as linguistics, evolutionary psychology, pragmatism and sociology itself (Habermas 2001c, 2002). However, the very importance of this empirical discovery depends upon its universal status, explicatively – this is how human communication actually works – as well as normatively – certain values, practices and institutions are to be universally favoured because they allow for the expansion of communicative rationality as central to our human condition. Both being equally real as forms of social life, the lifeworld is to be preferred normatively to the systems because its social reproduction takes place through the 'condensation' but never the 'replacement' of the normative orientation of linguistic interactions (Habermas 1987: 264–7). This paradigmatic shift from consciousness to language is surely Habermas's long-lasting legacy and contribution to modern social science and philosophy (Outhwaite 1994). Yet it does not fundamentally alter the picture we have drawn so far, as Habermas's linguistic turn requires that his conception of human language and social interaction can count, equally and simultaneously, with philosophical and empirical backing (Habermas 2002: 21). The discovery of human language's orientation to understanding matters scientifically as much as it does philosophically: it is metaphysical and postmetaphysical at the same time.

Not too dissimilar from the tension we encountered above between the liberal and the republican versions of natural law, normative arguments with a universalistic intent need simultaneously to be founded on subjective agreement and be held as objectively valid. Habermas reworked Kant's categorical imperative through two principles that retain, but in a transformed way, the universalistic and open-ended nature of Kant's original formulation. The first universalisation principle (U) states that '*[a]ll* affected can accept the consequences and the side effects its *general* observance can be anticipated to have for the general satisfaction of *everyone's* interests' (Habermas 1990a: 65). This is complemented by a second, discourse principle (D), that now explicitly centres on the communicative realisation of moral reasoning as moral discourse: '[o]nly those norms can claim to be valid that meet (or could meet) with the approval of all affected in their capacity *as participants in a practical discourse*' (Habermas 1990a: 66).[16] Habermas (2003b: 85) thus speaks about the 'transformation of Kant's "ideas" of pure reason into "idealising" presuppositions of communicative action' and explicates this modification in four planes: (1) Kant's cosmological idea of the unity of the world becomes 'the pragmatic presupposition of a common objective world'; (2) Kant's idea of freedom in terms of practical reason is revised on the basis of 'the pragmatic presupposition of the rationality of accountable agents'; (3) Kant's totalising idea of reason becomes the 'unconditionality of the validity claims raised in communicative action'; and (4) Kant's idea of reason, which is also 'the highest court of appeal', is now transformed into 'rational discourse as the unavoidable forum of possible justification' (87).

To be sure, this detranscendentalisation aims to leave the problems of Kant's first philosophy behind and Habermas understands these developments as the postmetaphysical paradigmatic shift that is provided by the linguistic turn:

> Giving up the background assumptions of Kant's transcendental philosophy turns ideas of reason into idealizations that orient subjects capable of speech and action. The rigid 'ideal' that was elevated to an otherworldly realm is set aflow in this-worldly operations; it is transposed from a transcendent state into a process of '*immanent transcendence*'. (Habermas 2003b: 92–3)

Kantian transcendental deductions are now counterfactual pragmatic presuppositions that work in terms of immanent transcendence. We will come back to this idea of immanent transcendence several times below, but crucially these pragmatic presuppositions of communication constitute the means by which description and normativity may eventually be brought to work together:

> these unavoidable presuppositions of argumentative practice, no matter how counterfactual, are by no means mere constructs. Rather they are *operatively effective* in the behavior of the participants themselves. Someone who seriously takes part in an argument de facto proceeds from such presuppositions. (Habermas 2003b: 107–8)

[16] Habermas's later formulation of the D principle in *Between Facts and Norms* widens the scope to which it can be applied, as it now refers to all rational discourses instead of to only practical ones: '[j]ust those actions are valid to which all possibly affected persons could agree as participants in rational discourses' (Habermas 1996: 107).

Whether this change is as radical as Habermas would like it to be remains, however, open to question – also in terms of his own account of his relationships with Kant:

According to Kant, rational beings think of themselves as agents acting on the basis of good reasons. With regard to moral action, they have an a priori knowledge of the possibility of actualizing the idea of freedom. In communicative action *we also tacitly start* with the assumption that all participants are accountable agents. It is simply part of the self-understanding of subjects acting communicatively that they take rationally motivated positions on claims to validity; agents mutually presuppose that they indeed do act based on rationally warrantable reasons. (Habermas 2003b: 96, my italics)

There are three main questions that remain as we assess Habermas's postmetaphysical arguments in relation to Kant's philosophy. First, for both writers the core of modern normative discourses lies more in their justificatory strategies than in their substantive content; we need to be able to account for the procedure with which we justify our decisions as normatively sound. Interestingly, however, the universality of the procedure is itself an act of deduction (transcendental in Kant, pragmatic in Habermas) that does not result from its application to itself: as metanorms, procedures are expected to be fruitfully applied to themselves but that is different from explicating their origins through that application.[17] At the same time, although the procedure must remain open ended, substantive decisions that would undermine its universality (human beings being treated as means rather than ends, to decide democratically on the suspension of democratic deliberation) are excluded by principle. Positive as this is in normative terms, procedures create justificatory challenges that potentially undermine their substantive purchase. Secondly, both Kant and Habermas face problems with a certain indecidability that arises when a decision between competing though equally universalistic norms or principles is at stake. The universalistic status of the procedure does not help when at stake is, for instance, whether freedom of speech may need to be preferred over the right to privacy in some cases, while the opposite conclusion may be

[17] This is accepted by Karl-Otto Apel (2004: 67): '[i]t is immediately obvious that presuppositions of this kind cannot be grounded in a formal-logic sense without *logical circularity*, that is, cannot be demonstrated. It is also equally clear that the existence of such presuppositions cannot be revealed *empirically* independently of the act of strict transcendental reflection.' See also Albrecht Wellmer's (1998: 50–1) justification of the '*procedural* core of democratic ethical life . . . [as] . . . a *way of dealing with* (irresolvable) dissent, heterogeneity, and conflicts which are structurally unavoidable in modern societies'. We will come back to these questions when we discuss Kant and Hegel's works in Chapter 5.

reached in other situations. These formulations allow for the mediation between particular instances and general principles but *not* between competing general principles. Thirdly, and arguably most importantly in relation to Habermas's self-description of his intellectual project, there is the question of how radical the linguistic turn is *vis-à-vis* Kant's monological arguments in relation to the rationality of the decisions thus reached. To be sure, the U principle explicitly opens moral decisions to all those potentially affected and although its participatory or even democratic content now becomes explicit, its fundamental insight in terms of inclusivity was arguably already built into Kant's categorical imperative. In relation to the D principle, it no doubt specifies the importance of collective decisions being the result of intersubjective deliberation, but no definitive argument has been given as to why intersubjective deliberation must *always and necessarily* be better equipped to arrive at sound rational decisions – not least, in Habermas's own account that modern public deliberation is subject to manipulation, hypocrisy and strategic action (Habermas 1989, 1992b). Neither the political desirability of democratic deliberation nor the counterfactual presupposition of rational discourses in the context of an ideal community of communication automatically translates into philosophical certitude.

Closing remarks

A universalistic orientation has been central to Habermas's work for over sixty years and it is this universalism that in my view makes his work stand out in contemporary social theory.[18] Universalism also connects Habermas's social theory with modern natural law and we saw that for Habermas the normative grammar of modernity, centrally represented

[18] I have consciously left out from this chapter Habermas's writings on cosmopolitanism, not only for reasons of space but also because they can be read as further expression, rather than as a radical reformulation, of the arguments on which I have concentrated. See, for example, the following formulation as expression of the built-in cosmopolitanism of Habermas's theory of communicative action in terms of a universalistic orientation: 'Only moral imperatives (and legal norms such as human rights that can only be justified morally) claim absolute validity, that is, universal recognition ... This explains Kant's demand that valid moral laws must be "universalizable." Moral norms must be able to command the rationally motivated recognition of all subjects capable of speech and action, beyond the historical and cultural confines of any particular social world. Thus, the idea of a thoroughly morally ordered community implies the counterfactual extension of the social world in which we find ourselves to a completely inclusive world of well-ordered interpersonal relationships: All human beings become brothers and sisters' (Habermas 2003b: 104). See also Habermas (1998, 2001a, 2006) and Fine and Smith (2003) for further discussion.

in the ideas of human rights and popular sovereignty, is couched in the language of rational natural law. Coming to terms with natural law is then not only a task for the intellectual historian but for social theorists themselves. *At its best*, modern sociology remains crucially connected with the natural law tradition: historically, because early sociology arose as a sublation of modern natural law; conceptually, because sociology is the social science that has remained most committed to its scientific and philosophical planes; normatively, because it allows sociology to transcend empirical description and to try also to address fundamental human concerns. Habermas's argument on postmetaphysical thinking needs then to be interpreted less as a claim about the definitive decline and overcoming of metaphysics and more as a way in which philosophical and normative questions are related to the empirical discoveries of scientific disciplines. The importance of the principle of impartiality in moral, legal and scientific discourses (but arguably also in other social arenas) is a major insight to which we will come back. Also, there is the question of immanent transcendence in terms of understanding the location of the normative in modernity: as a tension between immanent justifications that make arguments rationally acceptable and transcendental grounds that make them binding. Expressed in the tension between description and normativity, social theory takes up the traditional philosophical challenge of the mediation between theory and praxis.

Yet the universalistic orientation in Habermas's work makes apparent what appear to be inescapable challenges. Modern universalism requires of standards of justification that are to be upheld transculturally and even suprahistorically while at the same time they need to be the result of free and autonomous deliberations in particular socio-cultural contexts. Habermas is fully aware of this challenge and the fact that his solutions remain tentative is, in my view, a mark of distinction that is inscribed in the attempt to keep descriptive/explanatory and normative/philosophical arguments working together. He combines them without eliding them and differentiates them without reifying them. Habermas's answers reflect challenges that are all too real: the connections between natural law and social theory are problematic yet worth exploring in detail. As they work as regulative ideas, universalistic proceduralism is bound to make visible potential new areas of conflict. The attempt to address these universalistic commitments *explicitly* becomes a symbol for social theory at its very best.

To be sure, the hypocritical use of normatively charged concepts in political debate makes apparent the dangers involved in our normative concepts being emptied and becoming shallow; indeed, they downgrade public political life itself. But at a more analytical level, an important task is that of critically investigating the patterns of change and stability of natural law arguments in modernity – whether and how their foundational role as well as normative appeal is constantly asked to reinvent itself. Although natural law ideas keep playing a relevant role in modern society – justice, fairness, equality, freedom, human rights are not values we want to do away with – changing socio-historical circumstances mean that new normative challenges emerge for and from them. Therein lies what I think is one of Habermas's key insights into what we may call the dialectics of modernity and natural law. Modernity's normative self-understanding is and remains fundamentally framed within the tradition of natural law, as many of our most meaningful notions remain enmeshed in its language and presuppositions. And yet the same justificatory strategies through which they were first introduced and explicated appear increasingly rigid and difficult to accept. Committed as it is to understanding modern society, Habermas's project no doubt belongs to the best tradition of social theory. But to the extent that he is also committed to a strong universalistic orientation, and that the modifications of his theoretical arguments need to be explicated with reference to challenges that are directly derived from this universalistic orientation, I have also been arguing here that his work belongs in the tradition of natural law. In depicting Habermas's social theory as a form of postmetaphysical natural law, I am also using it to set up the general tone of the historical, conceptual and normative enquiry that will now follow.

2 A natural law critique of modern social theory: Karl Löwith, Leo Strauss and Eric Voegelin

The previous chapter argued for the contemporary relevance of looking together at both social theory and natural law and did so on the understanding that Habermas is fundamentally committed to the renovation of modern social theory. I should now like to turn this angle of observation upside down and reconstruct a series of twentieth-century critiques of social theory from the point of view of natural law broadly understood. Although not directly or explicitly, Habermas's reconstructive effort may be seen as a reconstructive response to the kind of 'natural law critique' of social theory that I discuss here.

The three writers to whom attention will be paid in the following pages were extremely critical of modern social thought as an intellectual tradition, of its more recent developments in modern social sciences and the role these have played in shaping modernity's self-image. It is therefore not altogether surprising that they are not widely discussed in contemporary social theory. In order to make their insights relevant to what is to come in the rest of this book, we will then have to read Karl Löwith (1897–1973), Leo Strauss (1899–1973) and Eric Voegelin (1901–1985) at least partly against the grain. I contend that their works can be profitably interpreted as a reassessment of some of social theory's blind spots and unwarranted presuppositions without, however, accepting their conclusions about social theory's aporias and somewhat inevitable decline. In their exasperation with social theory's lack of understanding of its own past, conceptual shortcomings and deficient normative awareness, Löwith, Strauss and Voegelin's critiques are highly instructive even if they became as extreme as the propositions on the definitive demise of natural law that they forcefully criticised.[1]

[1] For my purposes in this chapter, there is no need to engage in the far less interesting debates with which they have become associated; namely, Löwith's 'Freudian' debt to his doctoral supervisor Martin Heidegger (Wolin 1995) and Strauss's 'esoteric' influence on American right-wing politics (Norton 2004).

They also share the experience of being *émigrés* who fled Nazi Germany (Löwith and Strauss) and Nazified Austria (Voegelin) in the 1930s and eventually landed in the United States. They belong to the same generation and remained in contact throughout their adult lives.[2] Similarities in context and broad intellectual orientation do of course account for some of the overlapping concerns to be found in their works, most of which point towards a critique of modernity in terms of its unfulfilled promises and the distance between sweet ideals and bitter reality: their assaults on the Enlightenment idea of progress, their critiques of modern culture in the form of historicism, relativism, positivism and indeed nihilism, the inability of liberal democracies to defend themselves against fascism and totalitarianism, their scepticism towards modern (social) sciences' belief in a strict separation between fact and value, to name a few. Moreover, the texts I shall be looking at more closely below – Löwith's *Meaning in History*, Strauss's *Natural Right and History* and Voegelin's *The New Science of Politics* – were originally written in English as their recently acquired academic language and were published at roughly the same time (they date, respectively, from 1949, 1950 and 1952).[3] None of these writers engaged systematically with contemporary sociological writings but all produced occasional accounts of certain aspects of modern sociology that we will also review in some detail. Max Weber was the figure who represented for all three the most sophisticated version of twentieth-century social science, so they examined Weber's work with a paradigmatic intention: coming to terms with Weber was no mere scholarly task but a way of reckoning with key developments in both modern social science and modern society (Roth 1965).[4] With his distinction between facts and values, his concern with Western rationality and also with his disenchantment thesis, Weber became the embodiment of everything for which social science strove but could never truly achieve: to become the empirical, immanent, free of metaphysical presuppositions and socially produced knowledge of social life that could eventually be used for social reform.

[2] See, for instance, the selected correspondence between Strauss and Voegelin (Emberley and Cooper 2004) and between Strauss and Löwith in *Constellations,* 16(1) (2009). On this count, though not of course in normative outlook, their works belong together with that of other prominent German *émigrés* such as Theodor Adorno, Max Horkheimer, Herbert Marcuse and Hannah Arendt who were all confronted with similar experiences of persecution and exile (Kielmansegg, Mewes and Glaser-Schmidt 1997, Wolin 2001).

[3] Strauss's and Voegelin's texts are the result of the same Walgreen Lectures they gave at the University of Chicago, Strauss in 1949–50 and Voegelin in 1950–1.

[4] See also the special issue of the *European Journal of Political Theory* (3(2), 2004) on different interpretations of Max Weber by German intellectuals in the USA at the time.

I am interested in a combined reading of these works because they point against conventional sociological wisdom on a number of central assumptions. But while there is clear compatibility between these writers' views on modernity and modern social theory, when it comes to explicating the connections between social theory and natural law I shall also be focusing on the different substantive results of their respective critiques. I suggest that by understanding the specific arguments that they raise against different aspects of modern social theory and, to repeat, by drawing some consequences they themselves would have disapproved of, their works allow us to reconsider the historical trajectory and contemporary challenges posed by the question of universalism. Löwith's secularisation thesis challenges the modernist historical imagination which mistakenly takes the radicality of its attempt at the critique of religion as an immediate expression of its success in having accomplished that task. Similarly, the modern faith in immanent progress as the basis of its claim to self-assertion must always be prepared to scrutinise the extent to which it remains rooted in the natural law tradition. Yet in his highly stimulating reading of Weber and Marx as philosophical sociologists, Löwith argues that these writers were initiating ground-breaking developments; it was now possible to advance a kind of social theory that was socio-historically informed – the salience of capitalism for understanding the whole of modern social relations – and philosophically sound – the fact that capitalism had become 'human destiny'.

For his part, Strauss argues that natural law (indeed natural right) is a perennial feature of our human attempts at understanding human events in purely immanent terms. Strauss's reconstruction of the natural law tradition as natural right gives due credit to the secular origins of modernity but at the price of withdrawing even more autonomy from modernity and social theory – the latter then becoming a mere appendix to natural law. The core of Strauss's outlook in this context is that there can be no meaningful enquiry into social and political problems beyond natural law. It is through a highly provocative interpretation of Weber that Strauss eventually argues that sociology's intellectual worth depends upon natural law presuppositions – presuppositions that cannot, however, be justified in terms that are internally acceptable to modern social science. Strauss is not against the *idea* of social science but does not believe that *modern* social science is prepared to take up the serious intellectual and normative challenges demanded by modern life.

Voegelin finally seeks to resituate the problem of the transcendental as a central dimension of any attempt – ancient and modern, religious and secular – at explicating what is truly human in social life. Through an analysis and critique of 'gnosticism', Voegelin explicates the main features of a long-lasting intellectual orientation that has wholly obliterated the transcendental; a process that in modernity has found its highest intellectual expression in positivism and its most dramatic political expression in totalitarian regimes. I shall reinterpret his attempt to reclaim the transcendental as a claim on the location of the normative in social life. The normative is no accidental dimension of social life but remains central to our conceptualisation of it – without a universalistic idea of the normative our common conception of humanity disappears. Voegelin's *New Science of Politics* is a highly instructive, though ultimately unsuccessful, attempt to recover our ability to think about the normative aspects of life in society as a transcendental domain that dwells, however, within social relations themselves. Starting from a similar critical standpoint – modern social theory ought to recognise its debt to natural law more decidedly – three different charges eventually emerge: Löwith *diminishes* social theory's intellectual worth on the basis of its absolute neglect of natural law, Strauss *dissolves* whatever remains relevant in social theory as merely the modern form of natural law and Voegelin *challenges* social theory for its neglect of transcendence as that inviolable moment of normativity without which our common sense of humanity is bound to dissolve.

Secularisation and philosophical sociology: Karl Löwith

Karl Löwith's long-term intellectual agenda is fundamentally marked by issues that connect modern social theory and natural law: the relationships between nature and history, the rise and consequences of 'European nihilism', the underlying normative preoccupations of the modern philosophical tradition from Hegel via Nietzsche to Weber. His sensibility when addressing these problems is sombre if not directly pessimistic – something which has also been described as a mark of his personality (Gadamer 1985). To be sure, the social and political events that marked Löwith's life go a long way to explain this, but in his writings this pessimism is more directly connected to the kind of intellectual difficulties that we face in modern times. Although they differ in their interpretations, in Löwith's rendition ancient philosophy based on cyclical conceptions of time, religious doctrines that believe in salvation, and Enlightenment social and political thought with its secular idea of progress are all equally inadequate for reflecting on the meaning of life under contemporary conditions. Löwith has no positive programme to offer instead, as the ultimately contemplative orientation of his work struggles to encompass the key aspect of modern life: uncertainty is the price we pay for the promise of moral autonomy, political self-determination and individual freedom (Wolin 2001: 98).[5]

In the preface to *Meaning in History*, Löwith (1964: v) states that although 'neither a providential design nor a natural law of progressive development is discernible in the tragic human comedy of all times', the most crucial intellectual conviction of modern times is precisely the *belief* in the purposeful character of history. A human concern with the meaning of history has been a permanent trait of Western thinking, based as it is on our 'basic experience of evil and suffering, and man's quest for happiness' (3). Löwith argues that the modern historical imagination first makes apparent, then criticises, but none the less fails to overcome the view that any meaningful understanding of history requires a point outside human history, 'a transcendent point beyond actual facts', whose justification is impossible to establish on sound philosophical grounds (5). Historical thinking is fundamentally linked to a universalistic idea of the human genre which, 'however, has not existed in the historical past, nor can it exist in any present. It is an idea and an ideal of the future, the necessary horizon for the eschatological concept of history and its universality' (18). This ambivalence is captured in the tone as much as in the content of his argument. Löwith's extremely eloquent prose is worth quoting at length:

> The significance of this vision of an ultimate end, as both *finis* and *telos*, is that it provides a scheme of progressive order and meaning, a scheme which has been capable of overcoming the ancient fear of fate and fortune. Not only does the *eschaton* delimit the process of history by an end, it also articulates and fulfils it by a definite goal ... It is only within the theological, or rather eschatological, scheme of the historical process that history became 'universal'; for its *universality does not depend merely on the belief in one universal God but on his giving unity to the history of mankind by directing it toward a final purpose* ... We of today, concerned with the unity of universal history and with its progress toward an ultimate goal or at least toward a 'better world', are still in the line of prophetic and messianic monotheism, we are still Jews and Christians, however little we may think of ourselves in those terms ... *We are neither ancient ancients nor ancient Christians, but moderns – that is, a more or less inconsistent compound of both traditions* ... It seems as if the two great conceptions of antiquity and Christianity, cyclic motion and eschatological direction, have exhausted the basic approaches to the understanding of history. *Even the most recent*

[5] I agree with Robert Pippin's (1999: 26) general argument that in order to renovate the modern project we ought to qualify 'modernity's exaggerated sense of historical autonomy'. But I depart from his interpretation of Löwith's argument on secularisation and, with the provisos I indicated at the beginning of this chapter, I take Löwith to be an essential resource to think through the modern claim to historical autonomy.

approaches at an interpretation of history are nothing else but variations of these two principles or a mixture of both of them. (Löwith 1964: 18–19 my italics)[6]

Löwith attempts to demonstrate the extent to which the modern historical imagination is fully embedded in religious presuppositions – both Christian and Jewish – which it can neither adequately justify nor fully control. But *Meaning in History* is an atypical book also in its structure. Its first substantive chapter focuses on Jacob Burckhardt and the book then moves backwards in history to end with the Bible, while in the process it revisits, always in inverse chronological order, conceptions of history in Marx, Hegel, Comte, Voltaire and Augustine, among others. The book then begins at that point in time that, somewhat paradoxically, marks the end of that long-term vision of history in terms of finis or telos. By the end of the nineteenth century, and best represented in the works of Burckhardt and also Friedrich Nietzsche, modernity had already lost its faith in secular progress without newer faiths having yet emerged (Löwith 1995).[7] The current state of knowledge about human affairs, as expressed in modern social science, is therefore a key aspect of the wider secularisation process that in Löwith's view is constitutive of modernity. The problem is that these modern disciplines have not fully realised what is involved in their debt to religion. This claim directly challenges modernity's self-understanding of its own historical emergence as a time of a radical epochal break marked precisely by the decline of

[6] As said, Löwith wrote *Meaning in History* in English while living in the USA and the book was first published in 1949. The book appeared in German in 1953, after Löwith's return to his home country. Two things are worth pointing out in that connection. First, by changing its title to 'World History and Salvation: The Theological Presuppositions of the Philosophy of History' (*Weltgeschichte und Heilgeschehen. Die theologien Voraussetzungen der Geschichtsphilosophie*), Löwith makes clear that his main goal in the book is to show that immanent and transcendental arguments on the meaning of historical events are fundamentally intertwined. Secondly, it was the then doctoral student Reinhart Koselleck who was commissioned to do part of the translation of the book from English 'back' into German under Löwith's personal supervision (Donaggio 2006: 175).

[7] Jeffrey Barash (1998: 75) summarises well the unresolved paradox that underpins Löwith's approach in *Meaning in History*: 'if Löwith seeks to overcome the illusory attempts by traditional philosophies of history to impose a Divine or a reasoned order on history, his attempt paradoxically depends on the identification of an ordered historical movement encompassing the great interpretations of history throughout the Western tradition'. The methodological challenge for Löwith is how to justify his own positioning *within* the flux of history but *beyond* what he himself diagnoses as the inescapable trap of historicism in modernity. I think this is the case not only in relation to Löwith but also to any proposition that seeks to uphold a claim to universalism. As said, Löwith has no positive answer to this problem, and I take the combined reading of Weber and Marx to be discussed below also as an illustration of the general proposition that while the question of universalism is the noblest of intellectual projects it is also, and at the same time, one that presents potentially unsolvable challenges.

religious influences – and this is also the main sense in which Löwith's critique of modernity has been read and criticised.[8]

But Löwith's unilateral critique of modernity in terms of unfinished – indeed unfinishable – secularisation is not the line of argument in which I am most interested here. His central insight is not that religious sources and influences remain ubiquitous in modernity – we have seen that Habermas is also prepared to grant this. The key is less Löwith's challenge to modernity's historical self-conception of having attempted a total break with religion and more his questioning of the extent to which modernity has successfully accomplished this goal: as it developed from unrecognised religious foundations, the modern idea of progress cannot be revised in terms that remain acceptable to modern philosophy and modern social science's claim to immanent and empirical knowledge.

There is another aspect to Löwith's thesis. If successful, modernity's critique of religion equally undermines its own normative foundations: modern social theory creates its own normative dead ends. The key challenge for modern social theory lies therefore in the fact that it is posited in between 'theology and philosophy', the fact that it is bound to 'ask questions that cannot be answered on the basis of empirical knowledge' (Löwith 1964: 3). Modern social and political thought has nowhere safe to go to as neither traditional religions, with their cyclic conceptions of time, nor Christian eschatology, with its hope for other-worldly salvation, nor indeed modern politics and science based on a teleology of immanent progress, can provide consistent as well as meaningful answers to the existential questions that are fundamental for our shared human condition. What constitutes us as human beings? Do we have a shared humanity? What makes a society fair? Is it possible to achieve firm normative standards? Does life have an ulterior meaning (and, if so, how do we get to know about it)? In terms of the integrity of its normative foundations, therefore, modernity compares poorly with previous epochs because it 'has not made up its mind whether it should be Christian or pagan. It sees with one eye of faith and one of reason. Hence its vision is necessarily dim in comparison with either Greek or biblical thinking' (207).

[8] Most saliently, of course, by Hans Blumenberg (1983: 30): '[r]egarding the dependence of the idea of progress on Christian eschatology, there are differences that would have to block any transposition of the one into the other. It is a formal, but for that very reason a manifest, difference that an eschatology speaks of an event breaking into history, an event that transcends and is heterogeneous to it, while the idea of progress extrapolates from a structure present in every moment to a future that is immanent in history.' The literature is of course extensive, but for further discussion see Barash (1998), Harrington (2008), Riesterer (1969), Syse (2000) and Wallace (1981, 1983).

Neither a one-sided interpretation of Löwith's secularisation thesis that defines modernity purely as a religious bastard, nor the opposite view of voluntaristically reaffirming modernity's complete separation from religion is, however, an adequate answer. Löwith's secularisation thesis is best introduced as the *Aufhebung* by which modern social and political thought is constituted by the simultaneous suspension and carrying forward of its natural law heritage. Löwith does not omit the differences between the modern historical imagination, for which ideas of future and progress are immanent, and the traditional eschaton that is always and necessarily transcendent. The key question for him is the difference that makes in terms of providing a real sense of meaning *in* history:

> A universal history directed toward one single end and unifying, at least potentially, the whole course of events was not created by Voltaire but by Jewish messianism and Christian eschatology, on the basis of an exclusive monotheism. Once this belief had been adopted generally and had prevailed for centuries, man could discard the doctrine of providence, along with that of creation, judgement, and salvation, but he would not return to such views as had satisfied the ancients. Man will seek to replace providence, but within the established horizon, by secularizing the Christian hope of salvation into an indefinite hope of improvement and faith in God's providence into the belief in man's capacity to provide for his own earthly happiness. (Löwith 1964: 111)

Historically, Löwith locates the intellectual transformations that were needed for the emergence of modern social theory firmly within the tradition of natural law. Giambattista Vico's *The New Science* is given special credit, as Vico would have been the first to argue that true historical knowledge was possible because history itself was human made. The natural sciences study a world that is materially self-sufficient, devoid of meaning and whose existence is independent of human intervention, so natural phenomena can never be fully comprehended by human means alone – 'nature necessarily remains opaque' (Löwith 1964: 118). The historical sciences can for their part be established on stronger ontological and methodological foundations because they are human disciplines devoted to the study of strictly human affairs (Löwith 1998: 124, 164). Vico represents a turning point in the rise of modern social thought: '*New Science*, which is at once a philosophy and a history of humanity, is possible because the "nature" of man and nations is in itself a historical human nature, not fixed by physical properties but becoming ... what it is by a historic law and development' (Löwith 1964: 120). Vico inaugurates a modern understanding of history, that is, a field of enquiry which offers endless opportunities but also great challenges because it is 'a world made by men and, at the same time, everywhere surpassed by something which is closer to fate than to free choice and action. History is not only deed and action but also and even primarily event and happening' (126). By being simultaneously committed to understanding history in terms of individual actions *and* fate, immanence *as well as* transcendence, Vico may be regarded as one of the earliest representatives of the secularisation process that is constitutive of the modern imagination. Vico's *New Science*, argues Löwith, 'was the first empirical construction of universal history – of religion, society, governments, legal institutions and languages – on the philosophical principles of an eternal law of providential development which is neither progressive nor simply cyclic and natural' (116).

It is the very radicality of modernity's critique of religion that leaves it heavily dependent upon its religious background. In its obsession with breaking free from religious tutelage, the modern historical imagination unintendedly mirrors the object of its critique. After revisiting Voltaire's *Essay on the Manners and Mind of Nations* as the first attempt to map out human history empirically – i.e. by systematically criticising the view that the Bible was a reliable historical source – Löwith turns decidedly to Hegel, whose philosophy of history is described as 'neither sacred nor profane' but 'a curious mixture of both, degrading sacred history to the level of secular history and exalting the latter to the level of the first' (Löwith 1964: 59). Hegel's dictum that 'the history of the world is the world's court of justice' makes apparent a fundamental tension: whereas only transcendent principles are able to make history truly meaningful – a conception of providence that works as the cunning of reason – modern history becomes fully immanent in terms of a radical conception of human freedom: '[t]he spirit, which, as world spirit dominates history, is negative vis-à-vis nature; that is, progress in the unfolding of the spirit toward freedom is progress in the liberation from subjection to nature' (Löwith 1967: 213). After Hegel, it is no longer possible to aspire to true historical knowledge via philosophical means alone – the universalistic underpinnings of Hegel's 'philosophical historical anthropology' point to the idea that the only remaining possibility for universalism is historical and immanent rather than transcendental (Riesterer 1969: 31, see also Chapter 5).

Questions and answers do change in modernity, but they are not radically different from those of previous times. What matters the most is the fact that the means by which traditional questions have to be answered are transformed; they start constituting a novel 'intellectual genre' that is neither purely philosophical nor purely empirical – something we may eventually call modern social theory (see Chapter 8). It is the rise of sociology in its original Comtean positivism that sublates, in the double sense of conserving and carrying forward, the problematic universalism upon which all ideas of history are based. In this newer attempt at transcending traditional religious frameworks, Löwith makes no secret of where in his view the dangers ultimately lie:

> Comte, like all philosophers of history, thinks in terms of generalities but not of individual persons. Since Comte has constantly in mind 'the whole human evolution,' where everything 'must be referred not to man but to humanity,' the universality of history and its continuity are overemphasized at the expense of the finite and personal character of human life ... This sociopolitical viewpoint is indeed inevitable for the historian because the primary subjects of secular history are not single individuals but communities, groups, and states. (Löwith 1964: 88)

Somewhat anachronistically, but surely of the highest importance for his own biographical and socio-political context, Löwith emphasises the totalitarian implications of this 'universalism' which, as it centres on collective agents rather than on individual human beings, is just not worthy of its name. Yet already in the early 1930s Löwith had singled out Max Weber and Karl Marx as two particularly salient figures who were neither traditional philosophers nor conventional scientists. Weber and Marx became the towering figures they eventually became because they went beyond, effectively *betrayed*, the plans they had set for themselves: '[w]hat ultimately shaped the scientific work of both arose out of an impulse which entirely transcended science as such. This was not only true of Marx, who was led from the academic career he had planned into politics, but also of Weber, who was led in the opposite direction from politics to science' (Löwith 1993: 46). In Weber and Marx, says Löwith (42–3), 'the sphere of their investigations is one and the same ... what is it that makes man "human" within the capitalistic world'. An understanding of 'man as such' was surely not the explicit goal of either writer but is none the less 'their original motive ... [o]ne must ultimately refer back to this idea of man if the "sociological" investigations of Weber and Marx are to be understood in their fundamental radical significance' (43). Whatever else their sociological contribution might have been, they were driven by the principle that 'the ultimate purpose of all human institutions is not the institutions themselves but man' (70). Löwith's argument is effectively that the underlying philosophical anthropologies of Weber and Marx were as important as their sociologies.[9]

Löwith praises Weber and Marx for differentiating their intellectual projects from both a first philosophy and positivistic science while at the same time remaining committed to a universalistic orientation.

[9] See along these lines Bryan Turner's (2013) assessment of the relationships between sociology and philosophical anthropology in the work of Alasdair MacIntyre.

Following Karl Jaspers's (1989) interpretation that sociology is the social science best equipped to continue the philosophical tradition but through modern and empirical means, Löwith (1993: 48) argues that 'sociology is a specialised science which in fact becomes universal. Like the "grand" philosophy of the past, it subsumes all within itself and fertilises all sciences, as long as these sciences ... are in any way connected with man'. Sociology's universalistic potential does not refer to the discovery of the unchangeable laws of social life; positivistic law-like statements were completely out of the question: 'it would be wholly mistaken to construe the fundamental universality of their sociological problematics as a mere "sociologism" exceeding the limits of sociology as a specialised discipline' (47). The critical question was rather to come to grips with the particular problems of our shared human condition as they unfold in modernity. Löwith finds acceptable the claim to universalism that it is based on modern sciences' empirical drive only to the extent that it does not lead to the neglect of ultimate questions. Weber's and Marx's insights and legacies are best served by sociology because it remains committed to asking these fundamental questions which are to be responded to not by pure philosophy but by philosophically informed social science – or modern social theory. Weber and Marx are founders of social theory because they tried to create a new intellectual genre that was able to grasp modern social life in a way that was, simultaneously, empirically comprehensive, conceptually sophisticated and philosophically sound:

> [b]oth Marx and Weber were *essentially* sociologists, namely, *philosophical sociologists*; not because they founded any particular 'social philosophy' but because they in fact, following the basic principle of their work in the face of the actual problems of our human existence, questioned the totality of the contemporary life situation under the rubric of 'capitalism'. Both provide – Marx directly and Weber indirectly – a critical analysis of modern man within bourgeois society in terms of bourgeois-capitalist economy, based on the recognition that the 'economy' has become human 'destiny'. (Löwith 1993: 48, my italics)

It is under this notion of 'philosophical sociology' that Löwith sought to capture the simultaneous scientific and philosophical orientation of Weber's and Marx's *œuvres*.[10] The paradox of his analysis of these two writers suggests that the greatness of their achievements equals their internal inconsistencies. Social theory cannot establish, in terms that are in the last instance acceptable to its own standards, the very claims to knowledge that are supposed to constitute its rational core. The intellectual

[10] Ferdinand Tönnies and Georg Simmel had already used the idea of philosophical sociology at the turn of the twentieth century. See, respectively, Chapters 6 and 7.

greatness of Weber and Marx depends upon the highly original yet also conflicting ways in which they combined, on the one hand, traditional natural law themes and concerns about the meaning of life and our common humanity and, on the other hand, specifically modern forms of scientific knowledge in their empirical analysis of capitalism and its institutions. The centrality of human destiny under capitalistic conditions is a theme that comes from outside their scientific requirements; it is philosophically anticipated. It certainly needs to be made compatible with the written word of their sociologies, but the importance of these sociologies lies in an understanding of the modern world that is

> [n]either a living cosmos nor a creation, nor is it the universe of mathematical physics. It is *our* world of selfhood and interhuman relations within an anonymous mass society – it is a world without nature . . . it is the negative experience that man has no definitive place and nature within the natural universe. (Löwith 1966: 103)

Weber and Marx faced the difficult modern questions about the immanent and transcendental condition of historical time, the relationships between social action and human fate, the disjuncture between existential concerns that we all share as human beings and the particular socio-historical conditions under which modern capitalism operates. There are no definitive solutions to these tensions in modernity and, in so far as they addressed these questions seriously, their substantive answers remained intractable *vis-à-vis* their explicit intellectual projects – to understand the unprecedented features of modern capitalism. But it is in this same struggle for consistency in terms of a strictly scientific understanding of social enquiry that their timeless originality lies: modern social theory's intrinsic intellectual value is diminished as it cuts itself off from ultimately irresolvable philosophical questions. The constitutive strain of the social theory they founded is that whereas it contains an internal drive to take up fundamental existential challenges, its scientific language and aspirations make it incapable of solving them because philosophical questions are pushed to the background and become unanswerable. Weber and Marx sought to take up the deep philosophical challenges that we in modernity inherit from natural law with the realisation that we now live in a world without nature, a world where social relations have become our nature and at the same time a world that in order to remain human needs to be *made* meaningful. A claim to universalism is central yet deeply problematic in modernity.[11]

[11] It must be noted that Löwith's appreciation of Marx's work grew increasingly unilateral and he eventually lost sight of the best insights of his own earlier assessment. Marx's

Positivism and immanence: Leo Strauss

Leo Strauss's coming to terms with the tradition of natural *law* starts with the argument that its adequate treatment must rather focus on the notion of natural *right*.[12] Strauss (1974: 120–64) distinguishes three main moments in the history of natural law. The first, which he traces back to Greek philosophy (mainly Plato and Aristotle), is based on an idea of natural virtue that seeks substantive answers to the question of the good life. The main aspect of this early tradition is that, although it pointed towards a teleological idea of natural virtue in immanent terms, there was still a cosmological element that ultimately underpinned it. Thus, to the extent that an idea of the individual can be said to have existed back then, it was different from the modern one as it presupposed the natural inequality of human beings whose ultimate worth depended upon either the polis's substantive ethical life or a transcendental notion of a natural cosmos. The second form of natural law thinking that Strauss identifies is Christian divine law which, best represented in the work of Aquinas, has at its core notions of duty and obedience to divine commands. Strauss rejects the idea of religious natural law on the basis that its foundation is located, outside the realm of nature, in the transcendentally unalterable and ultimately unknowable will of the divinity. Given that this is the type of natural law that tends to attract most attention in the field, Strauss is adamant in firmly separating his

political economy was dissolved into a rather crude version of religious natural law in disguise and the antagonism between the bourgeoisie and the proletariat was read thus: 'one class is the children of darkness and the other the children of light . . . the final crisis of the bourgeois world which Marx prophesies in terms of a scientific prediction is a last judgement, though pronounced by the inexorable law of the historical process' (Löwith 1964: 44).

12 While I have not followed Strauss's view on this and used 'natural law' throughout, my treatment of it as an intellectual tradition which is based on a universalistic orientation regarding questions of human knowledge and human justice is however 'Straussian' in this fundamental sense: 'all natural right doctrines claim that the fundamentals of justice are, in principle, accessible to man as man' (Strauss 1974: 28). I shall none the less prefer the idea of natural law (even when referring to Strauss's own argument on natural right) for three reasons. First, because there are wider implications to be discussed and derived from natural law's religious overtones – most saliently in relation to the presence and role of transcendental factors when understanding history in general and the modern idea of progress in particular. Secondly, because there is a liberal and even modernist bias in the idea of natural right, not least in a sense of absolute rupture with previous natural law theories, which goes against the type of analysis I am interested in pursuing: there is little point in replacing the religious bias of natural law with the liberal bias of natural right. Thirdly, because the prevalent view in the literature is to understand natural law as a generic term that captures both traditional natural law and modern natural right. I discuss further some of Strauss's views on this in Chapter 3 below.

own natural right doctrine from traditional religious doctrines. The third and last form of natural law he introduces is modern natural right. The importance we just saw that Löwith attributed to Vico in creating the basis for our modern understanding of history in terms of purely human affairs, Strauss (1952, 1988a) gives to Machiavelli and Hobbes, on the basis of a purely immanent understanding of politics, and also to Spinoza, in changing the terms of the dispute between secular reason and religion. An outlook to be elaborated fully only a century later in the writings of Locke and Rousseau, the core of the modern doctrine of natural law lies in the notion of subjective individual rights. It is only with the rise of modernity that we encounter a conception of fully 'egalitarian natural right ... [in which] ... all men are by nature free and equal. Natural freedom and natural equality are inseparable from each other' (Strauss 1974: 118). It is only in modernity that the view emerges of 'the historical process as a single process in which man becomes human without intending it' (Strauss 1989: 90).

Strauss contends that an immanent orientation to human affairs is central to natural law and therefore it neither emerges in nor is specific to modernity. My main goal in this section is thus to explicate how Strauss sees the relationships between natural law and the modern social and political sciences as they share this immanent understanding of social life. His critique of the modernist bias of contemporary social science is instructive in this context because, while Strauss seeks to recover a sense of wisdom to be found in the philosophical tradition, he accepts that modern conditions change the terms under which this is possible. Modern social sciences' rejection of natural law in the twentieth century is for Strauss also an indication of their own difficulties. With the traumatic experience of the Holocaust in mind, Strauss argues that the social sciences have fallen below the critical threshold once achieved by their natural law predecessors:

> After the experience of our generation, the burden of proof would seem to rest on those who assert rather than on those who deny that we have progressed beyond the classics. And even if it were true that we could understand the classics better than they understood themselves, we could become certain of our superiority only after understanding them exactly as they understood themselves. Otherwise we might mistake our superiority to our notion of the classics for superiority of the classics. (Strauss 2004a: 55)

To be sure, Strauss is no friend of modernity, but as we shall see below he is not interested in its outright rejection either (Pippin 1999, Rosen 2009, Tanguay 2007). His problem is with what he considers is the reductionist self-understanding of modernity as a self-positing historical period, and in tackling this problem Strauss suggests that we need to reassess the way in which we see the connections between modernity and the long-term development of Western civilisation. Modernity's current crisis is marked for Strauss by its descent into barbarism in World War II and the difficulties associated with reconstituting normative standards afterwards. Strauss (1997a: 94–100) argues that this is now most apparent in the transition from a substantive *idea* of progress that was able to orient political action to a mere *belief* in it that can be upheld or discarded at will. But while recent events made the Western crisis all too apparent, at the intellectual level these difficulties are more difficult to grasp as they come out of the West having lost sight of its constitutive normative strain, the split between 'Athens' and 'Jerusalem', 'or, to speak in a nonmetaphorical language, the Bible and Greek philosophy' (104). On the one hand, both traditions 'agree regarding the problem of justice, the difficulty created by the misery of the just and the prospering of the wicked' (106). But, on the other hand, they disagree about what the content of morality is and ought to be:

> [t]he one thing needful according to Greek philosophy is the life of autonomous understanding. The one thing needful as spoken by the Bible is the life of obedient love. The harmonizations are possible because Greek philosophy can *use* obedient love in a subservient function, and the Bible can *use* philosophy as a handmaid; but what is so used in each case rebels against such use, and therefore the conflict is really a radical one. (Strauss 1997a: 104)

The sources of this clash belong to the past; yet they remain of the highest importance because in this normative split lies 'the core, the nerve ... of the vitality of Western civilisation' (Strauss 1997a: 116). The crisis commenced as we lost sight of the fact that this was in fact a dramatic conflict, that this was still a relevant problem for us and that it could not be solved definitively. In language that evidently echoes Weber's rendition of this dilemma as a modern dilemma – no individual can be a true scientist and politician at the same time because these two activities are inspired by different and mutually competing values – Strauss also posits the problem in terms of irredeemable decisionism and tragic personal choices. It is impossible to be a philosopher and a theologian at the same time and there is no third possibility that can produce their synthesis: '[b]ut every one of us can be and ought to be either the one or the other, the philosopher open to the challenge of theology, or the theologian open to the challenge of philosophy' (117).

Below we will come back to the decisionist implications of this argument, but for the time being this matters to us in the context of

Strauss's views on the fate of twentieth-century social science. As said, he does not reject the social sciences *per se* but is very much against their current positivistic mainstream (Behnegar 2009). Social sciences' main problem is to have lost sight of the centrality of the conflict between Athens and Jerusalem as the most challenging of normative questions: 'it is this difficulty which is at the bottom of what in the social sciences is called the "value problem": that philosophy or science, however you might call it, is incapable of giving an account of its own necessity' (Strauss 1997a: 131). The problem of trying to answer these questions by purely immanent means is not particularly modern; rather, it is constitutive of intellectual work as such: '[t]he question is whether there is a pure grasp of truth as an *essential human possibility*, quite regardless of what the conditions and *actualization* of this possibility are' (Strauss 2004b: 66). The project of a purely immanent science that is devoted exclusively to the study of social life marks the point at which modern social theory and Strauss's reconstruction of natural right intersect. This is precisely the kind of intellectual task that modern social theory has been able to undertake at its most lucid moments (similar, therefore, to Löwith's depiction of Weber and Marx as philosophical sociologists).[13] Thus conceived, the social sciences surrender even the aspiration of trying to grasp the location of the normative in social relations: they have relinquished the most crucial insight that normative questions are central to understanding social life. Serious intellectual endeavours are on the contrary marked by their attempts at understanding how human beings want and ought to live their life in common. Crucially, positivism turns these shortcomings into virtues and rejoices in its inability to speak about the most fundamental normative problems:

A social science that cannot speak of tyranny with the same confidence with which medicine speaks, for example, of cancer, cannot understand social phenomena as they are. It is therefore not scientific. *Present-day social science* finds itself in this condition. If it is true that present-day social science is the

[13] If we take a restrictive view of Löwith's secularisation thesis, then Strauss's position is radically different because he rejects that Christianity is central to understanding modernity. But if we take Löwith's position to be that Greek conceptions of cyclical time and Christian eschatology exhaust the possibilities of conceiving history, then Strauss's vision of the struggle between Athens and Jerusalem is much closer to Löwith's. As I have been arguing, however, rather than questioning modernity's explicit will to break with religion, it is the constant reappearance of natural law themes and concerns that challenges the view that modernity has actually succeeded in definitively accomplishing that task. This last interrogation is something that all three writers I discuss in this chapter share and thus creates the space for a combined reading of their works without any of them losing their specificity, nor indeed having to accept their somewhat conservative implications.

inevitable result of *modern social science* and of modern philosophy, one is forced to think of the restoration of *classical social science*. (Strauss 2004a: 49, my italics)[14]

Note that here Strauss counterpoises modern or present-day social science with classical social science rather than modern social science with classical philosophy. In fact, in the introduction to *Persecution and the Art of Writing* he even describes his own project as a sociological one. Strauss (1997b: 417) refers to his interest in understanding 'esoteric' and 'exoteric' teachings in the history of philosophy as falling 'within the province of sociology of knowledge'. A particularly important chapter of this sociology of knowledge is for Strauss 'the sociology of philosophy' that could *only* emerge in societies which no longer 'took for granted the essential harmony between thought and society, or between intellectual progress and social progress' (417). While this mismatch between intellectual and social trends may have been exacerbated in modernity, there is clearly nothing particularly modern in it. Rather, it reflects the perennial situation in which intellectual work is not welcome and intellectuals are not allowed to speak their minds freely. To be sure, much has been made of Strauss's obsession with 'esoteric' or 'multilevel' writing in terms of its elitist, cultic and conservative implications (Norton 2004, Drury 1985). But a simpler methodological case can be made for Strauss seeking to avoid the modernist bias by which the freedom of speech that Western democracies seem to afford to intellectuals is mistakenly seen as the transhistorical condition of all intellectual work. In Eugene Sheppard's (2006: 54–80) convincing interpretation, this is what makes the notion of exile crucial to understanding the different levels that are at play in Strauss's work. *As an intellectual*, Strauss is interested in exile because, right from Socrates' experiences, speaking the truth has proved dangerous and scholars have had to pay with silence, emigration and indeed their own lives. *As a teacher*, the idea of exile allows Strauss to assess whether students are prepared to leave their comfort zone and endure the rigour and solitude of serious

14 Compare how similar the underlying sensibility is in relation to Hannah Arendt's (1958: 445) well-known claim that '[t]o describe the concentration camps *sine ira et studio* is not to be "objective," but to condone them; and such condoning cannot be changed by condemnation which the author may feel duty bound to add but which remains unrelated to the description itself. When I used the image of hell, I did not mean this allegorically but literally . . . I think that a description of the camps as Hell on earth is more "objective," that is, more adequate to their essence than statements of a purely sociological or psychological nature.'

intellectual work. *As a Jew*, Strauss accepts the condition of exile as one permanent feature of Jewish life (not least Strauss's own). The relativism of contemporary mass culture has closed itself against the idea that it is possible, let alone desirable, to reflect normatively on how people ought to live their lives. It is this last point that crucially marks all that is wrong with the practitioners of modern social sciences – they see their task as that of having to 'overcome' what is rather the most important of intellectual challenges:

> I have never met any scientific social scientist who apart from being dedicated to truth and integrity was not also wholeheartedly devoted to democracy. When he says that democracy is a value which is not evidently superior to the opposite value, he does not mean that he is impressed by the alternative which he rejects, or that his heart or his mind is torn between alternatives which in themselves are equally attractive. His 'ethical neutrality' is so far from being nihilism or a road to nihilism that it is no more than an alibi for thoughtlessness and vulgarity: by saying that democracy and truth are values, he says in effect that one does not have to think about the reasons why these things are good, and that he may bow as well as anyone else to the values that are respected by his society. Social science positivism fosters not so much nihilism as conformism and philistinism. (Strauss 1988a: 20)

Strauss's most systematic engagement with the connections between modern social sciences and natural law takes place via his discussion of Max Weber. Although he reads Weber as a radical contradictor of natural law (Behnegar 1997), he does not spare words and calls Weber 'the greatest social scientist of our century' (Strauss 1974: 36). He rightly sees Weber as part of the German historical school but concludes that Weber departs from the conclusions of that school 'because it had preserved natural right in an historical guise, instead of rejecting it altogether' (37). But the idea of *historical natural right* is a contradiction in terms and Strauss correctly explicates that that was not Weber's position. If Weber's project were simply just another rejection of natural law, however radical, his work would hardly deserve close scrutiny. Weber's paradigmatic importance for twentieth-century social science becomes apparent as we reflect on how he conceived 'values' and thus tried to address normative questions in modernity.

It is well known that for Weber historical materials are the subject matter of the social sciences. The selection of these materials is always directed by present concerns, which of course are also historical; this is how social scientists decide what to study. Yet Weber equally held the view that there was something transhistorical not so much in the findings of the social sciences – their empirical discoveries were bound to be superseded by future research – but in their very knowledge claims.

Weber surpassed the limits of his own explicit framework as he effectively operated with presuppositions that led him closer to the universalistic standpoints of the natural law tradition – at least in relation to the principles that govern the social sciences' methodological procedures. Although they vary hugely according to time and place, there are some 'concrete and historical value ideas' that are, however, of 'trans-historical character: the *ultimate values are as timeless as the principles of logic*. It is the recognition of timeless values that distinguishes Weber's position most significantly from historicism. Not so much historicism as a *peculiar notion* of timeless values is the basis of his rejection of natural right' (Strauss 1974: 39, my italics).

Strauss's argument is that no serious intellectual endeavour is meaningful or even possible without some natural law presuppositions – even if they are unreflectively reintroduced, as Strauss believes they are in Weber. No absolute separation between (empirical) social science and (normative) natural law is actually possible. Strauss accepts that in modernity all claims to ultimate values are problematic, although he does not concede that ultimate values are, in the last instance, unknowable or irrational. He explicates that Weber's rupture with the German historical school is based on the latter's pseudo-natural law thinking under the guise of cultural relativism and, more dramatically, extreme nationalism (see Chapter 7). But Strauss then discovers an internal ambivalence in Weber's thinking because the central premise on which his empirical research is predicated – the historicity of knowledge – is itself a statement that seeks transhistorical validity. Weber's distance from both historicist relativism and natural law metaphysics obtains from his ontological belief that, although ultimate values do exist, they are part of an irrational realm about which no true knowledge can ever be achieved. Weber's preference for an ethically neutral social science ascertains 'that there cannot be any genuine knowledge of the Ought' (Strauss 1974: 41) and that values pose conflicts that 'cannot be resolved by human reason' (74). The conclusion is that Weber was unable to come up with a satisfactory solution to the conundrum arising from a historicist understanding of social research as guided by the concerns of the present, a variant of ontological irrationalism in relation to the existence of ultimate values, and a methodological framework whose rules and procedures seek to stand before the tribunal of different historical periods and cultures. An incisive child of modern times, Weber paid the heavy price that is put on those who strive for consistency within modernity's attempts at self-foundation. Weber, says Strauss:

> [w]as inclined to believe that twentieth-century man has eaten of the fruit of the tree of knowledge, or can be free from delusions which blinded all earlier men: we see the situation of man without delusions; we are disenchanted. But under

the influence of historicism, he became doubtful whether one can speak of the situation of man as man or, if one can, whether this situation is not seen differently in different ages in such a manner that, in principle, the view of any age is as legitimate or as illegitimate as that of any other. He wondered, therefore, whether what appeared to be the situation of man as man was more than the situation of present-day man, or 'the inescapable datum of our historical situation'. Hence what originally appeared as freedom from delusions presented itself eventually as hardly more than the questionable premise of our age as an attitude that will be superseded, in due course, by an attitude that will be in conformity with the next epoch ... What claims to be freedom from delusions is as much and as little delusion as the faiths which prevailed in the past and which may prevail in the future. (Strauss 1974: 73)

The definitive resolution of this aporia cannot be worked out within Weber's framework, Strauss contends. Rather, it requires Strauss's own idea of natural *right* that we introduced above – the discovery of those fundamental principles that are rationally 'accessible to man as man'. Weber's insufficient understanding of how much his social science belongs to the wider intellectual tradition of natural law prevents him from arriving at a solution which, although it was not actually far from his standpoint, was none the less unacceptable to him. To the extent that '[s]ocial science is human knowledge of human life' or, to put it differently, once we accept that the social sciences' 'this-worldly understanding of human life, is evidently legitimate' – both statements that Weber would have accepted – there is then little ground for separating modern social science from natural law (Strauss 1974: 71). But the idea that modern social science and natural law belong to the same intellectual tradition is something that Weber rejected. The grounds on which Weber 'refused to grant that premise' is that, for him, 'science or philosophy rests, in the last analysis, not on evident premises that are at the disposal of man as man but on faith' (71). Weber's problem is that he cannot have it both ways: either he accepts modern social sciences' claim to valid knowledge as legitimate, in which case value-decisions can be apprehended as rationally as questions in any other area of society, and hence his own contribution to the social sciences is closer to natural law than he would otherwise admit; or else he rejects all possible connections with natural law and accepts that his own scientific work is based on irrational faith, in which case nothing of what Weber actually achieved scientifically remains meaningful for the study of human affairs – both methodologically and substantively. In rejecting any possible connection between his sociology and natural law, Weber renders his lifetime's work meaningless.

But Strauss sees through this apparent contradiction and takes Weber's idea of modern social science as the highest point of an intellectual trend that, although it has sought to undermine the natural law tradition, may have become one of its main vehicles in modernity. In his attempt at simultaneously rejecting traditional natural law and new cultural relativism (dogmatic metaphysics and naive positivism), Weber was carrying out precisely the kind of intellectual endeavour that he thought was no longer viable. The more consistent Weber was in building up his scientific framework upon historicist premises, the more he fell victim to his own success: the transhistorical validity of his cognitive enterprise was discarded in principle but imposed itself in its actual practice. Strauss read Weber as the most sophisticated attempt at developing a 'presuppositionless' science of the social that, in order to become fully established, required a universalistic orientation even in spite of itself. Weber was unable to reconcile his scepticism towards universalism on the basis of his diagnostic of the differentiation of value spheres and the need to uphold the universalistic foundations that his own sociology needed to be at all meaningful.

Beyond Weber, Strauss's conclusion is that, rather than a thorough rejection of the tradition of natural law, the project of the modern social sciences is one that has a much deeper connection with it; the modern social sciences have natural law elements built into them *from their very inception*. It is not only the straightforward thesis of sociology having broken away from natural law that Strauss rejects. It is the notion that sociology's intellectual value depends upon its deep yet also problematic connections with the natural law tradition that is particularly interesting, though unsettling, for our more conventional self-understandings in contemporary social sciences and social theory. Their intellectual worth, we can now say echoing Strauss, lies in whether they can become aware of their debt to the universalistic core of the natural law tradition, and then make it relevant for modern times in order to avoid the risk of becoming *just* another type of natural law. The salience of social and political thought in modern times seems to lie in how deeply it is able to grasp the old questions of the tradition of natural law, and then translate them into the social scientific formats that have become acceptable for us in the present.

Gnosticism and the problem of the normative: Eric Voegelin

Eric Voegelin locates universalism at the centre of his understanding of natural law but, in so doing, he rejects the view that this universalistic core is a particularly Western idea. He conceives universalism as an original development of early Eastern empires that entered into the

'Western' intellectual orbit only by 500 BC (Voegelin 2000b: 382). What makes universalism truly 'universal' to Voegelin is the fact that, as an intellectual orientation, it developed independently in different socio-cultural and historical contexts, geared as it was towards the creation of a sense of belonging that went beyond any group's definition of sameness. As he built on Karl Jaspers's idea of the axial age, Voegelin's preferred notion was that of an ecumenic age, 'a period in the history of mankind that roughly extends from the rise of the Persian Empire to the fall of the Roman empire' (167). The main feature of this ecumenic age was the tensional relationships between the political and military power of these early imperial formations, which sooner or later had to come to terms with their own territorial limitations and eventual decline, and the worldviews from which they drew legitimacy, whose foundational ontologies were firmly universalistic:

> The builders of empires and the founders of religions in the age we have called the Ecumenic Age were indeed concerned with the society of all mankind that had become visible beyond the confines of the former concrete societies; they were concerned with the order of a human mass that had been drawn into the vortex of pragmatic events; and in the symbolism of an ecumenic order in the making they both met. (Voegelin 2000b: 197)

As an institutional power but above all as the bearer of a quest for transcendental meaning, religion plays the most important role during the ecumenic age. But in this first religious universalism we encounter a notion of humanity that receives rather than produces its own sense of universality. How far this humanity extends, what its main features are and, above all, how it will deal with the inconsistencies that are bound to emerge, are issues that all point to a passive notion of humanity:

> Universal mankind is not a society existing in the world, but a symbol that indicates man's consciousness of participating, in his earthly existence, in the mystery of reality that moves towards its transfiguration. Universal mankind is an eschatological index. (Voegelin 2000b: 376)

The modern idea of universalism will to some extent remain an ideal projection if compared to the actual conditions of socio-political life. But, as we will see in the rest of this book, with the rise of modernity a more active sense of humanity begins to emerge: human beings actively creating universalistic ideas, working through their internal contradictions and focusing more on proceduralism than substantive content. The slow but marked crisis of religion that is experienced as the decline of the transcendental is characterised by a concomitant rise of 'gnosticism' – a process that culminates, in modernity, with a wholly restrictive secular worldview.

But before we address the question of Gnosticism, we still need to discuss Voegelin's views on the development of the Western tradition of natural law. Similarly to Strauss, Voegelin distinguishes between three major periods in Western philosophy, the climactic achievements of particular authors marking the specific nature of the social and political crises of their respective epochs. The first period centres on the works of Plato and Aristotle as they reflected on the Hellenic crisis; the second one focuses on Augustine and refers to the crisis of Rome and rise of Christianity, and the third and final period, best represented by Hegel, marks the commencement of the Western contemporary crisis (Voegelin 2000a: 89). Crucially, what matters to Voegelin are the limits and dangers that are involved in thinking about human affairs by claiming that immanence is all that there is to know about human beings. And although Voegelin is actually much more of a historian of ideas than Löwith and Strauss, his work contrasts with theirs because Voegelin is not primarily interested in reassessing or indeed correcting the ways in which the moderns (mis)represent their own philosophical tradition. His most pressing concern is instead explicitly normative: trying to overcome the ontological reduction by which the moderns in particular have come to believe that human life can be adequately conceptualised as devoid of any sense of transcendence.[15] Though not particularly modern, an outright rejection of the transcendental has become one of modernity's most dogmatic prejudices: 'if we wish to master the past in the sense of mastering the present, we are confronted with the task of clearing out all the ideological junk in order to make the *conditio humana* visible once again' (Voegelin 1999: 72). The tasks of modern social theory are inadequately understood, indeed they misrepresent themselves, because they do not consider the transcendental as a fundamental aspect of what is involved in human experience. Modern positivism arose out of the decline of the Hegelian system and has become the definitive expression of the modern worldview in which

[15] To be sure, Voegelin's massive work as historian of ideas – his five volumes on *Order and History* and eight volumes on *History of Political Ideas* – is modern in terms of the empirical and critical standards with which it is pursued. However religiously inspired his normative agenda may be, there is no space in his work for mystical experiences or methodological theologism: '[i]t takes time . . . to acquire the empirical knowledge that inevitably lies at the basis of an understanding of the historical process, and still more time to penetrate the accumulated materials analytically . . . today, fifteen centuries after Augustine, even though the ecumenic horizon has become global and the temporal horizon has expanded into unexpected depths, *the empirical knowledge of the process is still so incomplete that every day brings surprises in the form of new archaeological discoveries, while the experiential penetration of the materials is badly lagging behind*' (Voegelin 2000b: 404–5, my italics).

'the consciousness of principles is lost' (Voegelin 2000a: 90). Several different strands composed the heyday of modern positivism in the half century between 1870 and 1920. They included the Comtean laws of humanity, Marxist materialism and Weberian sociology, and in Voegelin's view these different schools of thought shared the idea that a fully fledged understanding of modern social life was only possible because they refused to make any reference to transcendental principles of human existence. As a system, positivism believes in the inherent virtue of the natural sciences, subordinates theoretical relevance to methodological consistency and reunites huge masses of otherwise unconnected empirical information under defective theoretical principles (90–5).

Similarly to Strauss's rendition above, Voegelin explicates further his critique of positivism through a discussion of Max Weber, who is also read as a positivist in spite of himself. But because the role that Strauss and Voegelin assign to the transcendental in understanding human life points in opposite directions, I none the less think it is important to examine Voegelin's engagement with Weber. Voegelin contends that Weber is the last positivist because he took positivism to its logical conclusion and also because the intellectual tools that may have been needed to overcome its limits, a study of the classical tradition that was not contaminated by a modernist bias, had been mostly forgotten by Weber's time. Also similarly to Strauss's argument, Voegelin contends that Weber was never fully able to make the substantive results of his research, which point beyond positivism, compatible with his own restrictive methodological proposals, which may have remained fully embedded in the positivistic mainstream of that time. Thus, for instance, Voegelin accuses Weber of being committed to a positivistic account of history similar to Comte's law of three stages in which history is teleologically guided by systematic increments in instrumental rationality. This teleology then translated into Weber's methodological preference for ideal types and into his substantive emphasis on the modern polytheism of values (Voegelin 2000a: 104–5).

But a key aspect of Voegelin's reading of Weber is his contention that the sociologist did not understand how far his selection of research areas was neither a result of idiosyncratic decisions nor dependent on his particular socio-historical context. Rather, it reflected a commitment to the tradition of natural law: antiquity and Christianity exercised pressures on Weber's decision to focus on the role of different religious ethics in economic behaviour (Voegelin 2000a: 101). Voegelin explicates thus the fact that Weber's sociology never fully succumbed to positivism; it is its connection with the natural law tradition that led Weber to choose issues that encouraged him to reflect on the transcendental. Weber's comparative studies of world religions are treated as an 'impressive performance' whose most relevant insights have not been adequately captured by commentators and were indeed not realised by Weber himself. What is ultimately missing in Weber's monumental sociology of religion is a subtler conception of the role that natural law actually plays in the project:

> [i]t has perhaps not been sufficiently observed that the series of these studies receives its general tone through a significant omission, that is, of pre-Reformation Christianity. The reason for the omission seems to be obvious. *One can hardly engage in a serious study of medieval Christianity without discovering among its 'values' the belief in a rational science of human and social order and especially of natural law.* Moreover, this science was not simply elaborated as a belief, but it was actually elaborated as a work of reason ... The horizon of Weber's social science was immense; all the more does his caution in coming too close to its decisive center reveal his positivistic limitations. (Voegelin 2000a: 103, my italics)[16]

Voegelin translates Strauss's charge of irrationalism at the level of ultimate values into the problem of defining values as fundamentally demonic; Weber misunderstood what values actually are and how they need to be theorised (Voegelin 2000a: 99). Weber's idea of value-free social science is the only consistent modern option when seeking to study social life because it is based on a restrictive understanding of values: 'the exclusion of the *scientia prima* from the realm of reason is not an increase but a decrease of rationalism' (105). But Weber could not have really meant that all values have the same dignity and Voegelin interprets Weber's elitism as a Nietzschean 'sensitiveness for excellence' that worked as a normative inspiration for the passionate scientist and the charismatic political leader. Weber was, however, unable to explicate these choices because he compulsively 'observed the positivistic taboo on metaphysics' (104). But as soon as this taboo is lifted and we allow ourselves to think about values as a legitimate object of intellectual enquiry a different picture emerges: values are located *in between* the immanent and the transcendental aspects of human life. Values are immanent because they reflect what human beings actually strive for but they are also transcendental because they place limits on what human beings can make of their own lives and institutions. An insight of this kind would have been open to Weber only 'on the level of a philosophical anthropology' but that was a task from which Weber just

[16] See Chapter 7 for further discussion on the role Weber gives to natural law principles in legal developments and legal reasoning.

'shied away' (100). Instead of Weberian value judgements, natural law elaborates, 'empirically and critically', on the position of the transcendental *vis-à-vis* human nature:

> Only when ontology as a science was lost, and when consequently ethics and politics could no longer be understood as sciences of the order in which human nature reaches its maximal actualization, was it possible for this realm to become suspect as a field of subjective, uncritical opinion. (Voegelin 2000a: 96)

The idea of values as wholly irrational or demonic is only acceptable because we have already rejected all notions of the transcendental when reflecting on the location of the normative in social life.

What makes positivism so problematic, and what the internal aporias of Weber's sociology make so dramatically apparent, is the fact that positivism fundamentally distorts our comprehension of human knowledge and reality. Our notions of what constitutes appropriate knowledge of human affairs change because 'the meaning of science as a truthful account of the structure of reality, as the theoretical orientation of man in his world, and as the great instrument for man's understanding of his own position in the universe is lost' (Voegelin 2000a: 91). In submitting what adequate knowledge is to the positivistic tyranny of the methods, there are aspects of human experience that become completely lost from sight. The more positivism advances, the less we are able to even give a name to that realm of human life which we ought to be studying: '[i]f I have lost certain sectors of reality from my range of experience, I will also be lacking the language for appropriately characterizing them. That means that parallel to the loss of reality … there is always the phenomenon of illiteracy' (Voegelin 1999: 90). Positivism is then the latest and most advanced expression of a reductionist account of social life that has no vocabulary to address normative questions. Because it has no terms left with which to reflect on the transcendental, modern social science has grown unable to conceptualise the location of the normative in social life.

Yet Voegelin's characterisation of the current state of social and political sciences is not altogether pessimistic. By the 1920s, and following his thesis on the connections between social crises and the development of new forms of intellectual enquiry, Voegelin argues that more philosophically aware forms of knowledge began to develop. He does not dwell long on these improvements but he none the less mentions such writers as Edmund Husserl, Ernst Cassirer and Karl Jaspers as intellectuals whose work very much points in the right direction as they offer 'important steps towards the restoration of theoretical relevance' (Voegelin 2000a: 96; 2000b 47–9). Husserl's (1970) phenomenology and influential critique of modern science, Cassirer's (1977) philosophical anthropology and theses on symbolisation processes and Jaspers's (2011) studies on the axial age are of importance because of their contribution to curbing positivism's excess and reinstating the normative as a legitimate domain of modern intellectual enquiry. Voegelin then sees his own *The New Science of Politics*, which was first published in 1952, as belonging to the same tradition. Indeed, what is new in Voegelin's *New Science* is the need to go back to the lost vocabulary of the normative. Its novelty, which 'will rather appear as a restoration', should allow us to reconnect our understanding of politics with substantive normative questions and thus help overcome the still prevalent positivistic reductionism (Voegelin 2000a: 88). Voegelin's new science seeks to retrieve our ability to reflect upon the transcendental aspects of human life and experience as immanent parts of social life. But his new science is also new because it is just impossible to go back to the same old contents when historical conditions have of course changed so greatly.

The most radical challenge that Voegelin poses to modern social science is therefore the need to accept that normative problems are the key to reflecting meaningfully about human life in society; they are central to understanding the location of the normative in social life. But as we accept this we also have to accept that thinking the normative is now only viable in strictly immanent terms; differently put, we need to think the transcendental beyond faith and the kind of religious experiences that in modernity have proved not to be universally available. Voegelin argues that both 'reason' and 'spirit' are constitutive elements of who we are as human beings (Voegelin 2000a: 215–17, 222–30). As we take them together, a vision emerges in which 'man experiences himself as a being who does not exist from himself. He exists in an already given world. This world itself exists by reason of a mystery, and the name for the mystery ... is referred to as "God"' (Voegelin 1999: 86). To be sure, the preference for a God with capital G reflects Voegelin's personal commitments but the insight into the importance of the transcendental can be reapproached without having recourse to his religious ideas. I rather suggest that we understand it as a more general focus on the transcendental dimension of human life that effectively points to the transcendental because we belong in a cosmos that precedes us and is universally experienced as an unsolvable problem.[17] Furthermore, in an argument that again highlights the centrality of the tradition of natural law, Voegelin does not entrust any particular church with having the monopoly on the right doctrines on the transcendental:

[17] In the apt words of a commentator, Voegelin's argument can be rendered as seeking to grasp the 'essential human capacity of participating in the timeless' (Purcell 1999: 30).

Because the church took over the worldly idea of order from classic and Stoic philosophy, this became a component of Christian theology, as for example in the *Summa theologiae* of Thomas. This had *disastrous consequences* for the later development of natural law, for, first of all, it became, as it were, Christian natural law and the church took on the role of guardian of natural law. However, *it is nowhere written that in the various historical situations church personnel are particularly suitable guardians of the natural law* ... there is a very considerable stock of knowledge of order coming from philosophy that is denatured and deformed in the theological field. (Voegelin 1999: 208, my italics)[18]

At stake here there is an idea of normativity as a key component of what we take the social world to be and an immanent idea of social order that in order to be conceptualised requires a meaningful representation of its internal transcendence. Indeed, even though they do not have to be read in a fully secular language, Voegelin's own formulations are not alien to this secular reading. Universalism is a key component here, as losing sight of the transcendental is losing part of our ability to conduct ourselves in our particular society, on the one hand, and in the whole society of humankind, on the other:

[t]he nature of man achieves fulfillment in the order of society and has to determine its order. But this insight is restricted, because the order only occurs within a limited community, so that the interests of the limited community in history enter into an amalgam with the general problematic order at the level of humanity. And the particular interests of a society can thus appear in the cloak of more universal formulations of humanity – and thereby again denature and deform humanity in general. (Voegelin 1999: 209)

I find this formulation consequential because it connects what we understand by social relations with what we take human nature to be. Voegelin understands representation precisely as the articulation of images of the human and society. The term moreover asserts a key additional move: while social order always takes place within restricted communities, the representation of that social order requires us to go beyond parochialisms and reach out to an idea of humanity in general. The transcendental is in this context the projection of the immanent, concrete social life, on to the transcendental, ideal images of the human that go beyond what takes place in actually existing communities in order to develop a sense of universal humanity. But the ultimate implications of Voegelin's idea of the transcendental only become

18 In fact, it has been rightly pointed out that for Voegelin Christianity is partly responsible for the rise of modern gnosticism. In its devaluation of philosophy in order to assert revelation, through the 'doctrinalisation' of its original teachings and in its exaggerated 'apocalypticism', Christianity becomes 'particularly vulnerable' to gnosticism. The end result is that '[b]elievers believe at the cost of their humanity' (Douglass 1976: 34–9).

apparent as we explicate what he understands by gnosticism, a social and intellectual programme whose core lies precisely in its reduction of the transcendental dimension of our human experiences:

> Gnostic speculation overcame the uncertainty of faith by receding from transcendence and *endowing man and his intramundane range of action with the meaning of eschatological fulfillment* ... The spiritual strength of the soul ... could now be diverted into the more appealing, more tangible, and, above all, so much easier creation of the terrestrial paradise ... the miracle was worked successively through the literary and artistic achievement that secured the immortality of fame for the humanistic intellectual, through the discipline and economic success that certified salvation to the Puritan saint, through the civilizational contributions of the liberals and Progressives, and, finally, through the revolutionary action that will establish the Communist or some other Gnostic millennium. *Gnosticism, thus, most effectively released human forces for the building of a civilization because on their fervent application to intramundane activity was put the premium of salvation.* (Voegelin 2000a: 193–4, my italics)[19]

Gnosticism is then the way in which Voegelin deals with the rejection of the transcendental as a relevant domain of human life. In modernity, positivism is its most salient intellectual expression (as we just saw), while totalitarian regimes became in the twentieth century its most dramatic political manifestation.[20] Voegelin (2000a: 192, 196) speaks repeatedly about the ninth century as the time in which Gnosticism began to emerge, but its fully fledged consequences only became apparent at some point between the mid-seventeenth and early nineteenth centuries – or, as he put it, in the period that goes 'from humanism to enlightenment' (185). The key transitional role that we have seen Löwith attribute to Vico and Strauss to Hobbes, Machiavelli and Spinoza in laying out the foundations of the modern social sciences, Voegelin also gives to Hobbes. It is fear of uncertainty that leads to the wholly understandable yet fallacious idea that human life can be apprehended as exclusively immanent (189). Hobbes's fundamental innovation comes together with his fundamental shortcoming because he

[19] This analysis is built on Löwith's secularisation thesis, to which Voegelin refers approvingly a few pages before this last passage (Voegelin 2000a: 185).

[20] This is not the space to offer an account of what Voegelin understands by totalitarianism – a theme to which he devoted a lecture course in 1964 in Munich and which then became his most famous book: *Hitler and the Germans* (Voegelin 1999). Voegelin's main thesis there is the connection between totalitarianism and exclusively immanent accounts of human life and social relations. The key problem in totalitarian regimes is that they offered an idea of humanity without limits, with no sense of the transcendental: 'there is no point, as is still so often done, in accusing Hitler of inhumanity; it was absolute humanity in human form, only a most remarkably disordered, diseased humanity' (Voegelin 1999: 108, see also Porter 2002).

> [s]implified the structure of politics by throwing out anthropological and soteriological truth ... things, to be sure, would be so much simpler without philosophy and Christianity. But how can one dispose of them without abolishing the experiences of transcendence that belong to the nature of man? (Voegelin 2000a: 218–19)

Hobbes's attempt at a solution only makes matters worse, because he asked man to be god and create a kind of being who would have no need of transcendental experiences. Hobbes, therefore, 'improved on the man of God's creation by creating a man without such experiences. At this point, however, we are entering the higher regions of the gnostic dream world' (219).[21] Without being essentially modern, gnosticism is how Voegelin describes the most fundamental traits of modern society: we 'recognize the essence of modernity as the growth of Gnosticism' (190). What is specifically modern is the fact that gnosticism is now equated with modern common sense; it has become the unquestioned way of considering the triumph of unrestricted immanence over transcendence. At the same time, gnosticism is particularly Western in the sense that only Western modernity stopped believing in the transcendental notion of universalism. The gnostic reduction passes as universal the idea that there is no need for the transcendental to understand social life, whereas in fact it is precisely the intuition of the transcendental that has actually proved closer to universalism. Gnosticism is in this sense another expression of Western or Eurocentrism.

But Voegelin's account is never unqualifiedly pessimistic and in fact he argues that however strong it may appear, '[g]nosticism, whether ancient or modern, is at a dead end' (Voegelin 2000b: 74). Gnosticism is self-defeating because its ignores the fact that the role of the transcendental in social life cannot continue *ad infinitum*: '[g]nostic politics is self-defeating in the sense that measures that are intended to establish peace increase the disturbances that will lead to war' (Voegelin 2000a: 227). Without a normative programme to offer, Voegelin is, however, adamant that we should not surrender to the reductionism that is central to gnosticism, either intellectually or politically. It is possibly his long-term view in the understanding of human affairs from which this *lack of pessimism* ultimately draws support. This is how Voegelin concludes his volume on *The Ecumenic Age*:

> If one realizes that we are still grappling today, and still inconclusively, with the problems set by the differentiations of consciousness in the Ecumenic Age, one

[21] See Chapter 4 for my interpretation of Hobbes's sublation of human nature with the rise of Leviathan.

may feel that nothing much has happened during the last 2,500 years. While it would be wrong to translate this sentiment into the doctrinaire conclusion that there is nothing new under the sun, the feeling has its importance as a safeguard against the human weakness of elevating one's own present into the purpose of history. (Voegelin 2000b: 405)

Closing remarks

This chapter explored the relationships between natural law and social theory from the point of view of three writers who are highly critical of the latter because of its neglect of the former. The selection of Löwith, Strauss and Voegelin is unconventional in the context of contemporary social theory (though not in contemporary political theory) and, because of their own shortcomings and limitations, their selection is potentially misleading for the project of making social theory's claim to universalism more contemporary. But a key insight that transpires from all three is that our modern disciplines, when successful in the task they explicitly set for themselves, not only end up thinking in universalistic terms but also try to answer precisely the type of philosophical or existential questions that they expect to have left behind.

In the case of Löwith, modern social theory's value depends upon its always inconsistent reliance on natural law. Arguably against Löwith's self-interpretation, it seems to me that the strongest version of his thesis is not that of questioning social theory's attempt at breaking free from religious influences but that we ought to revisit continuously how successful these attempts have actually been. And even though this is an insight that was lost in his later writings, there is a fundamental contribution in his reading of Weber and Marx as philosophical sociologists who were concerned with how universal human questions are felt and develop under modern capitalistic conditions. Strauss's project is that of a fully immanent attempt at understanding social life. He did not have much time for modern social science and found it arrogant as well as ignorant, myopic as well as dull. Even Weber, the greatest social scientist of the past century, was unable to recognise and overcome the limitations of the positivistic framework within which he was working. And yet Strauss's notion that rational knowledge about society implies both explanatory as well as normative statements, that these statements were to be justified by immanent means and immanent means alone, and, ultimately, that the intellectual problems we now face are constitutive of the human condition, are all insights that help us in our reassessment. Voegelin shares their dissatisfaction with positivism and the current state of affairs in the social sciences. But in contradistinction to Strauss and

Löwith he places more emphasis in the centrality of the transcendental as a constitutive domain of our experience as human beings; he reflects more explicitly on the location of the normative in social life. In so far as it relies on religious experiences, his argument cannot be accepted without much re-elaboration. But I have tried to show that Voegelin's reference to the transcendental does not imply beliefs that are irrational, mystical or salvational. Rather it highlights the real struggle to come to terms with what it is that makes human beings members of the same species *within* our particular socio-historical contexts and *beyond* our shared physical constitution. An idea of humanity, he argues, is simultaneously immanent and transcendental; it is lived in the particular but can only be duly articulated as universal.

The strategic of goal of this chapter in the wider context of this book was to demonstrate that a systematic neglect of natural law is damaging for the development of modern social theory. Rather than exploring the extent to which social theory has actually been able to break free from natural law, I suggest that such an attempt may never be completed. It is wrong to keep running away from a serious engagement with natural law under the questionable premise that it is old fashioned and dogmatic metaphysics. But to interpret the criticisms we have advanced here as the last word on how to understand social theory's debt to natural law is equally problematic; we rather have to look directly at their interrelationships with all their real problems, complications and indeed highly ambivalent results. We now turn directly to modern natural law (Part II) and classical social theory (Part III).

Part II

Natural law

3 Natural law and the question of universalism

The historical trajectory, philosophical foundations and variety of meanings of natural law are not issues commonly discussed in contemporary social theory. This chapter offers a review of different conceptions of natural law which, although it will not be exhaustive, can help us in this book's reconceptualisation of the role of natural law in the development of social theory. This revision will be informed by a variety of subject areas: political theory, legal theory, socio-legal studies, the history of ideas and of moral philosophy as well as social theory itself.

My central proposition in this chapter is that universalism is natural law's central and most enduring feature. The intellectual core of the natural law tradition lies in its universalistic orientation and the first part of the chapter is directly devoted to demonstrating that a universalistic orientation underwrites the enormous variation to be found within natural law theory. As we are interested in how this universalistic orientation will translate into modern social theory, we will also be assessing the ways in which natural law universalism responds to some of the most common charges that have been raised against it: its 'Western' origins and its potential inability to deal with normative conflict and socio-cultural variation. I will concentrate on the secular variant of natural law thinking but some mention of its religious roots will also be made as we explore whether the connections between universalism and particularism are conceived as instantiations of natural, cosmological or religious forces that have the ability to intervene in human affairs or, rather, they are understood in strictly immanent terms as human actions that sediment as social and cultural structures. We have already seen, and will encounter again below, that the distinction between transcendental and immanent strategies is central for modern social theory's rendition of previous natural law concerns. The second section of this chapter focuses on the Enlightenment's highly ambivalent relationship with natural law and revisits some of their interconnections. It reassesses the somewhat conventional thesis that the Enlightenment conceived itself as playing a pivotal role in the decline of traditional natural law, a process which was then of critical importance for the eventual rise of modern natural law and subsequently social theory. I will, however, argue that we need to concentrate on the period of the early Enlightenment in the second part of the seventeenth century in order to make sense of the transition from traditional to modern natural law (an insight that is then substantiated in the next chapter). Continuities as well as discontinuities will then be considered: while both types of natural law acknowledge the ubiquity of social change, it is only with the Enlightenment that a modernist imagination emerges in which historical change is explicated through the separation of neatly discrete periods. Similarly, the issue of how immanent intellectual strategies gained increasing salience will be referred back to the importance that the modern sciences started to achieve at the time.

The centrality of universalism

I define natural law as a general framework that centres on the ways in which peoples have imagined, and sought to foster, a sense of common human identity and belonging that includes all human beings. Underwriting all internal discrepancies, universalism remains natural law's defining feature – universalism constitutes the core of the tradition of natural law in its different versions and throughout history.

Defined as 'a system of laws' which, since the time of 'Justinian's lawbooks', has had a 'claim to universal validity', Alessandro P. d'Entrèves (1970: 23) suggests that 'the real significance of natural law must be sought in its function rather than in the doctrine itself' (35). The sociological relevance of this functional argument is further explicated as we see natural law as 'one of the most creative forces' of Western thought which, through such twentieth-century innovations as the universal declaration of human rights and the idea of crimes against humanity, can duly claim 'to have served the cause of humanity well' (18). Whether it takes the form of descriptive/explanatory statements on the historical development of a certain set of political or legal institutions, or of anthropological/normative claims about what are the most stable components of atemporal human nature, the fact remains that natural law is inseparable from a universalistic orientation: '[n]atural law theorists would never have admitted that law is merely the expression of the standards of a particular group or society. They believed in absolute values, and they conceived of law as a means to achieve them' (79).

More recently, and in a wholly different context, Marxist legal theorist Costas Douzinas offers a 'negative' definition of natural law. He also pursues a functional reflection on natural law through the role it has performed in the history of social and political thought: '[n]o political philosophy or version of natural law was worthy of its name, if it was not grounded on universal principles or did not aim at universal ends' (Douzinas 2000: 67). The fact that highly conservative versions of natural law have been salient during the twentieth century is not alien to Douzinas but, quite rightly, he challenges the view that natural law is always and necessarily conservative. Rather, he argues that it is precisely its universalistic claim that makes *the tradition* of natural law normatively relevant for critical social theory. In the footsteps of Ernst Bloch, then, the argument is made that

> Natural law represents a constant in the history of ideas, namely the struggle for human dignity in freedom against the infamies, degradations, and humiliations visited on people by established powers, institutions and laws ... Its tradition unites critics and dissidents more than any other philosophy and political program. (Douzinas 2000: 15)

Although it remains mostly negative, the claim that natural law is a constant in the history of ideas is itself a conventional way of explicating its connections with the universalistic orientation of different intellectual traditions.[1] Natural law's universalistic orientation is now fully ingrained in our way of understanding the world and of making judgements about what we may want the world to be: '[t]he law as reason that begets the world pushes toward an, admittedly abstract, fraternity of all humankind. In this latter aspect, Stoic natural law remains one of the most honourable chapters in the history of ideas' (Douzinas 2000: 53).[2] Analytically as well as historically, the point to emphasise here is that ideas of natural law keep coming back because of their universalistic orientation – there is something universal in the need to think about human beings as members of the same human species.

A similar view is expressed in modern moral philosophy. J. B. Schneewind (1998: 17) opens his reconstruction of this tradition by defining natural law as '[t]he belief that human action should be guided by natural laws that apply to all people, no matter what their race, sex, location or religion'. Or, as he concentrates on the natural law elements of modern social and

[1] A much more problematic formulation of the same argument is the claim about the eternal recurrence of natural law: 'the idea of natural law is immortal ... there is manifestly something invincible and eternal about that body of spiritual and moral ideas which for thousands of years has been called natural law and is once more coming back into honour' (Rommen 1998: 118–19).

[2] Jürgen Habermas (2010: 469–70) has recently argued that the idea of *human dignity*, whose history goes back to Roman and Christian notions of the intrinsic value of the human person, can work as 'the "portal" through which the egalitarian and universalistic substance of morality is imported into law'. On Habermas's views on natural law, see Chapter 1 above.

political thought, Norberto Bobbio (1993: 1) argues that, from 'Hobbes (who is its fountainhead) to Hegel ... all the major political philosophers of the modern age employ this model' of natural law. In the next two chapters I will be explicitly taking up the task of disentangling the natural law elements to be found in Hobbes, Rousseau, Kant and Hegel, but for now the question of universalism is still about defining what makes it possible to reconcile natural law's internal intellectual diversity with its treatment as a single tradition:

> Cutting through all the cautious qualifications and scholarly hesitations to which the sheer variety of natural law theories inevitably gives rise ... the central intuition of the natural law tradition ... [is] that human beings through the diligent use of their reason do have access to norms of justice that are in some profound sense natural and universal rather than conventional and provincial ... *natural law was the principal carrier in the Western intellectual tradition of universalist or 'species-centered' as opposed to 'ethnos-centered' moral aspiration.* (Oakley 2005: 18–19, my italics)

Indeed, convergent definitions are found in a varied array of twentieth-century writers. We have already mentioned Marxist philosopher Ernst Bloch, who connected questions of natural law with those of a search for human dignity.[3] German legal theorist Hans Kelsen,[4] historians of ideas Anthony Pagden[5] and Richard Tuck,[6] and natural law theorist John Finnis,[7] have all offered similar accounts about the centrality of universalism for natural law.

The idea of universalism as a meaningful intellectual orientation that lies at the centre of the natural law tradition thus co-emerged with the

3 As 'the Greek law of the community ... became too restricted; a universal law, common to all Greeks, had already begun to develop before the time of Alexander (parallel to the Roman *jus gentium*). From this there arose an extremely broad, and so extremely universal, theory of law as a theory of right' (Bloch 1996: 14).

4 'The natural-law doctrine undertakes to supply a definitive solution to the eternal problem of justice, to answer the question as to what is right and wrong in the mutual relations of men' (Kelsen 1949: 481).

5 From Aristotle and Aquinas to modern natural law theorists, 'the project was to create a political philosophy which could be fully accountable in terms of a set of rationally conceived, and thus universally acceptable, first principles' (Pagden 1987: 4).

6 To Tuck, the modern school of natural law theorists of the seventeenth century attempted 'a radically simplified and "minimalist" universal morality ... [in which] self-preservation was a paramount principle and the basis for whatever universal morality there was' (Tuck 1999: 5).

7 Finnis (1980: 23) defines natural law as comprising the following three elements: '(i) a set of basic practical principles which indicate the basic forms of human flourishing as goods to be pursued and realized, and which in one way or another are used by everyone who considers what to do, however unsound his conclusions; (ii) a set of methodological requirements of practical reasonableness ... which distinguish sound from unsound practical thinking ... [and] (iii) a set of general moral standards'.

historical fact of the existence of different conceptions of natural law. Differently put, there is no contradiction between the *belief* that there is such a thing as a single human species which is governed by a universal set of laws that are valid irrespective of place, time or culture, and *the historical realisation* that peoples think and act in hugely different ways depending on time, place and culture – not least, as the same kind of diversity is itself expressed in natural law's internal variation. There is something more fundamental at stake here than affirming that universalism and particularism are intertwined and presuppose one another. I should like to argue that the universalistic orientation of natural law, which is usually presupposed as a matter of principle, implies its factual recognition as highly varied and heterogeneous. This is not a question about particular natural law doctrines being assessed as 'progressive' or 'conservative' in their normative standpoints. Heinrich Rommen, a conservative Catholic lawyer soon to flee Nazi persecution in the late 1930s, traced the emergence of natural law *vis-à-vis* divine law precisely as the quest for understanding why human life and norms are so varied and changeable:

> The idea of a natural law can emerge only when men come to perceive that not all law is unalterable and unchanging divine law. It can emerge only when critical reason, looking back over history, notes the profound changes that have occurred in the realm of law and mores and becomes aware of the diversity of the legal and moral institutions of its own people in the course of its history; and when, furthermore, gazing beyond the confines of its own city-state or tribe, it notices the dissimilarity of the institutions of neighboring peoples. When, therefore, human reason wonderingly verifies this diversity, it first arrives at the distinction between divine and human law. (Rommen 1998: 4)

The quest for universalism that is central to natural law presupposes neither a single philosophical tradition nor peaceful, stable and harmonious socio-historical processes. The opposite is in fact the case: as an intellectual orientation, natural law is only possible because it begins by looking at divergence and conflict as the most basic of socio-historical facts. It is because of the prevalence of conflict, variation and change that natural law seeks to envisage potential answers that can be held universally valid. If the argument on the connections between universalistic beliefs of unity and actual experiences of conflict and disagreement can be shown to have religious backing, it is even less surprising to find it also in more secular versions of natural law. The need for thinking in universalistic terms can be seen as a way of addressing the challenges posed by the highly varied and changeable expressions of social life itself. A universalistic orientation imposes itself on natural law – and this is an argument that will prove crucial also for modern social theory – not because it takes harmony, or indeed a single way of 'being human' as necessary, but precisely as a way of understanding change, variation and disagreement in social life. This is in fact a feature that is consistently mentioned as a key component of natural law as a long-term philosophical tradition. Throughout history, natural lawyers were of the view that:

> [c]ontroversy, disagreement and a tendency to conflict are ineradicable among human beings, who nonetheless want or need to live with one another . . . Whatever their differing explanations, the natural lawyers agree in holding that the tendency to conflict cannot be removed by any means within human reach. Since we want nonetheless to live in company, the problem is to control the propensity to conflict. The solution to this problem, in its most general outline, is what natural law provides. And it is understandable that duties and rights, and the obligation to live within the constraints they impose, should be in the foreground of a view that sees the human condition in this way. (Schneewind 1993: 57)

Natural law emerges and becomes meaningful because there is variation, diversity and transformation in social life: there is something 'natural' in the idea of natural law as it emerges out of the real challenge of having to understand the multiplicity of ways in which human beings experience their lives in common. The universalistic orientation that constitutes the intellectual core of natural law presupposes, and indeed seeks to offer additional support, to notions of transhistorical and transcultural validity. Sociologically speaking, then, it can be said that natural law's contribution lies less in trying to devise the best and one-size-fits-all solution to common problems and more in seeking to find the widest possible common ground between human beings for the solutions to common problems to be universally considered as fair and just. We shall briefly see below that universalism cannot be reduced to Western natural law but that natural law has offered a particularly friendly environment within which to advance a universalistic orientation. If I can now put it in more analytical terms, the idea of universalism emerged because it has encountered, sought to understand and tried to offer solutions to questions of: (a) *socio-cultural variation*, in the sense that different human groups do things and organise themselves differently; (b) *historical change*, as the realisation that worldviews and institutions do not remain stable but evolve over time; and (c) *normative disagreement*, that is, that different groups value things differently and justify these valuations according to differing criteria.

As he reconstructs the historical development of natural law, Ferdinand Tönnies's general definition is similar to those we have discussed so far: natural law is 'the law common to all mankind, established by natural reason among human beings and therefore observed by all peoples in the same way, and even referred to as the "common law" or the *jus gentium*' (Tönnies 2001: 212–13). We will discuss the role of natural law in Tönnies's social theory in Chapter 6 below, but it is now worthy of mention that he rejects the view that this universal orientation ever constituted the general framework from which particular legal systems actually developed. Rather the opposite: he argues that this universal idea of natural law 'came *later* than particular law; it was not its basis or underlying presupposition, but its sequel and antithesis' (213). The sociological rationale for rejecting a 'deductive' approach to natural law is that the early expansion of commerce in Greek times required a legal framework that made economic exchanges universally possible: 'it was essential for everyone to be able to *trade* and form *relationships* with one another as and when they wished. Everyone was to have total freedom, apart from obligations undertaken, contracts made, or relationships entered into, of his own free will' (214). The obstacles that blocked these developments, the legal arrangements that prevented the free flow of goods and people were thus seen as 'barriers *contrary* to the dictates of nature' (215). Natural law, Tönnies argues, 'served the needs not of relations between cities or between citizens, but of everyone against everyone else, as naked individuals shorn of their different civic costumes' (213). Throughout the ages, from the Stoic rejection of Greek city-states' legal particularism to the rise of Christian natural law and all the way down to seventeenth-century modern natural law, Tönnies contends that as an intellectual tradition natural law fundamentally kept 'its integrity as a formal system'. Owing to its key features 'of great clarity, simplicity and logical consistency', natural law appeared to be 'the "written word of reason" itself' (219). In spite of all its changes and of its definitively contentious character *vis-à-vis* state enacted positive law, natural law 'understood as the idea of justice, is an eternal and inalienable possession of the human spirit' (221). But even as the argument explicates the idea of natural law as '*aeterna veritas* – an eternal truth', it remains the fact that natural law is a human construction:

> [a]n ideal that could just as well be located in the distant future as in the past. To say that such a 'common' or 'general' law actually existed at any one time is not a view about what has happened in the historical past; it is a convenient hypothesis that will serve to translate the concept into reality in the future. Such a useful fiction is made more convincing by the notion that some element of universal humanity forms the kernel of all diverse practices and customs. (Tönnies 2001: 213)

It may then not be altogether surprising that Ernst Troeltsch decided to make questions about the Christian and Stoic traditions of natural law *the* main theme of his address at the opening meeting of the German Sociological Society in 1910. He argued that natural law was a convenient label to refer to the doctrines of such a variety of writers as Hobbes, Grotius, Puffendorf, Spinoza, Locke and Rousseau. But in addition to this relatively minor role he emphasised that natural law was found in all doctrines that 'believe in an eternal and divine Law of Nature, the Equality of man, and a sense of Unity pervading mankind, and who find the essence of Humanity in these things' (Troeltsch 1958: 204). The main task of a sociology of natural law in that context is thus defined by the challenge of comprehending 'the circumstances of the sharply differing opposition that occurs between the goals of the ideal legislation [i.e. natural law] and the conditions of life, which are rarely completely extinguishable' (Troeltsch 2005: 112). A sociology of natural law would then have to explicate the connections, but also the gaps, between ideal normative doctrines that uphold a universalistic conception of humanity and the imperfections in their actualisation in the variety of socio-cultural contexts from which sociology draws empirical observations.

If we now turn our attention to the question of the historical origins of natural law, we soon realise that a secular understanding of natural law is historically more adequate than a religious version. The historical roots of natural law are found in the philosophical tradition of Greek Stoicism rather than in Christian natural law. We can see that Catholic writers themselves accept the proposition that its origins need to be traced to before the rise of Christianity, and Greek Stoicism is thus credited with having transformed 'the original tribalism and formalism of Roman law' into 'a universalism which fitted it "to survive, as a world law, the life of the nation in which it had originated"' (Rommen 1998: 22). In the liberal tradition, Schneewind similarly argues that rather than 'Judaism and Christianity', the true initiator of the natural law tradition is to be found in Cicero. It was he who held the conviction that, because of its 'agreement with nature, [natural law] is of universal application, unchanging and everlasting' (Schneewind 1998: 18). For Cicero, moreover, 'the supreme symbol is Justice (*ius*), which can only be one and is therefore not a matter of dictatorial or tyrannical arbitrariness; this is one justice based on the one Law (*lex*), which is the Right Reason (*recta ratio*); and the Right Reason is Nature (*natura*)' (Voegelin 2000b: 93). A main consequence of asserting its secular credentials is that the intellectual means with which natural law universalism was being discovered and deployed became grounded in human rationality rather than in faith or revelation: the programme of natural law is a rationalist one. While we have already argued that its universalistic orientation is predicated upon socio-cultural variation, historical change and normative disagreement, a most problematic presupposition of early natural law is, however, the way in which it explicated the substantive causes of social change. Social change is not yet understood in immanent terms, as human interventions into human affairs, but as external or transcendental interventions into social life. Early natural law explicated socio-historical changes as responsive to the non-human designs of god or nature.

Leo Strauss has arguably put forward the most influential version of this argument. In Chapter 2 we have already discussed Strauss's claim that it is only by tracing the origins of natural law back to classical Greece that we can fully realise its most fundamental feature: that 'the discovery of nature is identical with the actualization of a human possibility which, at least according to its own interpretation, is trans-historical, trans-social, trans-moral and trans-religious' (Strauss 1974: 89). Strauss emphasises that an increasingly immanent understanding of human affairs through human means brings natural law closer to philosophy and removes it further from religion. Philosophy 'comes into being when the quest for beginnings is understood in the light of the idea of nature' (Strauss 1997a: 111) and this natural law becomes the essentially human attempt at understanding what is essentially human: 'all natural right doctrines claim that the fundamentals of justice are, in principle, accessible to man as man' (Strauss 1974: 28). His main proposition is that it is the actual variety of human attitudes towards good and evil throughout history, rather than the existence of a single conception of it that comes from outside history, that becomes the constitutive problem of the natural law tradition:

> [k]nowledge of the indefinitely large variety of notions of right and wrong is so far from being incompatible with the idea of natural right that it is the essential condition of the emergence of the idea: realization of the variety of notions of right is *the* incentive for the quest of natural right . . . there cannot be natural right if the fundamental problem of political philosophy cannot be solved in a final manner. (Strauss 1974: 10 and 35)[8]

For my general purposes here, a softer formulation of this argument is that the natural law foundations of modern social theory lie in how the latter takes up the former's insistence on the relevance

[8] To be clear, I do not think that Strauss, or any other writer, succeeds in making this strong case of natural law in terms of definitive answers to questions which are however *fundamental* in a strong sense – nor are commentators greatly impressed by the extent to which Strauss actually accomplishes this goal (Drury 1987; Pippin 1992; see also Chapter 2 above).

of posing questions about the nature of life in common *as necessary questions that involve thinking universalistically about ourselves as members of the same human species.*

If the question of natural law's secular credentials does not prove particularly controversial, a familiar objection we still need to address is that the Western origins of both natural law and universalism make them fundamentally ethnocentric and hence flawed. An initial clarification in this context is that, whereas we have seen that natural law theory is indeed Western, at least in terms of carrying a sense of historical identity to a highly complex of web of intellectual traditions, this is not automatically the case in relation to the idea of universalism. I will not discuss this in any great detail, but there are at least good indications that whatever else may have evolved 'endogenously', and can then be termed as particularly Western in the early natural law tradition, its universalistic orientation was not one of these elements. Eric Voegelin (1962) has thus argued that a universalistic orientation was central to all known world religions in antiquity and, in the context of our previous discussion of the Stoic roots of natural law, he suggests that 'Stoic thinkers were not Greeks but came from the eastern part of the empire' (Voegelin 2000b: 90).[9] He contends that 'from c. 800 to 200 B.C., with a concentration about 500 when Confucius, the Buddha, and Heraclitus were contemporaries', the idea of universal humanity developed somewhat independently in its respective cultural settings (382). He goes even further and claims that the idea of universalism was already present in non-Western contexts before the axial age and was in fact imported into the West: 'the idea of a universal God, for instance, achieved its specific purity through the mystic philosophers, but its existence, imbedded in a compact cosmological myth, is attested by Egyptian inscriptions for about 3000 B.C.' (Voegelin 2000a: 215). In other words, even if natural law universalism were to be rejected, this could not be simply justified on the basis of its 'original' Western roots. We ought to avoid the fallacy of origins whereby natural law, universalism and indeed Western philosophy are unduly construed as particularly Western although they emerged well before the idea of 'the West'. The problem with any fallacy of origins is that the alleged as well as real historical roots of a certain

[9] Karl-Otto Apel (2004: 61) draws the philosophical implications of this claim when he argues that 'it should not be overlooked that, at least since the modern Enlightenment – *but in fact already implicitly since the emergence of the great world religions* – people have tended to identify themselves fully with a particular political system of self-preservation in the name of an *essentially universalistic ethico-religious form of legitimation*' (my italics). On non-Western universalism, see Shijun (2009).

intellectual development are taken as the reason why it cannot deal with phenomena that come from different socio-historical contexts.[10]

A secular account of the trajectory of natural law is then relatively consensual in the literature, and the argument that universalism is intrinsically ethnocentric should at least be treated more carefully historically, analytically and normatively. Yet beyond these considerations we still need to address two additional problems that in the next two chapters will prove key in explaining natural law's impact on the rise of modern social theory. First, there is the question of the relationship between natural law and philosophical anthropology; that is, whether 'changing ideas of natural law have to do with changing ideas of nature' (d'Entrèves 1970: 17). The argument is that natural law universalism depends on what we define as our fundamental human properties which, in turn, make certain institutions, values or sets of practices normatively preferable *because* they contribute to enhancing those essential human features. The connections between human nature and natural law will prove crucial in the modern natural law that we will revisit in the next two chapters. Both Hobbes and Rousseau explicitly make the argument that the transition from the state of nature to civil life depends on the creation of social institutions that fundamentally correspond to the sublated actualisation of human beings' 'natural' asociality (Hobbes) and sociality (Rousseau). In turn, Kant and Hegel show how problematic this recourse is, as ideas of human nature have proved extremely unstable throughout history and hence provide no secure, let alone universal, justifications for social institutions. Secondly, there is the question of whence the normative force of natural law ultimately derives; we have seen that while historically speaking the discovery of natural law was an immanent enterprise – natural laws were to be grasped through the use of human reason – the traditional normative appeal of natural law lay in its transcendental reference point: traditional natural law is human beings' rational discovery of the non-human sources of morality. In fact, by the seventeenth and eighteenth centuries, natural law theorists were still battling over:

> [t]he old problem of whether natural law had moral force for humanity because it was God's will or whether in addition it had independent moral authority with us.

[10] Although she does not problematise the historical origins of universalistic ideas, Seyla Benhabib's (2002: 24) critique of the holistic fallacy of treating 'societies', 'cultures', 'ethnic groups', or indeed whole 'civilisations' as homogenous and undivided wholes is appropriate in this context: '[t]he suggestion that universalism is ethnocentric often also presupposes a homogenizing view of other cultures and civilizations, neglecting elements in them that may be perfectly compatible with, and may even lie at the root of, the West's own discovery of universalism.'

Few disputed that natural law *existed* because of God's will; the question was rather whether or not there were moral values shared by God and humanity which entailed the moral obligations of natural law independently of our regard for God's willing this to be so. (Haakonssen 1996: 6)

For the transition from traditional to modern natural law and then to social theory to take place, the question of the intrinsic normativity of social life still has to be fully explicated. We have already encountered this problem in the previous chapters, for instance, in the claims about immanent transcendence in Habermas and Voegelin, and it will also reappear several times in what follows. If I now try to unpack the argument so far we can see that, cognitively, the discovery of natural law was mostly a rational enterprise that sought to reach as far as human reason would make possible – hence its universalistic orientation. Normatively, however, traditional natural law has systematically made its authoritative force depend on a transcendental will – cosmological, natural or divine – that is uncritically ascertained because it is as absolute as it is unknowable. The increasingly procedural, internalist and open-ended nature of modern universalism will eventually confront the dogmatism with which traditional natural law sought to achieve substantive normative purchase. For social theory to emerge, both dimensions will have to be disentangled: cognitive universalism will be fully incorporated into its deep-seated conceptual structures so that the empirical can start to play an ever-greater role; and normative transcendentalism will become less substantive and more reflexive. It is thus not wholly surprising that while a universalistic orientation was being offered and promoted in traditional natural law, all kinds of prejudice, essentialism and forms of domination also came with it.

Furthermore, we have already touched on the tension between the actual historical conditions of change that made the appearance of a universalistic horizon necessary and the explicit admission that no definitive resolution of such conflicts will be possible in practice. Universalistic ideas emerge out of awareness of diversity and conflict rather than of peace and stability. Universalism can of course be assessed differently in normative terms, but a key point is that its relevance does not depend on one or another ideal conception of human nature, or on actual socio-historical conditions corresponding to a somehow definitive sense of political unity or cultural homogeneity:

The Stoic legal and social philosophy is, like the entire Stoic ethic, a product of the disintegration of the ancient polis and the world-kingdom of a created cosmopolitan horizon. In place of positive law and morality emerges the ethic derived from a universal, law-abiding reason. In place of the national interests of his native country, the individual is fulfilled by God's reason; in place of the single political connection is the idea of humanity that lacks differentiation in terms of state and place, race and colour. From this human ideal comes a fully free *Gemeinschaft*. (Troeltsch 2005: 118)

Universalism is then best seen as a necessary way of recreating a sense of unity, a way of imagining the fundamental equality between human beings, in the context of having to respond to dramatic socio-historical events. This early sense of universality was possible not against but because of the acute sense of crisis that became apparent in the historical 'disintegration of the ancient polis'. At the same time, universalism developed with a certain self-propelling capacity: the more it was able to recognise differences empirically, the more it sought to foster the belief in universal equality.

Reinhart Koselleck has explored the gap between newly born universalistic ideals and the realisation that they will be impossible to implement in actual socio-political life. He explicates how Stoic philosophy developed an ever sharper *conceptual* universalism while its *political* character remained mostly underdeveloped. However strong its universalistic agenda may have been, this early natural law programme did not have the idea of a unified political project such as, for instance, the constitution of a world state. At stake was mostly the question of a foundational principle that could illuminate philosophically our understanding of who we are as human beings – the idea of a singular species that is constituted through the awareness of its particularity and diversity. This new form of imagining a universalistic sense of human belonging was still dependent upon a strict separation between fields of human action that were susceptible to at least partial human intervention and design – not least among them political life itself. But following our argument above, it also presupposed that transcendental normative authority was beyond the reach of human intervention:

The Stoics considered the cosmos, governed by *logos*, as their home in which all humankind – freeman and slave, Hellene and Oriental, just as much as the gods and the stars – had a part. Political agencies were built into the cosmopolis, although *the Stoics could never have identified the supervening with the empirical order* ... We do not have here mutually exclusive concepts but rather supplementary concepts of varying magnitude, which are intended to *mediate between the political tasks of the day and the general philosophical apprehension of the world*. (Koselleck 2004: 167, my italics)

This early universalistic orientation favoured the overcoming of differences between different social groupings at a higher level, in the realm of thinking instead of in actual political life. Socio-cultural particularities were being conceived as naturally or divinely construed, so these arguments remained highly dogmatic and unmediated. To the extent that human history remains a part of natural or divine history, the rational understanding of human affairs does not fully translate into rational programmes for political action – and least of all in history itself conceived as a strictly 'social' domain. Early ideas of universal human belonging were justified in hierarchical terms; they were the result of natural or divine designs rather than being humanly construed and hence subject to purposeful transformations through human intervention. It has thus been suggested that when Cicero 'talked about "the common society of the human race", he may have meant little more than this: that there is a kind of mutual recognition between men which differs from the relationship between men and the rest of the natural world' (Tuck 1999: 38). We shall see below that both Hobbes and Kant still thought it necessary to distinguish explicitly between different kinds of entity depending on how their rationality and will was actualised: animals *or* beasts which possessed no rational powers, human beings, who were capable of rational action but were not only rational, fictitious pure rational beings whose actions were based exclusively on rational volition, and finally god himself who was neither rational nor irrational but the possessor of an absolute will. In other words, while a truly universalistic idea of the human species was already built in as a logical possibility, to the extent that universalism remained a dogmatic reflection of particular cultural attributes or socio-historical circumstances, it was still possible to exclude certain parts of the human species. This offered a number of options for universalistic conceptions that were, however, not universalistic enough: 'writers of the Hellenistic and Roman period were unhappy with the fully fledged Aristotelian account of the natural slave, but they were quite prepared to argue for the forcible enslavement of those who violated the common code of mankind' (40).[11]

Because its universalistic orientation worked mostly at the level of ideas, hierarchies among different fields of life or indeed among whole populations were common in traditional natural law. There was always a tension between vertical outlooks that sought to give priority to certain groups and horizontal ones that favoured the fundamental equality of all human beings irrespective of their social position, ethnic origin or cultural accomplishments. A key step forward in this context was given when hierarchies were no longer being upheld through transcendental or naturalistic arguments but now entered into

[11] The problematic connection between *philosophical arguments* about universalism and their *political implications* in terms of slavery and empires is of course at the centre of the contemporary postcolonial critique (Connell 2007). This is of course an intrinsic challenge, a permanent source of concern, though not at all a necessary flaw.

realms that were subject to strictly human intervention. Hierarchical stratifications remained but particular forms of life and identity, indeed all kinds of socio-cultural differences, were now seen as socio-culturally produced – hence potentially subject to self-reflection and self-criticism. They were the result of human action and, because of that, were susceptible to human change. Some particular cultural, religious or ethnic contents were still given undue priority, yet now for historical rather than divine or natural reasons: vertical particularism and horizontal universalism began to be treated as equally immanent. Koselleck explicates this transition with a reference to Diogenes, who thus 'coined the universalistic "cosmopolite" with the object of transcending the usual dualism' between Hellenes and barbarians. But complications remained because even within this newly attempted unity previous hierarchical principles were recast rather than abandoned altogether. The distinction between Hellenes and barbarians:

> [t]hat had formerly been made spatially came to be deployed horizontally as a universal criterion of differentiation: 'Hellene' was a person with sufficient education, whether Greek or non-Greek, who merely had to be able to speak proper Greek; the remainder were Barbarian. Thus, this new antithesis, which was organized around education, no longer derived from natural qualities: to this extent, the counterconcepts were denaturalized and stripped of all spatial connections. (Koselleck 2004: 165)

The problem of the mediations between egalitarian universalism and hierarchical particularism is not overcome, but the boundaries between those who qualify as full human beings and those who do not can start to be explicitly addressed because they are now a result of human practices. New exclusions are created and older ones still remain, but a key result is that traditional cosmological justifications find themselves under pressure. The answer to the question of who counted as a human being no longer depended automatically on the individual's natural features, or on his position within a preordained cosmological order. The critical threshold that becomes progressively though possibly never definitively overcome is that while the hierarchical justification of particularities remains built into these universalistic arguments, there is now a clearer awareness that these arguments are grounded on human action (though not yet on social relations as such). They are still able to provide justifications for slavery or imperialism, but at the same time it became apparent that what counts as universal will change historically and socio-culturally. For these modifications to make universalistic arguments actually more inclusive the modern proceduralist turn still needs to be inaugurated; the universal is still equated with the substantive adoption of a particular form of education, set of values and institutions. But because these particular socio-cultural contents are understood as something human made other human beings can learn them, make them their own and even excel at them. No socio-cultural practice is axiomatically beyond the reach of a particular group of human beings and this of course makes justifications for treating particular historical traditions as automatically superior or inferior much more problematic. Without recourse to a procedure with which to assess the universalistic orientation of competing answers, the more powerful groups were simply able impose their superiority. But to the extent that the cultural contents to be apprehended were themselves created by human beings, access to them was now potentially open to all: the human species could now *commence* conceiving itself as one. The dogmatism of these early formulations will then be worked through at two different planes. First, the procedural turn in modern natural law theory will offer a stricter separation between form and substance in universalistic propositions and a more decisive internalist standpoint (these will be central in Chapters 4 and 5). Secondly, universalism will have to be brought 'down to earth' and pay more attention to historical and empirical developments (a key theme in the rise of social theory, as we will see in Chapters 6 and 7).

Enlightenment, early Enlightenment and natural law

I commenced this chapter with the proposition that although there is an important degree of heterogeneity within natural law, universalism is in fact its intellectual core. Far from being a static or homogenising approach, universalism emerges out of experiences of social conflict, historical change and normative disagreement. The historical origins of natural law were then traced back to the Stoic philosophical tradition and we used this to reject the charge that universalism was intrinsically ethnocentric and a purely endogenous Western development. We also distinguished between the discovery of natural law universalism that was mostly a rational and immanent enterprise and the sources of its normative authority that were transcendental. I should now like to take the discussion forward in historical terms and address the role of the Enlightenment and the early Enlightenment in the internal transformation of the tradition of natural law. My goal in this section is to assess the fundamental transformations, the radicalisation, of the ways in which universalistic arguments were then being introduced and justified.

One major trend we need to account for is that the distance between the immanent and the transcendental dimensions of earlier natural law universalism increased. On the one hand, the old transcendental normative authority of natural law will have to start reckoning with an incipient yet hugely consequential new sense of normative immanence. We can look at this from a Straussian viewpoint and equate the transition from transcendental to immanent propositions, from the religious to the secular, with the transition from traditional natural law to modern natural right.[12] On the other hand, the traditional cognitive status of universalistic claims is also being questioned: rationalistic strategies, however immanent, will now have to start accepting and incorporating the empirical – logically as much as socio-historically. Justificatory strategies about what constitutes acceptable rational explanations now had to deal with the problem of demonstrating their empirical evidence: self-sustained rational knowledge was now being constituted *also* through empirical experience. Both arguments come together because while the tension between transcendental and immanent arguments has always expressed the two souls of natural law, the idea that empirical knowledge will have a potentially decisive role is difficult to accommodate within either variant. The Enlightenment becomes salient in this context because this rejection of exclusively rationalistic, deductive or a priori arguments will be central in its position *vis-à-vis* the rise of modern social theory: explicating the causes of social change will now require more than the deduction of the fundamentals of human nature. To that extent, social theory surely is, and must continue to be, a sustained critique of natural law. But in so far as social theory has always sought to offer more than the empirical register of modern social life, it has also found it necessary to keep connected to the kind of philosophical questions that it has otherwise sought to debunk: cognitively, because questions about the ultimate nature of strictly social relations can only be answered philosophically; normatively, because modern social theory has remained interested in the meaning of social life under modern conditions – what makes human life human in modernity.

The starting point of Ernst Cassirer's classic work on the Enlightenment is that its original claim to knowledge sought the strongest possible foundations for the nascent social or moral sciences and, by the eighteenth century, those foundations were to be developed by

[12] The question of distinguishing between natural law and natural right has proved taxing for the literature we reviewed in the previous section. Thus, for instance, John Finnis's (1980) and Francis Oakley's (2005) works have both terms in the title but do not fully explicate their interrelationships. Heinrich Rommen (1998: 59) offers a line of enquiry when he argues that there is a potentially intractable ambiguity here because already 'the Late Scholastics employed the terms *lex naturalis* and *ius naturale* as synonyms'. See also note 12 in Chapter 2.

replicating successful advancements in the natural sciences. Both realms, the natural and the social, were thought to be governed by the same principles and in either case particular instances were to be subsumed under the universal:

> The path of thought then, in physics as in psychology and politics, leads from the particular to the general; but not even this progression would be possible unless every particular as such were already subordinated to a universal rule, unless from the first the general were contained (...) in the particular. (Cassirer 1979: 21)

The idea of a unified philosophical programme that can describe all realms of life and experience is of course very much consistent with what natural law has always stood for. Continuity is also found in the objectivist type of argumentation that the Enlightenment inherited from previous natural law. Knowledge about events in the physical as well as the social world was equally based on external laws that were justified objectively. But as both continuities and discontinuities are being considered, Cassirer argues that 'enlightenment universalism' does not represent a radical break with the natural law tradition that preceded it:

> [i]f we compare the thought of the eighteenth century with that of the seventeenth, there is no real chasm anywhere separating the two periods ... The difference in the mode of thinking does not mean a radical transformation; it amounts merely to a shifting of emphasis ... the basic assumption remains; that is, the assumption that between the two realms of thought there is no opposition but rather complete correlation ... The self-confidence of reason is nowhere shaken. (Cassirer 1979: 22)

Peter Gay uses a different language when he depicts the philosophes as 'modern pagans' but the substantive argument is similar. Enlightenment thinkers, he thought, offered 'a dialectal interplay of their appeal to antiquity, their tension with Christianity, and their pursuit of modernity' (Gay 1970: 8). He explains this further by looking at how the philosophes saw themselves in relation to previous intellectual traditions: '[t]he philosophe was a cosmopolitan by conviction as well as by training. Like the ancient Stoic, he would exalt the interest of mankind above the interest of country or clan' (13).[13] This does not stop Gay from also acknowledging that, as the old priority of traditional

[13] The connection between the Enlightenment and earlier cosmopolitan thinking is also found in Pierre Bayle, whom Cassirer describes as 'the spiritual leader of the Enlightenment' and cites as follows: 'I'm neither a Frenchman, nor a German, neither an Englishman nor a Spaniard, etc. I am a citizen of the world; I am not in the service of the Emperor, nor in that of the King of France, but only in the service of Truth. She is my queen, to her alone have I sworn the oath of obedience' (Cassirer 1979: 209).

moral philosophy had begun to fade, the languages and procedures that were now expected to serve as models were those of the natural sciences. More precisely, it is the automatic cognitive privilege with which previous natural law was credited that loses its centrality at the hands of the apparently non-normative language of the natural sciences. Yet the Enlightenment attitude towards scientific developments is full of ambivalences and tensions. On the positive side, there is the promise that science will deliver truly new insights into what we have so far been able to discover about social, moral and psychological questions. In challenging superstition, religiosity but also traditional metaphysics, the Enlightenment was committed to what was truly novel in scientific sensibility:

> If the scientific method was the sole reliable method for gaining knowledge in a wide variety of contexts, from the phenomena of the heavens to the phenomena of plant life, it seemed plausible and in fact likely that it could be profitably exported to other areas of intense human concern where knowledge was as primitive now, and disagreement as vehement, as it had been in physics a century before – the study of man and society. Even if facts and values were distinct, even if science was not the source of all past values, a bridge could be built between facts and values and the scientific method might become the instrument for the creation of future values. (Gay 1977: 164)

There was also, however, a more sceptical side to this attitude. The philosophes were aware of the fact that a certain intellectual impoverishment was in store if human affairs were now merely studied as a kind of human or social physics. The idea of a social world devoid of normative meaning was problematic for these writers, even though that seemed the potentially unavoidable conclusion of their own strong faith in science. Neither full continuity nor total rupture between transcendence and immanence, between philosophy and science, is then the answer that they (and we) are after. There is substantive continuity in terms of the need for a unified theory of knowledge but also radical discontinuity in relation to the kinds of foundation that would be needed to secure this unified approach. The fundamental challenge that remains, and the one that I think warrants an interpretation in which natural law and the Enlightenment remain fundamentally entangled, is that a wholly mechanistic idea of human action and social life had already proved not to be enough. Social physics makes for poor social science because, cognitively, there is more to learn about human life than the predictions that empirical sciences allow for. And it is also normatively insufficient because the very purpose of social enquiring becomes pointless if it gives up on the 'most pressing questions – What must I do? And, even more significant – Who am I?' (Gay 1977: 162).

The Enlightenment idea of social physics, with its insufficient conception of the normative and its restrictive idea of scientific explanations, makes all too apparent the original connections between the Enlightenment and positivism – not least in Comtean sociology. Although it surely reflects a more conspicuous commitment to immanent forms of knowledge, it is not necessarily less dogmatic than some of the arguments we reviewed in the previous section. In relation to the discussion in Chapter 1 on the postmetaphysical status of modern claims to knowledge, the question now is that previous cosmologies become increasingly problematic, although they do not disappear as acceptable forms of making sense of the world: the clash between philosophy and science has now been officially declared and will accompany us throughout the rest of our journey. A better sense of the continuities and discontinuities between natural law and the Enlightenment should allow us to reassess the conventional idea that a radical break marked the transition between the highly 'metaphysical' status of natural law all the way down to the end of the seventeenth century and the increasingly rationalistic and empirical orientation from the century of lights onwards.

In the previous section we discussed the gap between beliefs and ideals, which in traditional natural law were thought of as immutable, and practices and institutions, which were understood as historically changing and susceptible to transformation. The search for transhistorical validity under conditions of socio-historical change, which has always lain at the centre of natural law universalism, is under increased pressure and has to grapple much more decidedly with historical materials and socio-cultural conditions that pose greater challenges to unreflective universalistic arguments. To the recognition that peoples do things differently and that their practices change over time, we now add the methodological difficulty of how to handle the empirical information that is required to account for these changes: it is the actual status of these materials that is now considered as problematic. The question is about the conditions of possibility of historical knowledge beyond and above the register of empirical facts.

Nothing is more stable than ideas of socio-historical change, but the Enlightenment works with the argument that the best way to understand socio-historical change is in terms of epochal transitions. This occurs because of both a shift from transcendental to immanent intellectual strategies and a need to combine deductive and rationalistic approaches with empirical knowledge. But the price to be paid for this enhanced empirical awareness of socio-cultural variation was to start looking at these transformations in terms of isolated and discrete periods whose changes are then depicted as historical transitions. Yet neither purely deductive strategies nor purely inductive ones will do. Nor will it be enough to admit the importance of the velocity of social change: it is the idea of social change itself, understood as epochal transition, which became in need of explanation. But this was a task that neither natural law nor the Enlightenment were able to confront adequately, and towards the end of the eighteenth century it became central to the historicist critique of the Enlightenment – not least in Hegel himself (Löwith 1967, Schnädelbach 1980). While the transitional role of the Enlightenment in relation to modern social theory does not lie in its self-conception of having broken free from natural law, a more problematic proposition is the insufficient way in which it historically thinks about itself as a historical development. The Enlightenment inaugurates the modernist imagination for which historical change is explicitly conceptualised in terms of epochal transition. But it also offers a deficient idea of history in the sense that it can only justify its location within its own bigger scheme in terms of a particular that is subsumed under the universal. Socio-historical change is ubiquitous but for natural law social change is flat because it had no need to think about how historical change occurs. It paid attention to socio-historical change but had no real concept of it; the more it concentrated explicitly on justifying its universalism, the less it was able to explain social change.

This leads us to another, more methodological issue, which refers to trying to make sense of *the* Enlightenment in an excessively homogenous and unified fashion. To be sure, an argument can always be made against the description of any intellectual movement as a single movement because this would do violence to its internal heterogeneity. But in this particular instance at least part of the difficulty lies in how, by speaking about the Enlightenment in the singular, it is mostly the agenda of one particular social group, however important or influential, that becomes equated with social and intellectual developments during a whole century.[14] As argued above, we must avoid treating intellectual movements or historical periods as fully discrete, homogenous and self-contained; we need also to account for continuities, discontinuities, overlappings and juxtapositions. For my substantive purposes in this book, there is something to be said about the role of the so-called early Enlightenment

[14] For normative variety during the enlightenment see Muthu (2003) and for different counter-movements, McMahon (2001). For an overview, see Outram (1995) and Yack (2006). Although this is not a line of argument that I will pursue in this book, see also Dan Edelstein's (2009) historical reconstruction of the political use of natural law arguments during the French Revolution and in particular the role played there by the idea of *hostis humani generis*, the 'enemies of the human race'.

in relation to the internal transformations of natural law, on the one hand, and the later rise of social theory, on the other:

> The concept of *Aufklärung* [Enlightenment] resists convenient definition largely because it is at one and the same time striving both to present an intellectual agenda and provide a description of the achievements of an historical epoch that is already in place. This applies all the more forcibly to the period of transition between 1670 and 1720 (now tentatively designated the *Frühaufklärung* [early Enlightenment]. . .) there is a continual tension between the stated ideals and the inadequate intellectual, institutional and political realities which must in time be clarified and reformed. Nowhere is this tension more clearly seen than in the field of contemporary natural law which claimed a metaphysical standing and validity outside time, while simultaneously writing up its own recent history and representing the history of ethics as in fact the history of natural law pure and simple. *Prescriptive and descriptive, profoundly self-aware of the history of ethics and yet deliberately and deeply unhistorical in its self-promotion, the paradoxes of natural law were also the paradoxes of the Frühaufklärung.* (Hochstrasser 2000: 37, my italics)

I will take the idea of the early Enlightenment seriously and although I will modify its starting date slightly in order to bring Hobbes in, a key part of my argument in the next two chapters will be that we need a deeper understanding of the philosophical developments within natural law theory to account for the rise of social theory. I will use Hobbes to mark the transition between the traditional natural law we have discussed so far and modern natural law. Hobbes definitively changes the terms with which to think the relationship between the immanent and the transcendental, individual human nature and social life, moral motivation and political obligation and he did this by consciously working through arguments about natural law. In starting with Hobbes I deliberately seek to seek to reduce, though not altogether obliterate, the radicality of the modern caesura in explicating the rise of social theory. At the same time, the modernist imagination that emerged in the early Enlightenment was surely to think historically, but the way in which it did so remained problematic: it reified ideas of radical transitions and neatly defined periods, on the one hand, and made use of too dogmatic conceptions of the universal, on the other. While it surely gained in terms of empirical precision, it remained unable to justify its own position historically and the best it could do was to assert somewhat dogmatically its sense of importance, superiority and historical novelty.

We have said that one of the fundamental motifs of the Enlightenment was seeking to transcend fully ahistorical and asociological ways of thinking about traditional natural law. But acknowledging that this was in fact the case still says little about our current assessment of how successful that rupture actually was. The realisation that a gap remains between the aspiration to leave a certain period or trend definitively behind, and later reassessments of how (in)complete those attempts have actually been, should allow us to reconsider ideas about socio-historical change. This is not at all to argue that, by the end of the eighteenth century, social, political and intellectual actors were wrong in conceiving their own situation as one of radically changing trends and events – events which they surely thought they could alter through social action even though they took place under conditions that were not of their own making. But neither should we take these actors' self-conceptions at face value. We ought to remain prepared to reassess the gap between what they tried to do and effectively achieved not because of greater historical hindsight but because we are never the best judges or interpreters of what we ourselves do.

Closing remarks

Natural law is a long-standing tradition that centres on a universalistic conception of humanity as something possible, positive and rationally justifiable. It is a continuous though far from unproblematic engagement with the ways in which human beings conceive of themselves as members of one and the same human species. However dramatic the modern caesura may be regarded, its sense of species-being speaks of a sense of transhistorical and transcultural continuity that goes beyond modernity.

Substantive definitions of what a human being is have dramatically evolved over time and the ways in which these kinds of enquiry have been carried through have evolved equally radically. But universalism is central to the tradition of natural law as a *problem*, a *cognitive outlook* and a *normative orientation*. As a problem, natural law engages with universalism as it tries to make it philosophically plausible in spite of all its difficulties, shortcomings and dead ends. As a cognitive outlook, it is a guiding principle that helps organise and give coherence to the intuition that the particularities of human life are to be understood as part of a single human species. As a normative orientation, finally, universalism allows us to imagine potential solutions to the all too real conflicts and disagreements to be found in social life. Natural law has certainly been used as a conservative strategy but it is not intrinsically conservative. The more its universalistic orientation becomes apparent the more salient its role as a critical standard for assessing different kinds of socio-political arrangement.

After having traced the historical emergence and main features of the universalistic orientation that is core to natural law in this chapter, the next two chapters of this part will reflect further on several of the issues that we have raised here: the early Enlightenment, natural law and natural right, the transition between the state of nature and the civil condition, immanent reason and transcendental authority, human nature and social life, the relationships between procedural justification and substantive content and between scientific and philosophical arguments. We shall do so by looking at four authors – Hobbes, Rousseau, Kant and Hegel – whose works have proved central in modern social and political thought. They will in turn help us explicate how modern natural law became important in explaining the rise of social theory.

4 Modern natural law I: Hobbes and Rousseau on the state of nature and social life

We start this Chapter where we left the previous one, with the importance of the early Enlightenment in the internal transformations within natural law. As traditional natural law started to be redescribed in terms of 'subjective natural rights', its focus moved away from questions about the cosmos and closer to an 'anthropological understanding of the individual'. There was also a renewed interest in how ideas of the state of nature played a role in general conceptions of humanity and a decline in the 'intellectual significance of epistemological discussions of the source of moral knowledge in God or man'. Neither complete rupture nor radical continuity was effected, rather natural law theory 'shifted its axis from delineating a vocabulary of duty to exercising an agenda of rights' (Hochstrasser 2000: 5–6). These are really the themes that will occupy us in this chapter: the rise of modern natural law as a language of rights, the recourse to arguments on the state of nature in the establishment of ideas of social life and humanity, and the location of the normative in social life beyond traditional conceptions of the transcendental. On the basis of a universalistic orientation that remains central, we now witness several transformations that mark the rise of modern natural law.

Hobbes

Although his moral and political philosophy is not based on thick normative presuppositions about how human beings ought to behave, Hobbes's work is none the less based on the kind of universalistic orientation that is central to the natural law tradition. The historical context within which his writing took place is marked, intellectually, by the rise of the modern natural law tradition that is associated with the names of Grotius and Puffendorf and, politically, by the early bourgeois revolution of the seventeenth century in the Netherlands and England.[1] Hobbes's starting point in *Leviathan* is that individual men, who are themselves a work of nature and belong in the realm of nature must, however, come together and through their purposeful and intelligent actions create the state as the most formidable of 'artificial' institutions. A Leviathan is defined as a work of art whose *art*ificiality does not undermine or stand in opposition to individual man's natural qualities but is rather a way of strengthening and improving on human nature. Indeed, it is in the nature of human beings to be able to improve on who they naturally are and what they naturally do:

> *Art* goes yet further, imitating that Rationall and most excellent worke of Nature, *Man*. For by Art is created the great LEVIATHAN called a COMMON-WEALTH, or STATE, (in latine CIVITAS) which is but an Artificiall Man; though of greater stature and strength than the Naturall, for whose protection and defence it was intended. (Hobbes 1996: 9)

Men are naturally rational and thus it is rational for human beings to create an institution that does not exist in nature but which, because it will be greater and stronger than any individual, will come to the defence and protection of them all. Hobbes offers no transcendental justification for human reason: 'there is no such *Finnis ultimus* . . . nor *Summum Bonum* (greatest Good) as is spoken of in the Books of the old Morall Philosophers' (Hobbes 1996: 70). He defines it simply as our human ability to relate things to one another: 'in what matter soever there is place for *addition* and *subtraction*, there also is place for *reason*; and where these have no place, there *Reason* has nothing at all to do' (32). Reason is then the mundane activity of being able to grasp what can be gained, and lost, in whatever course of action individuals may decide to pursue. Interestingly, however, for Hobbes reason is both natural and artificial. While reason is an innate ability that all human beings possess naturally, Hobbes argues that not everyone is able to put reason to good use to the same extent. Reason is not one of our senses, it does not develop thanks to experience alone; rather, it is 'attained by Industry' (35). Reason requires individual application but also social conditions to bring about its fruits. Individually, it presupposes industrious, patient and constant practice but socially it needs cooperation and peaceful coexistence.

[1] Norberto Bobbio (1993: 149–58) claims that it is Hobbes rather than Grotius who offers the key transformations that mark the rise of modern natural law: methodologically, because of the deductive nature of his system and his wholly operational (rather than substantive) concept of reason; ideologically, because of his secular idea of human nature and the way in which he distinguishes natural law and natural right in terms of duties and freedom.

Below we shall see that it is on this idea of reason as the ability to add and subtract that Hobbes will base the strictly rational grounds for the Leviathan to emerge. But it is also worthy of mention that Hobbes is unable to consistently define reason as fully devoid of ulterior meaning and being independent of its potential contribution towards higher ends. He thus suggests that reason offers human beings possibilities for the 'Encrease of *Science* ... and the Benefit of man-kind' (Hobbes 1996: 36) and then connects this to his own intellectual programme where reason plays a key role in the discovery of 'Morall Philosophie ... the science of Vertue and Vice ... the true Doctrine of the Lawes of Nature, is the true Morall Philosophie' (111).[2] This tension between one thin and rather instrumental idea of reason and another thick and more moral notion is instructive. In fact, they are not wholly incompatible. First, because it is through this modest reckoning with things in terms of adding and subtracting that human beings are led to the realisation that it is better for them to abandon their condition of continual warfare and move towards a peaceful and civil state. To the extent that this decision can be termed as rational in this modest yet fundamental sense, the rise of a stable social order will prove to be *universally* positive. Being based simultaneously on a universalistic orientation, instrumental and substantive reason, descriptive and normative reasons, work in relation to one another. Secondly, because the instrumental idea of reason that Hobbes introduced at the beginning of *Leviathan* was supposed to depict what happens to human beings before the emergence of a commonwealth and, after the Leviathan has been established, what the dangers would be if they were to fall back to a situation of pre-social anarchy. While in the state of nature reason is nothing but an individual ability to take advantage of what is good to me and to preempt potentially harmful courses of events, inside the commonwealth reason is now also to be put to good social use. Reason can be deployed for strictly social tasks: science emerges, industry flourishes, tolerance improves, true moral philosophy develops, natural laws that favour peaceful coexistence are discovered.

While the question of the religious foundations of Hobbes's work is relatively problematic, not least because the last third of *Leviathan* is devoted to the Christian commonwealth, the secular implications of his thinking are beyond doubt. Knud Haakonssen (1996: 29) offers a

[2] It is at the end of this same paragraph, in which Hobbes draws his discussion of natural law to an end, that he has recourse to God in order to justify the claim that 'These dictates of Reason ... are properly called Lawes' (Hobbes 1996: 111). I will come back to the question of the role of religious arguments in Hobbes's theory below.

nuanced interpretation as he argues that the key question that both Hobbes and Grotius had to address 'was that human beings have the ability to understand what is good and bad even without invoking God but have no obligation proper to act accordingly without God's command'.[3] Differently put, to the extent that we learn about natural laws by immanent means only, immanence is fully granted only at the cognitive level: reason is all we need in order to know about right and wrong. But the normative force of natural law is far from wholly immanent yet, as its obligatory component still derives a great deal of its binding force from its (admittedly increasingly remote) divine origin. We have encountered this before, and I will not settle it here, but Hobbes argues for instance that divine commands offer the *only* justification for resisting a tyrannical sovereign (Hobbes 1996: 245). But Hobbes also describes god as absolute power and will. God is essentially arational, and therefore is not concerned with truth and cannot be the object of science; god is to be feared and revered but left outside the realm of rationality (Hobbes 1996: 246–52). Given the centrality that Hobbes gives to human beings' use of reason to decide what is best for themselves, in making god all powerful and arbitrary and indeed arational he also makes god irrelevant for the resolution of moral and political questions. The more powerful god's will is, the less we can count on it to secure our institutions and settle social strife. Beyond Hobbes's personal religious beliefs, therefore, he expected his philosophy to work cognitively as well as normatively in rational terms that were independent of religious support. The discovery of the laws of nature and the ascertaining of their normative binding power were equally immanent processes.

Hobbes's universalism is fully apparent in his understanding of human nature. The same passions, he says, are present in all human beings and while passions are universal, the objects to which they are directed are not: 'I say the similitude of *Passions*, which are the same in all men, *desire*, *feare*, *hope*, &c; not the similitude of the *objects* of Passions *desired*, *feared*, *hoped*, &c' (Hobbes 1996: 10). Hobbes's universalism is thus equally predicated upon universal human nature, passions and particular human ends, the objects that drive these passions. Universal human nature

[3] Hobbes's work can be described as offering a type of 'minimalist Christianity not unlike the one Grotius expounded' (Schneewind 1998: 98). The reference to Grotius points to his famous contention that natural laws would be valid even if we concede what is obviously impossible, that God does not exist (see Schneewind 1998: 73–100 and Haakonssen 1996: 26–35). A wholly immanent interpretation of Hobbes is found in Strauss (1974: 198): 'Hobbes's is the first doctrine that necessarily and unmistakably points to a thoroughly "enlightened," i.e., a-religious or atheistic society as the solution of the social or political problem'. See also Strauss (1988b).

requires a stable and immutable core whose actual empirical expression is multiple and contingent. In turn, this reflects a strong sense of individuality on Hobbes's part: while human beings, as members of the same species, all have the same passions, specific ends change from one individual to the next. Hobbes has no role for socio-cultural factors to explicate the causes of these variations, yet he can hardly be criticised for a lack of sensibility towards individual preferences. Individuals have different inclinations – wealth, fame, sensual pleasure – and different abilities to pursue these in terms of wit, imagination, steady character, among others (50, 99). These preferences are what they are, and change in the way they do, only because of individual differences:

> [t]he voluntary actions, and inclinations of all men, tend, not onely to procuring, but also to the assuring of a contented life; and differ onely in the way: *which ariseth partly from the diversity of passions, in divers men*; *and partly from the difference of knowledge, or opinion each one has of the causes, which produce the effect desired.* (Hobbes 1996: 70, my italics)

But arguably the stronger aspect of Hobbes's universalistic understanding of human beings lies in what he describes as the natural equality of men: 'Nature hath made men so equall, in the faculties of body, and mind' (Hobbes 1996: 86). There is, he argues, an 'equality of hope' in men as they seek to achieve their particular ends, although this also has the additional consequence that 'if any two men desire the same thing, which neverthelesse they cannot both enjoy, they become enemies; and in the way to their End . . . endeavour to destroy, or subdue one another' (87). We thus arrive at the conventional, and to an important extent also fair, depiction that power is the core of Hobbes's philosophical anthropology: '*Naturall Power*, is the eminence of the Faculties of Body, or Mind' (62). He includes such issues as 'riches', 'fame', 'reputation', 'success', 'affability', 'nobility', 'eloquence', 'honour' as the kinds of thing to which human beings aspire, but then reduces them all to power as their single common denominator (62–5). And this is also the context for his best known formulation that 'without common Power to keep them in awe, they [men] are in that condition of which is called WARRE; and such a warre, as is of every man, against every man' (88).[4]

But this is not the end of what Hobbes has to say about human nature. In addition to continual war and the striving for power,

[4] To the extent that this is the inherited interpretation we have of Hobbes, I should like to say that I find this highly reductionist as a philosophical anthropology. Power is not an adequate depiction of who we are and what we do as human beings – *the human cannot be reduced to power*. But I will immediately argue that this is only half of the story for Hobbes.

Hobbes introduces the idea of liberty as central to what also takes place in that continual state of war: '*A* FREE-MAN, *is he, that in those things, which by his strengths and wit he is able to do, is not hindered to doe what he has a will to*' (Hobbes 1996: 146). This is liberty in a strong sense because, in addition to pursuing one's ends, Hobbes includes the right to self-defence as a 'Right of Nature' (92). Liberty and self-defence are fundamentally interconnected as natural rights. In the more extended formulation of his idea of natural right, the argument is presented as follows:

The RIGHT OF NATURE, which Writers commonly call *Jus Naturale*, is the Liberty each man hath, to use his own power, as he will himself, for the preservation of his own Nature; that is to say, of his own Life; and consequently, of doing any thing, which in his own Judgement, and reason, hee shall conceive to be the aptest means thereunto.

By LIBERTY, is understood . . . the absence of external Impediments: which Impediments, may oft take away part of a mans power to do what hee would; but cannot hinder him from using the power left to him, according as his judgement, and reason shall dictate to him. (Hobbes 1996: 91)

The situation of continual war on which Hobbes has concentrated so far, including the natural right to pursue one's ends and self-defence that he describes as freedom, is pre-social if not actually asocial. Hobbes's state of nature is one in which individuals have not yet been affected by, or benefited from, fully fledged social institutions.[5] Before the establishment of the commonwealth, 'there is no place for Industry . . . no Culture of the Earth; no Navigation . . . no account of Time; no Letters; no Society; and which is worst of all, continuall feare, and danger of violent death; And the life of man solitary, poore, nasty, brutish, and short' (Hobbes 1996: 89). All these features that Hobbes emphasises in the state of nature do point to an idea of human nature that is centred on power, but they also characterise the state of nature as an asocial condition of human existence: 'men have no pleasure, (but on the contrary a great deale of griefe) in keeping company, *where there is no power able to over-awe them all*' (88, my italics).

[5] It is worth mentioning that, although his argument undoubtedly points in that direction, in *Leviathan* Hobbes does not explicitly use the expression 'state of nature' – most probably, in order to differentiate himself from Grotius' argument of men's natural sociality and previous conceptions of it in scholasticism (Bond 2011a: 1183). It remains an open question, however, whether Hobbes understands the state of nature as a purely analytical construct or whether he credits it with historical existence. I come back to the question of the conceptual status of the state of nature in the following section on Rousseau.

Hobbes has no altruistic conception of human nature, but this gloomy depiction of human life as selfish, fearful, hapless and lawless applies only until the rise of the commonwealth because what takes place in the state of nature does not automatically translate into how individuals will behave when living peacefully under a common authority. This state of continual warfare is unable to accommodate the impulse to sociality that is *also* a part of who we are and what we do as human beings. Furthermore, as we just reviewed, differences in the objects to which passions and impulses are directed are explained by reference to individual rather than any kind of social, cultural or historical factor. The argument can thus be made that although for Hobbes these asocial conditions are surely 'natural' in the sense of reflecting key aspects of human nature, they do not suffice to constitute the whole of human life. For our full humanity to express itself, social order is required. The pleasure of living next to one another, the personal enhancement that results from cooperative relations and indeed a wholly new form of strictly social improvement, only begins to emerge after certain conditions are met: we require a sense of stability and predictability in social life that is based on mutual trust. This desire for sociability is artificial in exactly the same sense as the Leviathan is also artificial: it is enhanced human nature rather than being against or anti-human nature.[6] In fact, this is precisely the kind of sociability – social relations, practices, institutions and regulations – that Hobbes calls 'manners', that is: 'those qualities of man-kind, that concern their living together in Peace, and Unity' (Hobbes 1996: 69). We shall come back to this idea of peace, but before we do this we can note that Hobbes contrasts natural right and natural law on the basis of this separation between an asocial state of continual warfare (the natural right to liberty understood as self-defence and the pursuit of one's interest), and the fully social condition that is the commonwealth:

> A LAW OF NATURE, (*Lex Naturalis*,) is a Precept, or a generall Rule, found out by Reason, by which a man is forbidden to do, that, which is destructive to his life, or taketh away the means of preserving the same, and to omit, that, by which he thinketh it may be best preserved. For though they that speak of this subject, use to confound *Jus*, and *Lex, Right* and *Law*, yet they ought to be distinguished; because RIGHT, consisteth in liberty to do, or to forebeare; Whereas LAW, determineth, and bindeth to one of them; so that Law, and Right, differ as much as Obligation, and Liberty; which in one and the same matter are inconsistent. (Hobbes 1996: 91)

[6] Thus, for instance, Norberto Bobbio's (1993: 2) use of the idea of 'artificial nature' when spelling out the key features of modern natural law theory. Also, see my discussion of social relations as artificial nature in Chapter 8 below.

This definition is hugely consequential. On the one hand, it expresses Hobbes's attempted rupture with previous natural law theory which allowed no distinction between an asocial state of nature and a fully social condition that has overwhelmingly positive consequences for human nature (Bond 2011a). On the other hand, Hobbes now defines the law of nature in strong normative terms as a general rule that, as found out by reason, binds people to behave in a certain manner (and forbids them to do things that are destructive to their lives). The argument I am trying to make is that for Hobbes natural right and natural law are equally universal, but they are also complementary because they apply to different situations: while the former is directed to what takes place in contexts of continuous war that can be depicted as asocial, the latter has priority in social life proper.[7] Both natural right and natural law have universal jurisdiction but within their own specific settings – the state of nature and the commonwealth, respectively. It is then worthy of further exploration that, while Hobbes does not elaborate further on the ideas of liberty and natural right, he does introduce nineteen different laws of nature one by one (Hobbes 1996: 91–111).

The first three laws of nature are surely the most important and are consistent with the other arguments we have discussed so far. Being the opposite of war, Hobbes makes peace the first law of nature: 'the first, and Fundamentall Law of Nature ... is, *to seek Peace, and follow it*' (Hobbes 1996: 92). The second law of nature connects the need for peace with the necessary conditions for the emergence of the all-powerful Leviathan – were I to seek peace, so must others: '*a man be willing, when others are so too ... to lay down this right to all things; and be contented with so much liberty against other men, as he would allow other men against himself*' (92). War being ubiquitous, nothing short of a comprehensive commitment to peace is required. The third law of nature that Hobbes introduces is justice, and he is careful not to associate justice with any particular state of affairs or substantive morality. He rather speaks of justice in procedural terms, as the obligation for men to meet the contractual obligations into which they enter:

7 Thus, for instance, in relation to the right to rebellion Hobbes (1996: 153) argues that '[t]he Obligation of Subjects to the Soveraign, is understood to last as long, and no longer, than the power lasteth, by which he is able to protect them. For the right men have by Nature to protect themselves, when none else can protect them, can by no Covenant be relinquished'. While full obedience is required under conditions of peaceful social coexistence, no such obedience is required when social peace breaks down. Admittedly, in this Hobbes breaks at least partly with the traditional claim that natural laws can offer grounds for the critique of positive laws (Schneewind 1998: 93).

[b]efore the names of Just, and Unjust, can have place, there must be some coercive Power, to compel men equally to the performance of their Covenants ... *Justice is the constant Will of giving every man his own* ... where there is no Common-wealth, there is nothing Unjust'. (Hobbes 1996: 100–1)

Of the remaining sixteen laws of nature given by Hobbes, the fifth is particularly important for my argument here. He calls it 'compleasance', which he explicates with proposition that 'there is in mens aptnesse to Society, a diversity of Nature, rising from their diversity of Affections ... The observers of this Law, may be called SOCIABLE' (Hobbes 1996: 106). Building on his argument on individual differences, Hobbes contends that not all individuals have the same appetite for sociability. Yet a general 'aptness' to life in society is none the less a law of nature because it is required for the establishment of long-lasting peace. While strife, fear and self-preservation are the constitutive elements of human psychology in the state of nature, after the rise of the Leviathan *sociability itself becomes a law of nature*. In fact, apart from the fourteenth law of nature on primogeniture that reads as increasingly idiosyncratic, all the other laws of nature are compatible with universalistic theories of social order. On the one hand, there is a first group that can be read as personality traits: gratitude (fourth), facility of pardon (sixth), avoiding cruelty (seventh), not showing contempt for others (eighth), avoiding pride (ninth), avoiding arrogance (tenth). On the other hand a second group resembles a sense of justice and procedural impartiality in terms of rational exchanges of argument and rules for deciding adjudication: appointed judges must uphold equity (eleventh), there must be regulations on the equal use of common things (twelfth, thirteenth), safe treatment for those who act as mediators (fifteenth), submission to arbiters (sixteenth), nobody can be his own judge (seventeenth), judges must be impartial (eighteenth) and witnesses must be truthful and be trusted (nineteenth).[8] This second group clearly points towards the kind of proceduralism that characterises modern scientific, legal and moral discourse (see Chapters 1, 5 and 8).

All of Hobbes's laws of nature have, then, two things in common. First, they refer to, and try to foster, sociability itself. They certainly seek to prevent a return to a state of continuous warfare, but they do more than that as they positively describe the kinds of behaviour and social institutions that can actively encourage sociability. Secondly, they are based on strong universalistic underpinnings: human beings, and human beings alone, are the focus of Hobbes's natural law. All the laws – peace,

[8] A similar list is also found in Hobbes (1999: 87–99).

justice, covenants, sociability – apply exclusively to human beings and how they ought to relate to one another. Hobbes makes this point explicitly as he explicates that the types of covenant he has in mind exclude pacts with all forms of non-human entities: 'To make Covenants with bruit Beasts, is impossible; because not understanding our speech, they understand not, nor accept of any translation of Right . . . To make Covenants with God is impossible . . . [as] . . . we know not whether our Covenant be accepted, or not' (Hobbes 1996: 97).[9]

For social life to emerge, a domain of radical immanence in which human beings recognise and treat each other as fully fledged human beings is essential. In turn, we need to develop a wholly immanent science of wholly immanent social life – not least because no real knowledge, but only faith or belief, is possible in the realm of the supernatural (Hobbes 1996: 103). Hobbes's moral philosophy then seeks to understand human action, and indeed social life itself, through immanent means alone, as knowledge of natural laws 'is the true and onely Moral Philosophy. For Morall Philosophy is nothing else but the Science of what is *Good*, and *Evill*, in the conversation, and Society of man-kind' (110). The function of moral philosophy in this general 'conversation' that is the 'society of mankind' is thus to enable human beings to know about good and evil. This depiction again contrasts quite radically with how Hobbes had described the poor, lonely and brutish life of human beings in the state of nature. To be sure, a strong universalism is central to bring his discussion of natural law to an end '[t]he Lawes of Nature are Immutable and Eternall; For Injustice, Ingratitude, Arrogance, Pride, Iniquity, Acception of persons, and the rest, can never be made lawfull' (110), and he eventually summarises the results of these nineteen natural laws with a reference to the golden rule: '[*d*]*o not that to another, which thou wouldest not have done to thy selfe*' (109).[10] While the seed of proceduralism is surely present here – not least in the formal and non-substantive way in which he has defined natural rights and above all natural laws – Hobbes does not do much with this formulation. Indeed, it may still be a somewhat automatic reflex in terms of the presence of religious arguments and influences in his work. But it is none the less interesting that Hobbes finds it adequate as a summary of his more extended discussion of the laws of nature. As we shall see, this will become a major thread in the engagement of Rousseau, Kant and Hegel with modern natural law.

[9] As we shall see in the next chapter, Kant had a similar concern with delimiting the realm of morality as an ambit of action that is exclusively human.

[10] Earlier in the text, he refers to the positive formulation of this argument in the Gospels (Hobbes 1996: 92).

Hobbes does not base the human need to leave the state of nature on any ultimate moral drive; rather, he is trying to explain it on the basis of what is actually inscribed in human nature. Human beings are the way they are, and treat each other in the way that they do, because this is their nature: this is Hobbes's descriptive claim about human beings. From there he derives a normative argument as to why it is rational for human beings to surrender their natural liberty and create the conditions that will make possible a stable social order. Crucially, then, Hobbes thinks that he has determined what the best normative order is by deriving it from his descriptive arguments about human nature. But the three aspects of human nature that allowed him to explain the rise of the Leviathan – the original natural rights to self-defence, the pursuit of one's interest and liberty – no longer suffice when seeking to account for how social life unfolds inside a commonwealth. Human beings' three natural rights are then transformed into nineteen different natural laws that: (1) favour the longer-term stability of the Leviathan; (2) create conditions for the impartial resolution of conflicts and, arguably most importantly, (3) foster sociability between human beings themselves. Hobbes's negative idea of human nature that centres on egoism and naked force, a human nature that is devoid of any appetite for society whatsoever, applies only to what happens to human beings *before the rise of the Leviathan* (or, indeed, as the Leviathan collapses and individuals are pushed back to a condition of continuous warfare). But the radical epochal change that is triggered by the erection of the Leviathan alters human beings to their core as they now develop an unprecedented appetite for society: they discover science, art, philosophy as well as the pleasures that come from peaceful human proximity. The stability of the Leviathan is the condition of possibility for its emergence and success, but for that to occur there are values, practices and institutions that cannot be explicated only by recourse to the 'natural' rationality of self-interest. Hobbes's own laws of nature depend upon certain universalistic commitments by which human beings recognise and treat one another as human beings, and for this to happen personal virtues as well as collective arrangements have to be in place: honesty, modesty, integrity, fairness, equality, trust, impartiality. Hobbes's strategy depends upon a radical separation between the asocial state of nature and fully fledged social relations in the commonwealth because radically different conceptions of human nature apply to each condition.

Rousseau

There is no single text that brings together Rousseau's views on natural law. But his most systematic treatment of such themes as human nature and the state of nature, his *Discourse on the Origin of Inequality*, offers a good place to start at least because its full title is 'What is the origin of inequality among men, and is it authorised by natural law?' (Rousseau 1993b). Yet neither in *Discourse* nor in *Social Contract* (Rousseau 1993c) is there a systematic treatment of natural law, so my goal below is to try to reconstruct his view on the arguments that we have seen are constitutive of the natural law tradition.

Early in *Discourse*, Rousseau asks rhetorically for the Aristotle of 'the present age' and replies that his enquiry is to lead him to design the right 'experiments' with which to 'discover the natural man' (Rousseau 1993b: 44). While the reference to experiments is arguably an expression of the growing legitimacy of the natural sciences by the mid-eighteenth century, the kind of experiments he has in mind remain philosophical ones. In fact, they explicitly engage with previous misrepresentations of human nature with the purpose that we are at last able to understand 'what is original and what is artificial in the actual nature of man, or to form a true idea of a state which no longer exists; and of which it is, nevertheless, necessary to have true ideas' (44). That state that no longer exists but without which we cannot think about human nature is of course the state of nature. A key theme running through Rousseau's engagement with natural law is then an explicit discussion with those philosophers of the previous century who, although they understood the real philosophical challenges, were none the less unable to address them adequately. In this connection, Rousseau repeatedly mentions Grotius, Spinoza, Puffendorf and mostly Hobbes. He praises their awareness of the need to have a clear concept of the state of nature as the philosophical procedure with the help of which to derive the best possible social and political institutions. Yet at the same time they have all developed mistaken conceptions of it. Seventeenth-century natural lawyers, argues Rousseau, 'have all felt the need of going back to the state of nature; but none of them has got there' and in fact they have all committed the same error (50). They mistake causes for consequences and endow human nature with what are effectively social attributes: 'every one of them ... has transferred to the state of nature ideas which were acquired in society; so that, in speaking of the savage, they described the social man' (50).[11] A wholly new way of approaching the old themes of the state of nature and human nature must be put in place so that human beings can begin to discern the fundamentals of human existence by themselves. Natural law is to be discovered not 'in all the huge volumes that moralists have ever written' but in human beings looking at

[11] Similar critical comments, devoted mostly but by no means exclusively against Hobbes, can be found in Rousseau (1993b: 26–7, 54, 71–2, 97; 1993c: 169, 176, 182–90).

themselves as how they really are – a task which he connects to the oracle of the Temple of Delphi: 'know thyself!' (43).[12]

We shall encounter this claim to originality and need for a fresh start several times in the next chapters and it is already apparent that the more Rousseau criticises the work of previous natural theorists, the more his arguments lie conventionally within the main tenets of the natural law tradition. Thus, in the best tradition of natural law, he contends that the noblest intellectual pursuit remains 'our very study of man' (Rousseau 1993b: 43), or equally he claims to 'confidently uphold the cause of humanity' because the most 'useful' but 'imperfect' of the human sciences remains that of the study of 'mankind' itself (49). At the opening of *Social Contract* he echoes Hobbes's own attempt to bring together descriptive and normative arguments as the challenge is understanding human beings 'as they are and laws as they might be' (Rousseau 1993c: 181).

But a first difference between Hobbes and Rousseau in relation to their conceptualisations of the state of nature is that the latter explicitly ponders on its conceptual and historical status. Rousseau argues that his reflections on the subject 'must not be considered as historical truths, but only as mere conditional and hypothetic reasonings, rather calculated to explain the nature of things, than to ascertain their actual origin' (Rousseau 1993b: 50–1). He is most probably here circumventing the still contentious issue of how to reconcile empirical historical research and biblical hermeneutics: 'it is clear from the Holy Scriptures that the first man, having himself received his understanding and commandments immediately from God, was not himself in such state [of nature]' (50). This first man of the Bible is already outside the state of nature because he had already been given god's laws, whereas in the state of nature he could have been aware of no laws at all.[13]

Rousseau's claim is also different from Hobbes's in that his arguments were supposed to work through a combination of inductive and deductive propositions. The inductive side is of course most apparent in the constant references he makes to the empirical developments in

[12] See, in Chapter 6, how Tönnies also uses this motto in describing sociology's normative task.

[13] Hobbes (1996: 25) argues similarly when he makes reference to Adam and the tower of Babel as historical facts. The recourse to the state of nature is anti-religious in both Hobbes and Rousseau to the extent that they reject the idea of natural sociality in 'natural man'. It is only by making the ideas of natural man and state of nature asocial that they can remain compatible, even if only in appearance, with biblical teaching (Strauss 1974: 271). See also Chapter 2 above, where we discussed Karl Löwith's claim that Voltaire is the first writer to make the methodological point that holy writings cannot be uncritically turned into historical sources.

anthropology at the time. This is the context in which Rousseau expresses his views on slavery, European expansion and the *bon sauvage*. Rousseau comments on how some practices and institutions of 'savages' are surely positive when compared with the corrupted practices and institutions of 'civilisation' and argues that 'our minds have corrupted in proportion as the arts and sciences have improved' (Rousseau 1993a: 8). The purity and simplicity of early times contrasts badly with the decadence of contemporary society, so much so that 'all subsequent advances have been apparently so many steps towards perfection of the individual but in reality towards the decrepitude of the species' (Rousseau 1993b: 91).

These comments are critical of contemporary developments and institutions but are by no means a general indictment of the highest kind of civilised life that human beings have been able to produce – a republic that is governed by a self-legislating people. First, Rousseau maintains that civil liberty is always to be preferred to natural liberty and all the depravities that human beings create as they come to live in society are more than compensated by the stimulation of faculties, new ideas, ennobled feelings and an uplifted soul as they live in society. As he realises these accomplishments, the individual 'would be bound to bless continually the happy moment which took him from it [the state of nature] for ever' (Rousseau 1993c: 195–6). Secondly, Rousseau also repudiates the crimes that, allegedly on behalf of 'civilisation', were carried out by European powers in their conquering endeavours. In a passage that Leo Strauss has connected to Kant's perpetual peace writings, for instance, Rousseau argues that 'you ought to have had the express and universal consent of mankind, before appropriating more of the common subsistence than you needed for your own maintenance' (Rousseau 1993b: 98).[14] Thirdly, and following Hannah Arendt's reading, while Rousseau's positive views on natural men and the state of nature do have the (critique of) colonial encounters in their background, even more important is the rise of the poor as relevant political actors in modern society. As we will discuss below, wealth figures highly in Rousseau's account of how civilisation negatively affects our natural goodness and in that context the contrast with the poor becomes all the more important: '[t]hat the wretched life of the poor was confronted by the rotten life of the rich is

[14] See Strauss (1974: 255). This kind of universalistic regulative principle refutes the highly unilateral statements in leading postcolonial theorising for which European thinking at the time was wholly racist and imperialist and could never think beyond the idea of *terra nullius*, a land without owners, as the 'sinister presupposition for social science' (Connell 2007: 47). For a general account of Rousseau's view against imperialism, see Muthu (2003).

crucial for an understanding of what Rousseau and Robespierre meant when they asserted that men are good "by nature" and become rotten by means of society' (Arendt 1965: 101). Finally, Rousseau contrasts what is beneficial for the individual in particular with what is beneficial for the species as a whole. While arguably this still reflects the tension between the cosmological and the anthropological foundations of natural law claims, his explicit argument leans towards anthropology: we need to know what human nature ultimately is because sound social and political institutions can be formed exclusively on its basis. In turn, the only way to understand human nature is to grasp human life at its barest, so towards the end of *Discourse* Rousseau's contention is in fact to have traced the origins of inequality:

> [a]s far as these are capable of being deduced from the nature of man merely by the light of reason, and independently of those sacred dogmas which give the sanction of divine right to sovereign authority. It follows from this survey that, as there is hardly any inequality in the state of nature, all the inequality which now prevails owes its strength and growth to the development of our faculties and the advance of the human mind, and becomes at last permanent and legitimate by the establishment of property and laws. (Rousseau 1993b: 116)[15]

Similar to Hobbes's argument, then, Rousseau's state of nature has no social institutions. It is a wholly individualistic condition within which, to the extent that people interact, their exchanges are sporadic and do not form stable social relations. Rousseau also argues that all human beings are equal in the state of nature and that their natural differences in terms of strength and abilities do not pose insurmountable problems. Real inequality emerges later and as a result of social relations. The task then is to understand the specific conditions of both natural equality and artificial inequality, on the one hand, and the causes that explain the transition from the former to the latter, on the other. Nature and society move in different directions and the plan is to 'reflect on the equality which nature has ordained between men, and the inequality which they have introduced' (Rousseau 1993b: 32). Rousseau also echoes Hobbes's views on how the rise of political institutions needs to be understood *vis-à-vis* what is natural and what is artificial in human life: '[t]he constitution of man is the work of nature, that of the state the work of art' (Rousseau 1993c: 260).

Rousseau does not clearly distinguish between natural right and natural law. For him they equally refer to first principles which, being discovered by reason, tell us about what human nature actually is.

15 As we shall see in the next chapter, this permanent and to a large extent also inconsistent attempt to combine inductive and deductive strategies will be central to both Kant's and Hegel's rejection of state of nature theories.

In relation to natural law, the argument only gains further specification as he speaks of 'two principles prior to reason, one of them deeply interesting us in our own welfare and preservation, and the other exciting a natural repugnance at seeing any other sensible being, and particularly *any of our species*, suffer pain or death' (Rousseau 1993b: 47, my italics). The way in which Rousseau elaborates on these two principles is worth exploring in greater detail because of what they tell us about his conception of human nature. A first thing to note is that Rousseau offers a more complex depiction of basic human drives in the state of nature than Hobbes did. There is more to human beings in the state of nature than liberty understood as self-defence and the pursuit of one's interests. A strictly *human* sensibility towards the suffering of fellow human beings is as natural a disposition in the state of nature as our self-interest. Human beings are the possessors of two foundational features that point in different directions, self-preservation *and* compassion; what matters, argues Rousseau, is whether and how these two impulses meet in actual human behaviour. The kind of long-lasting social institutions that humans beings will eventually build to address these two basic human drives cannot be anticipated. Equally, whether aggression or cooperation ensues will depend upon the situation and neither can claim logical or ontological priority:

> [l]et us not conclude, with Hobbes, that because man has no idea of goodness, he must naturally be wicked . . . that he always refuses his fellow-creature services which he does not think they have a right to demand, or that by virtue of the right he justly claims to all he needs, he foolishly imagines himself the sole proprietor of the whole universe. Hobbes had seen clearly the defects of all the modern definitions of natural right: but the consequences which he deduces from his own show that he understands it in an equally false sense . . . he ought to have said that the state of nature, being that in which the care of our own preservation is the least prejudicial to that of others, was consequently best calculated to promote peace, and the most suitable for mankind. (Rousseau 1993c: 71–2)[16]

[16] First published in 1755, Rousseau's *Discourse on Inequality* follows the criticism of Hobbes that Montesquieu had advanced a few years earlier, in *The Spirit of the Laws* (1748). Instead of domination and struggle, which are social rather than asocial, fear would in fact be a more appropriate representation of the original state of nature because it would actually prevent most forms of social interaction: 'Hobbes gives men first the desire to subjugate one another, but this is not reasonable. The idea of empire and domination is so complex and depends on so many other ideas, that it would not be the one they would first have [in the state of nature]' (Montesquieu 1989: 6). Incidentally, in relation to the religious references that we discussed in note 13 above, in contradistinction to both Hobbes and Rousseau, Montesquieu claims in the same page that divine law is the first natural law in 'importance', although it is not the first to be discovered in the state of nature.

With Hobbes, Rousseau's idea of human nature is individualistic as no real principle of sociability is accepted in the depiction of the state of nature; against Hobbes, Rousseau claims that human nature is complex because it also contains a dimension of compassion. Rousseau will then add a new feature that will prove crucial for his most famous argument on the general will: the individual's 'character as a free agent' who, as such, is able to 'act of free will' (Rousseau 1993b: 59). Another element is the human capacity for 'self-improvement' and this 'perfectibility', this human ability to learn and improve, will prove crucial in the transition out of the state of nature (60). Rousseau then elaborates further on compassion as the sensibility toward the suffering, pain or death of the fellow members of our species. He describes compassion as 'universal and useful to mankind' (73) and, being a 'natural feeling', its goal is

> [m]oderating the activity of love of self in each individual, contribut[ing] to the preservation of the whole species . . . it is this which in a state of nature supplies the place of laws, morals, and virtues, with the advantage that none are tempted to disobey its gentle voice. (Rousseau 1993b: 76)[17]

Rousseau's argument on compassion is important because he makes it central to his rendition of the golden rule that we have seen was also part of Hobbes's views on natural law. It is compassion that is the motive that provides the kind of proceduralisation that is needed for social relations to function on the basis of what we have discovered about human nature. Rousseau (1993b: 76) suggests replacing that 'sublime maxim of rational justice, *Do to others as you would have them do unto you* . . . with that other maxim of natural goodness, much less perfect indeed, but perhaps more useful; *Do good to yourself with as little evil as possible to others*'. Self-interest and compassion regulate one another: the 'good' to which he refers here can in fact be read as a combination of both. With this new rendition of the golden rule Rousseau makes even clearer his separation from traditional religious teachings, and arguably even more important for us is the fact that, as a procedure, it needs to prove useful in orientating social action rather than seeking logical correctness for its own sake.[18]

Rousseau's argument on compassion is thus made in terms of human beings' natural disposition. It is general compassion directed to fellow members of our species rather than a particular feeling towards particular members with whom one may share one or more features: 'what is generosity, clemency, or humanity but compassion applied to the weak,

[17] See Arendt (1965: 70–94) for further discussion on Rousseau's idea of compassion.
[18] As in Hegel's classical critique of Kant's categorical imperative. See Chapter 5.

the guilty, or to mankind in general?' (Rousseau 1993b: 75).[19] This idea of universal compassion towards fellow species members develops alongside the other dimensions of human nature – self-preservation, freedom and self-improvement – and is still individualistic. But arguably there is an inherently social side to natural compassion as it requires some kind of empathic understanding: either the state of nature is fully individualistic, in which case compassion can hardly be found there, or else we need to accept that there is a social dimension in the state of nature. Rousseau's argument is complicated because, with the rise of fully fledged social relations, human beings begin to develop all kinds of negative drives and traits: jealousy, envy, competition, deceit, vice, vanity, contempt (90). Social life puts pressure on the primordial psychology of natural men so now it becomes in their own interest 'to appear what they really were not. To be and to seem became two totally different things' (95). But Rousseau thus distinguishes four main ways in which people create a sense of hierarchical esteem among themselves: 'riches, nobility or rank, power and personal merit' (111). These are not, however, of exactly the same importance because, in an argument that resembles Hobbes's unification of different types of social esteem into one all-encompassing view of power, for Rousseau wealth is really 'the one to which they are all reduced' (111).

To be sure, the importance Rousseau attributes to wealth reflects the rise of the bourgeoisie and the wider socio-economic transformations of the eighteenth century. But Rousseau offered a more complex vision of natural human psychology in the state of nature than Hobbes: where Hobbes only saw self-preservation and had a rather minimal view of freedom as the absence of external impediments, Rousseau added more substantive dimensions such as free will, self-improvement and, even if inconsistently, also compassion.[20] Yet Rousseau's depiction of social life after human beings have abandoned the state of nature is arguably more problematic. For Hobbes, power relations are only ubiquitous in the state of nature whereas all types of virtuous institutions and practices begin to develop inside a peaceful commonwealth. In contrast,

[19] A similar attitude is found as Rousseau argues that it is only from feelings towards fellow countrymen that an adequate cosmopolitan horizon can be construed. At the same time as he favours this kind of cosmopolitan universalism he warns against 'boast[ing] love of the whole world so as to have the right to love no one at all' (Rousseau 1993d: 175).

[20] Skinner (2008: 124–77) offers this minimalist interpretation of freedom in Hobbes in contrast to the more substantive republican freedom in Rousseau. A free will as essentially self-legislating is central to Rousseau in a way that is alien in, if not directly opposed to, Hobbes.

Rousseau's depiction of social life itself is rather grim; compassion has not fully disappeared but now coexists with all these other negative traits that only emerge fully in social life – they are themselves constitutive of human sociality. An idea of unsocial sociability, which will also reappear in Kant, becomes key to Rousseau's conceptualisation of social relations:

> Our needs bring us together at the same time as our passions divide us, and the more we become enemies of fellow-men, the less we can do without them. Such are the first bonds of general society; such are the foundations of that universal benevolence which seems to be stifled in our hearts just when our minds recognize the need for it. (Rousseau 1993c: 169)

Law becomes the most important institution through which human beings regulate social interaction. Law sublates men's *natural* equality, as it is found in the state of nature, into *human* equality – equality before the law as expressed in the participation of all individuals in the sovereign. Indeed, participation in law-making processes is constitutive of Rousseau's idea of freedom. As they leave the state of nature, peoples organise themselves as self-legislating units, they form human communities in which everyone has the same say in the creation of political institutions and the general regulation of social life. A people becomes a people only through the law: 'when the people decrees for the whole people ... is what I call law' (Rousseau 1993c: 211). Rousseau's social contract is not a contract between the people and the government or the state; it is rather a contract between the people themselves. Only the people as a whole, united as a general will, can duly make the laws and because laws always refer to the general interest and never to particular interests, 'no one is unjust to himself' (212). Rousseau's well-known argument about the limitations of representation equally follows from this: '[l]aw being purely the declaration of the general will, it is clear that, in the exercise of the legislative power, the people cannot be represented' (267). While as a political principle this critique of representation is problematic or even unrealistic, its internalist component has become one of our major normative intuitions in modernity: when their personal life options are at stake, individuals ought to be able to make their own decisions. A radical legal constructivism arguably becomes the logical conclusion of Rousseau's argument, as he effectively blurs the distinction between positive and natural law: the general will is the only and true source of all law, so whatever the people will as law must become the law. He puts it thus: 'there is in the State no fundamental law that cannot be revoked, and not excluding the social compact itself; for if all the citizens assembled of one accord to break the compact, it is impossible to doubt that it would be very legitimately broken' (273). He eventually takes the final step that we have somehow been waiting for all along. By entering into a condition of full social relations where civil laws apply, at stake is effectively 'changing human nature, of transforming each individual, who is by himself a complete and solitary whole, into part of a greater whole from which he in a manner receives his life and being' (214).

The idea of individuality that Rousseau had deployed in his depiction of the state of nature has begun to crack – indeed, as Durkheim (1970: 101) has argued, public autonomy takes precedence over private autonomy in Rousseau's thinking (see Chapter 6 below). When it comes to the establishment of stable political institutions, absolute individual renunciation is as key in Rousseau as it is in Hobbes. But for Rousseau the recipient of this renunciation is the body of citizens themselves, the general will, rather than the state as a body that is separated from the people, as is the case in Hobbes. For Rousseau, then, while the individual remains central *vis-à-vis* the question of representation, she is pretty much left unprotected *vis-à-vis* the will of fellow citizens; Rousseau favours, therefore, 'the total alienation of each associate, together with all his rights, to the whole community' (Rousseau 1993c: 191). Rousseau's well-known remarks about individuals being forced to be free are then a logical conclusion to Rousseau's struggle and ultimate inability to see how central the individual was to become and remain in modern society both descriptively and normatively.[21]

Closing remarks

In their different ways, the theories of both Hobbes and Rousseau share a concern with what we may call the preconditions for the rise of social relations. On the one hand, they see individuals and the state of nature as primary and social relations as secondary. On the other hand, a wholly human life only begins to develop as individuals abandon the state of nature and engage decidedly in social relations. The artificiality of

[21] Rousseau's (1993c: 195) formulation reads as follows: 'whoever refuses to obey the general will shall be compelled to do so by the whole body. This means nothing less than he will be forced to be free'. In Löwith's (1967: 233–42) reading, Rousseau is the first philosopher to see in the differentiation between man and citizen, and between universal religious faith and particular political affiliations, the impossibility of unification that is constitutive of modern society. Rousseau being the first to have grasped this tension, Löwith contends that it was Hegel who eventually drew its more general implications. The authoritarian tendencies in this claim on the primacy of public autonomy may also explicate, for instance, Habermas's justified insistence in the co-originality and co-dependence of public and private autonomy in modern constitutional states (see Chapter 1 above).

social life effectively creates a new environment for human beings and both philosophers sought to weigh up the relative influence and autonomy of individual/natural factors *vis-à-vis* social/artificial ones. A problem then emerges for both writers because two mutually contradictory propositions are equally needed: at the same time as a radical caesura is supposed to mark the transition between the state of nature and social life, and stable human life is only possible in the latter, the very transition needs to be explicated on the basis of the natural properties that individuals leave behind in the state of nature. Hobbes and Rousseau equally argue that these natural properties are cancelled precisely at the moment in which men leave the state of nature. Society's *second* nature, social 'artificiality', is the sublation, the suspension and carrying forward, of men's natural qualities: the latter constitute the base that makes social life possible but then our human potential is radically transformed through social life. The artificiality of the Leviathan, as much as that of the general will, effectively transforms who we are as human beings. While they strengthen and enhance our human potential, natural qualities are pushed to the background without, however, disappearing altogether. Natural qualities are sublated because those features that were the condition of possibility for social relations to have emerged are turned into their exact opposite.

Hobbes's egoistic and suspicious individuals lead a nasty, poor and brutish life that only knows about self-preservation and the pursuit of their own ends. As they form a commonwealth, however, sociability becomes a major force in the re-shaping of their fundamental human traits. Individuals are now regulated by a complex web of natural laws, all of which point to the preservation and widening of their newly born sociability. It is only as social life emerges that we learn about such higher institutions and practices as science, morality or the rule of law. For their part, Rousseau's natural men have a wonderful innate sociability that, although it accepts a certain primacy of self-interest, crucially includes self-improvement and compassion. As these natural men enter social life, however, these positive qualities weaken while such traits as jealousy, envy, deceit and vanity all begin to take centre stage. The unsocial sociability that thus emerges makes 'civilised' life less pleasurable and more demanding than life in the state of nature, but this loss of natural equality is eventually compensated by the decisive transformation that legal equality brings with it. It is only as they abandon the state of nature that individuals have at least the opportunity to become free and to start calling themselves *human* beings – the highest prize of all being the actualisation of individual and collective freedom as equal members of a self-legislating people. Even though the substantive properties they attribute to the state of nature and social life are actually inverted, Hobbes's and Rousseau's arguments operate in the same way: the natural qualities that were the preconditions for social life to have emerged and for human qualities to have developed are eventually downplayed. They are the necessary conditions for the rise of a social life that can then be called human – and yet are unnecessary in social life itself. In turn, the more society comes to the forefront in their thinking, the more their anthropology goes to the background. This is a general movement that fundamentally marks the relationships between natural law and social theory.

In the next chapter we shall see how Kant and Hegel will pick up on the inconsistency that is implied in a procedure that, while it was supposed to grasp individuality at its barest lent itself, however, to views as radically opposing as those to be found in Hobbes and Rousseau. But as we try to establish the relevance of these arguments *vis-à-vis* the rise of modern social theory, let me finish by highlighting three additional issues in which the influence of their arguments is clearly felt.

(1) Hobbes and Rousseau are among the first to reflect on the complicated connections between anthropological arguments on our shared humanity and sociological ones on what makes the social an autonomous domain. The anthropological focus of their reflections on the state of nature is inverted first, and then pushed to the background, as the influence of society is explicitly introduced. They are also among the first to consider the transition from the state of nature to civil life as a radical caesura in which social life itself takes centre stage, human nature is transformed, and there are different laws of nature in each case. In Grotius, Puffendorf, Montesquieu and Locke, there is continuity between the state of nature and the civil condition: human nature does not change and the same natural laws apply (Laslett 1988: 67–122). One question that remains is whether, as a radical caesura, the transition from the state of nature to civil life was supposed to work analytically and/or historically. A distinction that has proved to be rich in conceptual, methodological, substantive and indeed normative implications, it has then been reinvented in modern social theory's key dichotomies of community/society and tradition/modernity (Bendix 1967). That the similarities between these strategies have not attracted much attention in the literature remains one of the most puzzling aspects of the history of modern social theory. Whatever the causes, however, this kind of dichotomising strategy for thinking about historical transitions is to be found throughout twentieth-century and contemporary social theory: industrial, post-industrial and then information modernity; first/second modernity; national/global modernity (Chernilo 2007: 129–33). We briefly mentioned

it in Chapter 1 with Habermas's distinction between system and life-world and we shall explore it more systematically in Chapter 6.[22]

(2) There is of course the question of universalism: both theories seek to grasp the general conditions that make possible the emergence of social relations as preconditions for the development of our fundamental human traits. All their main notions like natural men, state of nature, social life, humanity are based on a universalistic orientation – not least, as they are introduced and explicated without recourse to essential cultural factors that would make particular groups or peoples radically different from others. Natural attributes were as universal as those that emerge in society, but the former only allow for a very basic form of mutual identification, for instance fear of each other. Only sociality, in its artificiality, allows for the creation and recreation of those feelings with which we actually recognise one another as members of the same species. A true sense of common humanity is only possible in a social context and thanks to that context. We have also seen that this universalistic orientation equally finds expression in how key terms and intellectual procedures are consistently defined and justified in wholly immanent terms – to the extent that they appear at all, religious arguments do not have an analytical role to play and have little normative purchase. Immanent normative questions about morality and justice, peace and freedom appear constantly and become increasingly central. Yet both writers hint at the idea that universalism does not have to be equated with transcendental moral values or substantive conceptions of the good life. Hobbes and Rousseau understood that difficulties ensued whenever substantive answers were attempted and thus they tried to connect their reflections to some incipient forms of proceduralism. We cannot yet speak of a modern procedural turn, to be sure, but the role of procedural arguments and justifications remains a main thread accompanying us throughout this book.

[22] It is worth pointing out that these reflections on the state of nature also developed in the context of discussions about international order at the time: whether social order at the 'domestic' and the 'international' levels operated through the same principles. The standard view of the so-called 'domestic analogy' is that order in international society was to be analogically derived from what took place in domestic society, an argument that is conventionally attributed to Grotius (Bull 1977). See, however, Richard Tuck's (1999) claim that the analogy was meant to work the other way round: political theories in the seventeenth century had a clear vision of the international society and were trying to derive the conditions of domestic (or national) order from the international arena. I have discussed the main features and difficulties of the domestic analogy from the standpoint of natural law universalism in Chernilo (2010). See also Boticci (2003) and Suganami (1989).

(3) A final methodological issue has to do with the ways in which these authors were trying to handle the relationships between philosophical arguments and the increasing importance of empirical developments (in Rousseau's case, even inductive strategies). The need to connect, but without eliding, descriptive and normative levels of analysis will become increasingly urgent. Regardless of why they thought that their descriptive strategies would work, these writers did expect to discover human nature as it actually was. It is on the basis of these descriptive convictions that they sought normative purchase for their claims. Normative arguments were surely key for them, but they had to be distinguished, and only then reconnected, with descriptive ones. Yet however salient these 'empirical' findings became, they were to remain controlled by philosophical reflections. Science and philosophy did not talk to each other on an equal footing and what passed as acceptable or legitimate empirical knowledge was still to be decided by explicitly philosophical arguments. The ways in which we are (un)able to differentiate or integrate philosophical, historical, normative and empirical arguments have surely remained a major challenge, but also a great opportunity, for modern social theory.

5 Modern natural law II: Kant and Hegel on proceduralism and ethical life

Kant

There is little doubt that Kant saw his own philosophical work as seeking to move beyond what he regarded as the inadequate natural law mainstream of his time. This was best represented in the theories of Grotius, Puffendorf and other natural lawyers, whom Kant dismissed as mere 'sorry comforters' as they failed to address the ugliness and lawlessness of war with a meaningful concept of right (Kant 1999: 103). Kant and his followers may well have been consciously exaggerating the extent to which his philosophical project owed no debt to seventeenth-century natural law (Hochstrasser 2000: 18–19). Neither passive reception nor complete rejection will then be my argument for understanding Kant's debt to natural law: he was transforming it. Kant's innovations lie less in what he claimed was original in his own work than in having advanced further a number of the key issues that we have already encountered as central to natural law theory. Kant took from natural law what he thought was 'the determining problem for practical philosophy. He did not accept their solution; but he thought they were essentially right in seeing one issue – *the issue of social conflict* – as the first issue for which morality had to be suited' (Schneewind 1993: 55, my italics).[1]

To locate the idea of social conflict at the centre of Kant's ideas of human nature and natural law is consistent with what we discussed in Chapter 3. Kant's moral theory also offers a wholly immanent approach to understanding morality both in terms of how we come to know about what constitutes a moral action and where the normative force of moral commands ultimately comes from: 'Kant's metaphysics of the will . . . seeks to organize the universal around principles legislated by humans (or by human reason) for humans (or for human reasons)' (Thornhill 2007: 102). Below I shall argue that the strength of Kant's radical immanence

[1] On Kant's engagement with modern natural law, see also Apel (2004), Gregor (1993) and Fine (2011).

lies, somewhat paradoxically, in its attachment to a transcendental conception of the human, but his emphasis on immanent procedures again reinforces the connections between his moral philosophy and the natural law tradition. Yet arguably the most salient feature of Kant's practical philosophy in relation to natural law is its commitment to universalism. All the major concepts of Kant's moral theory – will, freedom, right, duty, virtue, justice – are defined and explicitly refer to a universal comprehension of human beings *qua* human beings. However much he may have transformed these areas of enquiry, then, his interest in social conflict, an immanent approach to moral issues and a strong universalistic orientation all locate Kant firmly within the natural law tradition. The question for us now is to determine the specific contribution of Kant's moral theory *vis-à-vis* both previous natural law theory and later modern social theory.

For our purposes in this chapter, two of Kant's texts stand out: his *Groundwork of the Metaphysics of Morals*, first published in 1785 (Kant 1997) and the *Metaphysics of Morals*, from 1797 (Kant 1996). The question of the philosophical status of Kant's arguments figures prominently in both texts and in that context he defines natural law in familiar terms: the '*systematic* knowledge of the doctrine of natural right (*ius naturae...*) must supply the immutable principles for any giving of positive law' (Kant 1996: 23). The problem for philosophy, argues Kant, is that it is now in a 'precarious position' because it must be 'firm even though there is nothing in heaven or on earth from which it depends or on which it is based'. If philosophy is to remain a form of knowledge worthy of its name and tradition, it is 'to manifest its purity as sustainer of its own laws' (Kant 1997: 35). Indeed, Kant was under no illusion about the popularity of his conception of philosophy at the time: 'if votes were collected as to which is to be preferred – pure rational cognition separated from anything empirical, hence metaphysics of morals, or popular practical philosophy – one can guess at once on which side the preponderance would fall' (21).

The a priori status that Kant claims for his philosophy is surely at the centre of what is now seen as problematic in Kant's project (see Chapter 1). Wholly a priori principles were, however, expected to do precisely what religious and cosmological foundations were thought to have achieved but never actually accomplished: to lay unshakable grounds upon which true knowledge about natural, individual and moral affairs could be established. We can perhaps better appreciate what Kant's aim was if we connect it to his criticisms of the ways in which Hobbes and Rousseau explicate what human nature is and how we come to know about it: for Kant too much has already been said about human nature for too little gain. Previous philosophers have moved in circles and argued pointlessly: it is 'perfection, now happiness, here moral feeling, there fear of God, a bit of this and also a bit of that in a marvellous mixture, without its occurring to them to ask whether the principles of morality are to be sought at all in acquaintance with human nature' (Kant 1997: 22). Kant thus rejects both the belief that we can determine positively the content of universal human nature *and* the view that moral commands can be deduced from whatever properties we endow human nature with: 'a metaphysics of morals cannot be based upon an anthropology but still can be applied to it' (Kant 1996: 10). The search for definitive conceptions of human nature has remained too substantive, a result which is based on the lack of clear principles with which to justify it as a philosophical enquiry. The study of human morality, 'has to do not with the matter of the action and what is to result from it, but with *the form and the principle* from which the action itself follows' (Kant 1997: 27, my italics). A more decided emphasis on justificatory strategies, on proceduralism, will be the path to follow.[2]

As we have seen, Hobbes and Rousseau had already made claims for the need for some kind of procedural turn for natural law to work in modern times: Hobbes by recourse to the golden rule and his nineteen laws of nature and Rousseau with his somewhat ambiguous formulation of 'doing good to yourself with as little evil as possible to others'. To an extent, Kant is here repeating what Hobbes and Rousseau had done before him: he takes his predecessors to task for their failure to realise that they are reproducing, rather than overcoming, the shortcomings of previous natural law arguments. Kant's innovation cannot be underestimated, yet he is building on what were by now relatively well-established arguments. His criticisms of previous state of nature theories actually mimic those we discussed in the previous chapter. Hobbes thought that he had put the idea of the state of nature on a firm footing by getting rid of the idea of natural sociality and replacing it with the idea of egoistic self-preservation. Rousseau accepted Hobbes's individualistic starting point but rejected the view that this necessarily led to conflict – compassion was equally if not more important in the state of nature.

Kant's handling of the idea of the state of nature remains somewhat perplexing. On the one hand, it is hardly mentioned in the early *Groundwork of the Metaphysics of Morals*, and indeed the centrality of the categorical imperative in that book is arguably an attempt to found

[2] This rejection of the contribution of anthropology to the derivation of human nature and then social institutions is one key aspect in which Kant departs from previous modern natural law.

secular morality without recourse to a fictitious asocial condition. On the other hand, in his later *Metaphysics of Morals* Kant not only discussed but made rather extensive use of the idea of the state of nature as part of his own arguments. He first refers to the state of nature at the end of Chapter 1 of the *Metaphysics of Morals* and in the context of the discussion about what is involved in having only provisional possession of something because no full civil condition has already been established.[3] Given the systematic construction of Kant's works, in which first principles are laid out right at the start, this reference to the state of nature comes late and can thus be interpreted as having relatively secondary status within Kant's moral theory. As he eventually elaborates on the idea of the state of nature Kant distinguishes between two different kinds. There is, first, an '*original* community' that, as an idea, 'has objective (rightfully practical) reality'; and there is also a second '*primitive community* ... which is a fiction' (Kant 1996: 40). He explicates this distinction further as follows: '[e]ven if one thinks (problematically) of an *original* community ... it must still be distinguished from a *primitive* community ... which is supposed to have been instituted in the earliest *time* of relations among human beings and cannot be based, like the former, on principles but only on history' (Kant 1996: 47).

What we have is two different types of states of nature, neither of which is wholly unproblematic, even though the idea of an original community can be said to have some objective utility as it is based on principles rather than being a mere historical fiction. Kant will not do much with this distinction later on in the text, but it none the less expresses his somewhat reluctant commitment to a notion that, even though he found it problematic, was still expedient in contemporary philosophy. In fact, when the idea of the state of nature is used again in the text Kant now counterpoises it to the civil condition in rather conventional terms for what we have discussed before:

> A rightful condition is that relation of human beings among one another that contains the conditions under which alone everyone is able to *enjoy* his rights, a condition that is not rightful, that is, a condition in which there is no distributive justice, is called a state of nature. (Kant 1996: 84–5)

While the contrast Kant draws here between the civil condition and the state of nature is to a large extent similar to those drawn by Hobbes and Rousseau, Kant's argument departs from theirs because it is not based

[3] Kant's formulation does not give much away yet: 'the way to have something external as one's own *in a state of nature* is physical possession which has in its favour the rightful *presumption* that it will be made into rightful possession through being united with the will of all in a public lawgiving' (Kant 1996: 46).

on any positive statement about human nature. Even though he does not fully reject it, Kant effectively downgrades the foundational role of the state of nature, which may now remain as a convenient strategy for thinking about social interaction outside an overriding legal framework but is no longer conceived as the radical caesura in which human nature is sublated as we enter social life. The state of nature is now a strategy for contrasting lawful and unlawful relations but neither human nature nor social life depends upon how the state of nature is conceived. Kant is still to make an additional move that separates him from Hobbes and Rousseau. If the concept of the state of nature is to be retained, it cannot be devised as fundamentally pre- or asocial:

> What is opposed to a state of nature is not . . . a condition that is *social* and that could be called an artificial condition . . . but rather the *civil* condition . . . a society subject to distributive justice. For in the state of nature, too, there can be societies compatible with rights (e.g. conjugal, paternal, domestic societies in general, as well as many others); but no law . . . The *civil union* cannot itself be called a *society*, for between the *commander* . . . and the *subject* . . . there is no partnership. They are not fellow members: one is *subordinated to*, not *coordinated with* the other; and those who are coordinated with one another must for this very reason consider themselves equals since they are subject to common laws. (Kant 1996: 85)

Kant breaks with previous ways of drawing the contrast that required a clear-cut separation between a pure individuality that is untouched by social factors and a fully socialised one. A civil condition and the state of nature are equally social: hierarchical command and horizontal coordination are both types of social relation. The sociological significance of Kant's formulation lies in the claim that legal coordination is based on our fundamental equality as human beings. While there is of course more to society than legal relations, peaceful social life presupposes this type of universal equality before the law. Hobbes had already argued that legal relations were only possible between human beings and Kant now extends this as he argues that, by clarifying the importance of distributive justice in social life, human beings effectively acknowledge their fundamental equality: social order requires us to accept and treat one another as members of the same species.

The closest we get to a definition of human nature in Kant is his idea of unsocial sociability, a notion with which he again depicts the hierarchical and horizontal aspects of sociality. Unsocial sociability points to our selfish and individualistic side alongside our cooperative one: the two pull in different directions but are equally real and constitutive of our humanity (Kant 1999: 44). In the *Doctrine of Virtues*, which is Part II of *The Metaphysics of Morals*, Kant again makes the point that the deduction of unsocial sociability comes from pure practical reason and not from empirical human nature. He then discusses whether our actions can have ends that we can regard as unconditional duties and whether, because of that, we can have 'a categorical imperative' that corresponds to them. Indeed we have two such goals: '[t]hey are *one's own perfection* and *the happiness of others*' (Kant 1996: 149–50). Human beings are both social and unsocial, and have an equal duty towards themselves, in terms of their own perfection, and to others, in looking after their happiness or well-being. Kant's dual notion of human nature depends of course on his double use of nature in this context. Human beings have a first or 'natural' nature but have also a second, indeed more profound, moral nature. Both are equally real, hence susceptible to their own different laws of nature, but they are not of the same worth: '[a] human being has a duty to raise himself from the crude state of his nature, from his animality ... more and more towards humanity, by which he alone is capable of setting himself ends' (151). Kant moves natural law theory away from naturalistic determinations and, by the same token, reintroduces a more fundamental idea of nature now in terms of the first principles of human reason that are needed for determining sound moral action and indeed rationality in general.[4]

In its classical formulation, then, the categorical imperative states: 'act only in accordance with that maxim through which you can at the same time will that it become a universal law' (Kant 1997: 31).[5] Its most decisive innovation is the offer of an explicitly procedural definition of moral action; it is a rule with which to determine whether any particular action can be deemed as moral. It is this proceduralism that makes it stand out in relation to previous universalistic arguments; morality is no longer defined through positive commands to act in a particular way and nor is it defined as a derivation from human nature's substantive

[4] Chris Thornhill (2007: 105) reconstructs this as follow: '[a]uthentic natural law, in short, is in fact law *against* nature, not of nature, for it is only where humans divest themselves of the "heteronomy" of (first) nature (i.e. influence by instincts, urges and impulses) and they institute universally binding laws, as autonomy, second nature, or "rational nature" ... Real natural law is the law of autonomy or of genuine humanity.' It is surely Kant's view that second 'moral' nature is more important than first 'natural' nature, but I do not think that the former is truly *against* the latter. As we act morally we learn to guide or even sublate our first instincts. I shall discuss below that for Kant (1997: 19–20) it is impossible to go against our natural instincts because they will always remain part of who we are as human beings. Kant's general cosmology is *also* populated by purely rational beings who have no such problems, but human beings are way too imperfect and do not belong in that category.

[5] A less often quoted yet simpler formulation is 'act upon a maxim that can also hold as a universal law' (Kant 1996: 17). For further discussion, see John Rawls's (2000: 162–216) close inspection of the different versions of Kant's categorical imperative.

qualities. Rather, it now depends on the *justifications* that are given for individual maxims or actions to be upheld as potentially universal. To this extent at least it can be argued that Kant brings to its logical conclusion the natural law insight that conflict, change and variation are central to social life. As attempts to determine positively the definitive contents of the good life have become more and more problematic – if not outright impossible – the philosopher's goal is no longer to adjudicate between competing cultural contexts, historical traditions or conceptions of the good life. Rather, his role is to establish rules with the help of which *individuals themselves* can assess with certitude the moral worth of different maxims and courses of action.

Following what we have been discussing in the previous two chapters, the claim that we need to think about the potential for generalisation of our moral maxims presupposes that individuals hold different views that have to be taken into account. The categorical imperative offers a way of thinking about moral issues in which no specific cultural content, set of rules or particular values is automatically accepted or rejected. Actions as well as maxims can be considered moral until the open-ended nature of the procedure requires us to revise the grounds on which they are being justified as potentially universalisable. Kant's world is one in which justifications on the basis of one's own cultural traditions can still be made but their claims to normative acceptance have to be justified through impartial procedural adjudication.[6] Interestingly, criticisms of general principles or specific institutional contexts are not to be raised on the basis of alternative general principles. They are instead assessed against particular interests or concerns that emerge historically and out of the specific conditions in which a universalistic orientation is being called into question: the end of slavery, equal pay for women, the widening of the political franchise, asylum laws. The categorical imperative connects our personal concerns, context and experiences with the widest possible sense of human belonging.[7]

[6] As a general rule to reflect on how to arrive at sound moral decisions, the categorical imperative replaces substantive recommendations with the reasons and justifications that must underpin moral actions. Indeed, as justifications and the procedure itself now become an explicit concern, Kant's moral universalism not only requires that we arrive at the same decisions but also that we do so for the same reasons.

[7] Kant was, however, aware of a problem that in Chapter 1 I argued remains present in Habermas's postmetaphysical claims; namely, what happens when there is a conflict between competing principles: '[w]hen two such grounds conflict with each other, practical philosophy says, not that the stronger obligation takes precedence, but that the stronger *ground of obligation* prevails' (Kant 1996: 17). Quite consistently, Kant argues here that the emphasis must always be on the rationality of the justifications,

The centrality of proceduralisation in redefining a universalistic orientation pushes Kant beyond what previous natural law had achieved previously. When Hobbes and Rousseau mentioned their procedures they still saw them as another way of justifying their substantive definitions of human nature and paid no attention to their actual performance *as procedures*. For its part, the categorical imperative is devised as the key with which to unlock the problem of the reification of particular socio-cultural contents *vis-à-vis* universalistic ideas: we do not prejudge whether a specific institution is better than another but leave such an assessment to the individual's deployment of a rule that will help her come to a rational view about that particular institution's worth in that particular context. In making the inclusion of the individual point of view a necessary component of the categorical imperative, Kant is offering another key innovation. The assessment of whether the maxim that informs a particular course of action can become a universal law must always be made in the first person: '[a]nother can indeed *coerce* me *to do* something that is not my end . . . but not to *make this my end* . . . I can have no end without making it an end for myself. To have an end I have not myself made an end is self-contradictory, an act of freedom which is not yet free' (Kant 1996: 146–7).[8] Kant's Rousseaunian moment is that individuals themselves bear the responsibility for justifying their actions as moral actions at all times. Philosophers and the clergy, doctors and educators, may all know more about a particular aspect of life and yet it is for individuals themselves to decide what maxims they find important in a particular context and then independently assess whether they can become universal law.[9] Furthermore, this is the way in which empirical knowledge enters into Kant's moral philosophy. While within its strict a priori structure Kant's philosophy seems to have nothing to learn from the real world, moral action is always and necessarily informed by what takes place in the real world through the moral dilemmas that individuals actually face.

Up to now I have emphasised that the categorical imperative was devised as a highly stylised procedure, indeed a meta-norm, with the

although it remains open to question how this will actually help in deciding between equally universalisable maxims.

[8] Earlier in the text, Kant had defined freedom as a regulative idea, that is, freedom as such will never be fully realised but modern ideas of morality and individuality cannot be thought of without a conception of freedom (Kant 1996: 14–18). See also note 10 below.

[9] Thus my argument in Chapter 1 that at this level at least it is not crucial whether this principle of inclusivity is carried out dialogically, as in Habermas, or monologically, as in Höffe (2002), Rawls (1999) or indeed Kant himself. What does matter is that only individuals are the ultimate agents of action and moral judgement.

help of which human beings ought to decide between alternative courses of action. Being a procedure that must always and necessarily be accredited by individuals themselves, it stands apart from more substantive forms of natural law. But Kant offered several formulations of the categorical imperative. One of them centres on the idea of humanity, which he understands as a key intuition that makes moral reasoning possible while, at the same time, humanity itself is not the subject of moral reflection: the idea of humanity is a regulative ideal.[10] Kant thus argues that human beings must be treated always as ends in themselves and never as means: '[s]o act that you use humanity, whether in your own person or in the person of any other, always at the same time as an end, never merely as a means' (Kant 1997: 38). By resorting to the idea of humanity in general, and above all through the injunction about treating other human beings always as ends and never merely as means, Kant is surely strengthening the normative purchase of his moral universalism: even if we cannot know for sure what human nature ultimately is, we must none the less assume that all human beings are endowed with certain inviolable features, a universal human dignity, which requires them to treat each other always as ends and never as means.[11]

But by introducing this clause Kant is also doing something more problematic. Moral decisions are now not only those that we can *will* to become universal laws, as in the first formulation. They are now also those *actions* that abide by the treatment of fellow human beings always as ends and never as means. There is now a thin formulation of the categorical imperative, in which moral judgements are defined in

[10] In *Critique of Pure Reason*, Kant introduces the idea of humanity precisely in the context of his discussion of regulative ideals (as opposed to constitutive ideals): '[h]umanity (as an ideal) in its complete perfection contains not only all the essential qualities which belong to human nature and constitute our concept of it – and these so extended as to be in that complete conformity with their ends which would be our idea of perfect humanity – but also everything which, in addition to this concept, is required for the complete determination of the idea' (Kant 1973: 485–6). On regulative ideas and regulative ideals more generally, see Emmet (1994).

[11] As in Chapter 1, I decided not to concentrate on Kant's cosmopolitan standpoint in this discussion. But by now the connections between his moral philosophy and cosmopolitanism should be apparent: in his rejection of standing armies, for instance, Kant's argument is not only that their very existence makes war more likely. More crucial is the dehumanising, thus immoral, side of standing armies, as 'the hiring of men to kill or to be killed seems to mean using them as mere machines and instruments in the hand of someone else (the state) which cannot easily be reconciled with the right of man in one's own person' (Kant 1999: 95). Kant's explicit concern with cosmopolitanism can then be read as the political programme that derives from his moral universalism. On Kant's cosmopolitanism, see Fine (2011) and also Chernilo (2012).

terms of a type of reasoning, and a thicker one in which moral deeds are performed whenever we follow a very specific course of action – the treatment of human beings as ends rather than means. To be sure, Kant's moral theory has thus gained in terms of normative purchase – the procedural guidance to one's will is now offered further orientation on how to act in order to be morally sound. But the additional orientation we have gained, even though its substantive content has been carefully chosen in terms of a universalistically oriented idea of humanity, none the less sets limits on the open-ended nature of the procedure. Our thinking about moral maxims is to be as open ended as possible and yet it still requires one major substantive restriction – that human beings are always to be treated as ends in themselves.

Kant's radically immanent project for securing the normative purchase of morality does then have a transcendental limit: a universalistic idea of humanity. On the one hand, Kant's human beings are not purely moral beings. He explicitly rejects the view that his universalistic theory of morality needs a purely rational or idealistic conception of human nature:

> [w]e like to flatter ourselves by falsely attributing to ourselves a nobler motive, whereas in fact we can never, even by the most strenuous self-examination, get entirely behind our covert incentives, since, when moral worth is at issue, what counts is not actions, which one sees, but those inner principles of actions that one does not see. (Kant 1997: 19–20)

On the other hand, our moral sensibility and imagination are a fundamental aspect of who we are and what we have become as a human species. This is in fact connected to an argument we also made in the previous Chapter: from whence does the obligatory force of moral arguments derive? For Hobbes, covenants are only possible between human beings as they decide to conform to normative requirements on the basis of what human nature pushes them to do. But Kant does not derive morality from human nature – indeed moral obligation commands all rational beings even if they are not human beings (Kant 1997: 20). Kant's conception of humanity raises the question of the transcendental immanence that is built into his moral theory.[12]

[12] Kant's recourse to ideas of nature and providence in his cosmopolitan writing raises similar issues. There he argues that although 'we are too short-sighted to perceive the hidden mechanism of nature's scheme', providence will none the less find ways to curb negative developments and guide humans towards 'a perfect civil union of mankind' (Kant 1999: 52 and 51). Kant's idea of history is that of a fully immanent course of events which at the same time requires a transcendental accreditation of its conception of providence as progress towards, say, a situation of perpetual peace.

Here I am not echoing Hegel's criticism that there is no such thing as 'substantive-less' procedures because they all superstitiously smuggle in cultural contents, historical traditions or material/ideological interests (see the next section). But these problems illustrate how embedded in natural law much of Kant's work still is. Or, to put it differently, Kant's difficulties express the very real challenges that are built into universalistic arguments also in contemporary social theory (Chapter 1). My central argument is that a universalistic orientation is built into the very possibility of moral thinking. This creates opportunities in terms of internal refinement, but also difficulties for justificatory strategies. Understanding the location of the normative in modernity involves a tension between immanent justifications that make arguments rationally acceptable and transcendental grounds that make them binding. As Kant makes fully apparent, as the former become more open, the latter grow uncertain. Modern proceduralism seeks systematically to justify itself, offers a critically important sense of impartiality and can only be accredited internally by individuals themselves. However imperfect, the proceduralisation that lies at the centre of the categorical imperative is a fundamental step forward not only in moral theory but also for a number of modern institutional developments such as the rule of law, democratic political participation and scientific knowledge. Here Kant's categorical imperative does depart from what the tradition of natural law had been able to offer before. But the fact that in order to enhance its normative purchase its open-endedness is eventually restricted in terms of a transcendental idea of humanity also shows that traditional natural law universalism is not simply overcome or left behind.

Hegel

For all his criticisms of previous forms of philosophising, the appeal of natural law remains visible in Hegel. It is well known that the subtitle of his *Philosophy of Right*, first published in 1821, is precisely *Natural Law and Political Science in Outline* (Hegel 1991). But already in 1802–3 young Hegel had published two relatively short essays, *The Scientific Ways of Treating Natural Law, its Place in Moral Philosophy, and its Relation to the Positive Sciences of Law*, which were directly devoted to assessing the modern tradition of natural law that we have been discussing (Hegel 1975). While *Philosophy of Right* has undoubtedly the advantage of expressing Hegel's thinking more systematically, the *Natural Law* essays show with particular clarity Hegel's assessment of previous moral and political philosophy. In fact, even though natural law appears in its subtitle, Hegel does not really discuss natural law in the *Philosophy of Right*. In the introduction, he defines natural law as a form of philosophical right that seeks to comprehend the legal form *vis-à-vis* society as a whole, and then credits Montesquieu with having first made this visible. This 'philosophical approach to right', Hegel then contrasts with Kant's formalism, on the one hand, and with a merely historical approach to right, on the other (Hegel 1991: §3).[13]

In fact, this dual critique of excessive formalism and insufficient historical awareness is precisely the basis on which the early *Natural Law* essays are organised. Hegel read the tradition of modern natural law as constituted by 'crude dichotomies' (Rose 2009: 58): the state of nature and the civil condition, reason and nature, the social and the individual, particular inclinations and universal laws, the formal and the substantive, the state and civil society. On the basis of what we have seen in this and the previous chapter, Hegel may have exaggerated the extent to which these dichotomies lacked any form of articulation, but he was surely right in arguing for these to be explicitly considered. It will be my main contention below that the question of *mediation* is Hegel's central insight into our understanding of natural law. Mediations are key to understanding Hegel's thought: *subjectively*, as the phenomenology of a natural consciousness that finds its way in the world and, as self-consciousness, apprehends that its own freedom relates to the absolute spirit (Hegel 1977); *objectively*, in terms of the development of a world spirit that, *in concept*, has the opportunity to be realised through the reunion between religion and philosophy and, *in practice*, can potentially be realised in the modern state (Hegel 1989, 1991). Hegel's thinking may be read as a project that sought to mediate between various intellectual traditions: classical – most notably Greek philosophy, Christian theology and German idealism (Löwith 1967). Against Löwith's interpretation, however, I shall not read Hegel as marking a radical caesura within modern social thought and, against Strauss (1974), I do not cut him completely adrift from natural law. I do not treat him as the definitive inaugurator of modernity's epochal self-consciousness (Habermas 1990b, Pippin 2004) and, in emphasising the problem of mediations, I also seek to avoid the idea of an ontology of negativity that effectively, though possibly unintendedly, reduces both our human life and social interaction to conflict and competition (Adorno 1994). Rather, I suggest that Hegel

[13] After this, natural law appears only marginally in *Philosophy of Right*: it is mentioned twice in relation to marriage (Hegel 1991: §§161–2 and 168) and in passing when discussing Karl von Haller (§258, note) and Johann Fichte (§273). I will follow the normal convention of using paragraphs '§' rather than page numbers to quote from *Philosophy of Right*.

remains wholly within the tradition of natural law that we have been reconstructing. Hegel's major contribution *vis-à-vis* natural law lies in how he mediated between its various limitations and its rational core: '[I]f Hegel had a normative political credo ... it is the need to learn to live with contradiction and ambivalence in the modern world' (Fine 2012: 55).[14] For the rest of the section I shall then concentrate mostly on the *Natural Law* essays and complement my presentation with the more 'definitive' formulations of *Philosophy of Right*.[15]

Writing at the turn of the nineteenth century, Hegel describes his approach to contemporary natural law as 'scientific' and considers it important to clarify its position *vis-à-vis* the new role of positive sciences in the modern world. A theme that has accompanied us throughout – Habermas still thought it worth raising in the late 1980s in terms of the postmetaphysical status of his social theory – Hegel argues that the justification of true knowledge remains a fundamentally philosophical task, but one that needs to be able to accommodate empirical discoveries in all domains (Hegel 1975: 117–24). Natural law is no different from other types of knowledge and he explicitly compares it with 'other sciences such as mechanics and physics' (55). Natural law is a true science that has its own object while at the same time remaining a form of philosophy. Hegel's definition of natural law here is not dramatically different from those we have encountered so far:

> [s]ince all things are interconnected, empirical existence and the condition of all sciences will express also the condition of the world ... natural law will do so in particular because *natural law bears directly on the ethical, the mover of all things human*; and, insofar as the science of ethics has an existence, it is under the necessity of being one with the empirical shape of the ethical... as science, natural law *must express that shape in the form of universality.* (Hegel 1975: 58, my italics)

Natural law seeks to understand the domain of ethical life as 'the mover of all things human' and in order to do so it must take into account their actual empirical forms, their interconnections and also their rational shape 'in the form of universality'. Natural law studies 'the ethical'

[14] I here also follow Robert Fine's (2001: 30) claim that '[i]n Hegel's philosophy of right we are presented with a radically incomplete drama of human struggle'. But admittedly I locate Hegel more firmly *within* the tradition of natural law and have a more critical interpretation of Hegel's attempts to anchor his normative insights into specific socio-historical instances. See also Wellmer's (1998: 77–133) reconstruction of how Kant, Hegel and Marx engage with natural law theory.

[15] See Burns (1996: 42–6), Fulda (2004: 32–4), Horstmann (2004: 211–18) and Rose (2009: 55–63) for the importance of the *Natural Law* essays in relation to Hegel's later work. Burns and Rose also provide particularly clear expositions of Hegel's main arguments there.

empirically because it needs to understand history as it actually is but also because, normatively, the ethical is the mover of all things human and its universal content can only be adequately apprehended philosophically. The main challenge when studying the ethical is then to grasp its mediations as an ideal that is also actuality, a socio-historical development with a bearing on universality. Hegel's understanding of the role of natural law in the study of human affairs then raises, as we have also seen before, the question of the location of normativity in social life.

Hegel is, however, critical of the way in which modern natural law has dealt with these issues. A first line of criticism is directed at those philosophies that have sought to understand social and political life by referring to the state of nature. Although they are never mentioned by name, Hegel has in mind Hobbes and Rousseau, whose theories he describes as scientific empiricism (Hegel 1975: 67). The problem with approaches that are based on a wholly fictional condition of asociality is that, as they 'posit the being of the individual as the primary and supreme thing', they are intrinsically unable to apprehend the ethical (70). They cannot justify how different aspects of ethical life are actually interconnected and offer gratuitous formal connections instead. The state of nature is composed of individuals wrongly conceived as monads who lack a sense of unity and thus 'are destined to be self-opposed and to be in absolute conflict with one another' (64).[16] Methodologically, these theories clarify neither their philosophical nor their scientific status. We do not know why certain features are constitutive of our humanity in the state of nature, why some fade away and why others are sublated as human beings abandon the state of nature. There are no clear criteria for 'drawing the boundary between the accidental and the necessary; i.e. for determining what in the chaos of the state of nature or in the abstraction of man must remain and what must be discarded' (64). This complete lack of method leads scientific empiricism to mistake its own creations for first facts and then to use the latter to construct fictional representations of both the state of nature and of social life: 'the governing principle for this *a priori* is the *a posteriori*' (64). The justification of what was arguably a priori – unalterable human nature as it 'actually' was in the state of nature – is in fact a posteriori – what 'proves' to have worked in bringing about social order. These theories leave us with the worst of both worlds, Hegel contends, because they ultimately have no consistent notion of individual human nature

[16] It is this emphasis on conflict that convinces Hegel that, although his approach remains flawed, Hobbes's 'war of mutual destruction' is the only consistent representation of the state of nature (Hegel 1975: 65).

and of social order. Not too dissimilar to Kant's critique, Hegel is here accusing Hobbes and Rousseau of reproducing the same problems that they sought to leave behind.[17]

After these criticisms, Hegel thought it more important to engage with a second branch of natural law theory, the critical philosophy or transcendental idealism that is best represented in the works of Kant and Fichte. Hegel (1975: 57) claims that to an important extent they had already moved beyond the shortcomings of state of nature theories and raises two separate charges against the preference for procedural formalism that is best represented in Kant's categorical imperative. First, formal procedures tend to explain away problematic situations as accidents with no real significance; secondly, in order to enhance their normative purchase, all procedures smuggle in substantive content for which no adequate justification has been given: 'formalism can extend its consistency so far as is generally made possible by the emptiness of its principle, or by content which has smuggled in; but thereby it is in turn entitled to exclude what lacks completeness from its apriorism and its science, and proudly revile it as "the empirical"' (62).[18]

Hegel's first line of criticism of empty principles resembles his previous argument on asociality. He rejects what he contends was Kant's and Fichte's radical individualism because it led to a solipsistic conception of social life. In Kant's case the reduction of moral reasoning to a single general formulation makes it so 'completely out of the question to speak of a system of morality that not even a plurality of laws is possible' (Hegel 1975: 75). Hegel equally rejects the 'one-size-fits-all' approach of proceduralism: 'it cannot be a good thing to apply a universally simple rule to what is never simple' (96). Instead of gaining access to real universality as found in 'the high Idea of absolute ethical life' (133), Hegel sees these formulations as a race to ever 'emptier abstractions ... such as freedom, pure will, humanity' (68). Even as he praises the importance of duty in Kant's moral theory, Hegel rejects what he regards as its fundamental intuition: a dichotomous logic that thinks in terms of two separate moments – the particular maxim *and* the universal law, in the first formulation of the categorical imperative, the individual person *and* the whole of humanity, in the second. Hegel criticises Kant's systematic 'production of tautologies' by discussing its problems through several examples: private

[17] Hegel was not altogether critical of Rousseau and acknowledged that the general will was an essential contribution to the understanding of the modern state (Hegel 1991: §258, Neuhouser 2000: 55).

[18] Procedural formalism was no exclusive prerogative of Kant, of course. As Hobbes and Rousseau also intimated it, I read Hegel's criticism as having more general implications.

property, to deny having received a deposit for which there is no proof and defending one's country against its enemies (76–80). He elaborates further on this with the following case:

> The maxim, 'Help the poor,' tested by being elevated into a principle of universal legislation, will prove to be false because it annihilates itself. If the thought is that the poor generally should be helped, then either there are no poor left or there are nothing but poor; in the latter event no one is left to help them. In both cases the help disappears. Thus the maxim, universalized, cancels itself. On the other hand, if the specific thing which is to be superseded (i.e. poverty) were to remain, the possibility of helps remains – but only as a possibility, not as the actuality envisaged in the maxim. (Hegel 1975: 80)[19]

We have partly discussed earlier in this chapter whether the categorical imperative has to smuggle in substantive determinations that it cannot justify. But while above I criticised Kant for restricting the open-ended nature of the categorical imperative with too strong an idea of humanity Hegel's difficulty with the categorical imperative is that it is not restrictive enough. Hegel's second criticism centres on his rejection of the very idea that there is such a thing as pure practical reason that is devoid of particular volitions. He then writes:

> [p]ractical reason is the complete abstraction from all content of will (*Wille*); to introduce a content is to establish a heteronomy of choice (*Willkür*). But what is precisely of interest is to know *what* right and duty are. We ask for the content of the moral law, and this content alone concerns us. But the essence of pure will and pure practical reason is to be abstracted from all content. Thus it is self-contradiction to seek in this absolute practical reason a moral legislation which would have to have a content, since the essence of reason is to have none. (Hegel 1975: 76)

The core of Hegel's critique becomes fully apparent as we put both criticisms together: universal laws are unable to orient moral action because, as they can adopt several substantive contents, they effectively leave moral decisions underdetermined. Hegel turns Kant upside down, as it were: it is the very generality of the procedure, which Kant thought was its main strength, that now becomes its fundamental shortcoming.

[19] Gillian Rose (2009: 56, 61–3, 78–87, 93–7) repeatedly argues, on the basis of these examples and of Kant's translation of Roman Law into his own moral and legal theory, that the core of Hegel's critique of natural law is to unmask the class ideology of nascent bourgeois society (which, incidentally, is the more or less conventional sociological interpretation of the relevance of Kant and Hegel for the rise of modern sociology and modern society). While illuminating in several respects, I depart from Rose's reading because I am interested in the deployment of the tradition of natural law *as a way of thinking* that is of course never independent of socio-historical processes but whose immanent core, in terms of its claim to universalism, can be assessed in its own terms.

The problem is not that the categorical imperative smuggles in too thick an idea of humanity but rather that all particular maxims appear to be equally universalisable; to the extent that 'every specific matter is capable of . . . constituting the content of the maxim of the particular will . . . there is nothing whatever which cannot in this way be made into a moral law' (Hegel 1975: 77). Kant thought that with the categorical imperative he put the universal and the particular in relation to one another, but according to Hegel this had only been done in form and the result was to have hardened their split and made impossible their *real* or *absolute* reunion. Hegel's critique concentrates on how the categorical imperative splits rather than articulates the relationships between the universal and the particular: universal laws remain empty and produce only tautologies; maxims that are universalised effectively cancel themselves. The idea of a free and autonomous will is self-contradictory because if it remains truly open its lack of substantive content prevents it from being actually useful and, if it allows for substantive determinations, its autonomy collapses as the will is now being ruled from the outside and becomes heteronomous. The problem in Kant is that real social relations were expected to surrender their autonomy to formal abstractions.

Hegel's critique misses a key part of what makes Kant's categorical imperative important in modern society, however. His demolition exercise seems to have been accomplished because it reproduces the formalism it criticises. Hegel does not fully address the fact that the categorical imperative is not a logical or conceptual syllogism; he is wrong to contend that the categorical imperative 'amounts simply to the familiar [principle of] formal identity and the law of contradiction' (Hegel 1991: §29). Rather, the categorical imperative was devised to orient normatively specific courses of action that take place under particular circumstances – indeed, practical reason has primacy over pure reason in Kant's thought (Rawls 2000: 162, Rose 2009: 49). If we come back to Hegel's moral dilemma of helping the poor, individuals may or may not take intellectual pleasure in the demonstration of its logical inconsistency or potential self-cancellation, but the categorical imperative was expected to orient individuals to what to do in practice and to offer rational grounds for favouring certain courses of action over others. The Kantian procedure is far from bulletproof but is able to offer guidance to individuals struggling with moral dilemmas. Indeed, it remains central to many of our key normative ideas: impartiality, equality, inclusivity, rationality, autonomy.

In order to understand what is really at stake we need to clarify that Hegel's opposition to the formalism of Kant's moral theory is not based on a rejection of its universalistic orientation. Hegel challenges what he considers is a formalistic rendition of universalism that, because it is *based* on the atomism of the individual will, results in hypostatised dichotomies. The positive side of Hegel's argument lies in his systematic attempt to grasp the movement between the two poles that Kant had distinguished but whose interconnections arguably he did not fully unpack. It is really Hegel who made their mediations a central question. More problematic, it seems to me, are Hegel's attempts to bring these normative insights into socio-historical life. There is no need to read Hegel as a political theologian who praises the state as an earthly god and searches for a new kind of Christian redemption, and yet there is something troubling in the logic that is behind his project: the arguably more sociological effort to connect moral intuitions with socio-historical events and institutions, Hegel's need to find in them some rational core, runs the risk of eventually devaluing both universal normative intuitions and social life itself. In the remainder of this chapter I will address these questions by looking at some of Hegel's formulations in *Philosophy of Right.*

Hegel's concepts of the state and of the individual are two poles in need of mediation for the rational content of modern social life to emerge and in their definition he *re*-renders some fundamental natural law ideas. Historically, Plato's concept of the state and the Christian idea of the individual are key sources (Löwith 1967: 240). Philosophically, this is reflected in the structure of *Philosophy of Right*: Part I on 'Abstract Right' opens with a short but highly consequential section on the idea of 'The Person' (Hegel 1991: §§34–40), and the book comes to an end, at the end of Part III on 'Ethical Life', with a long and equally meaningful section on 'The State' (§§257–360). The section on the person opens with an individual will that achieves self-consciousness only as it learns about its freedom and rights. It is in the self-awareness that results from the combination of rights and freedom that the individual becomes a person: the 'individual enjoys the status of personality . . . on the basis of its universality as the self-consciousness of freedom' (Quante 2004: 89). A development that occurs only in modern times (Hegel 1991: §35), a person is always a 'pure personality' but is equally 'completely determined in all respects'; a person is simultaneously 'contentless' and 'wholly determinate', is the mediated reunion of 'the sublime and the wholly ordinary' (§37). For the idea of the person to emerge universal self-consciousness is not enough, the person is also *particularity* and *singularity.*[20] Particularity refers to the strictly subjective side

[20] In order to avoid confusion with the idea of the individual, here I follow Quante's (2004: 86, 95) rendition of *Einzelheit* as 'singularity' instead of 'individuality' as translated in Hegel (1991).

of one's individuality – 'desire, need, drives, contingent preference, etc.' – that are always directed to specific objects in the world (§37). Particularity is the domain of the subjective, of self-satisfaction, of choice, of the heteronomous. Singularity, for its part, refers to how the personality positions itself in a world 'which it encounters before it' (§39). Singularity is self-conscious reflection on one's specific socio-historical context and can thus be connected to such determinations as class, cultural background, religion, etc. The most dramatic institutional development to which this conception of the person gives rise is legal equality, and here Hegel's debt to Kant becomes apparent: '[t]he commandment of right is therefore: *be a person and respect others as persons*' (§36). As human beings recognise and treat each other as human beings, in their particularity and singularity, the formation of the person becomes possible *only as it takes place from the standpoint of universality*: '[t]he highest achievement of a human being is to be a person' (§35).

The modern state is the system of rights that makes possible the turning of bare human beings into fully developed personalities that are simultaneously universal, particular and singular. But Hegel's idea of the state sees it as more than a passive object; the state is itself a subject or indeed a personality with its own universality, particularity and singularity. Hegel introduces the idea of the state in its three moments of constitutional law, international law and world history and we can see that they correspond, though presented in inverse order, to the same moments of *singularity*, the state's constitution as its own internal environment; *particularity*, the state's relationship with other states as a collision of wills; and *universality*, the idea of the modern state in relation to the history of the species as a whole (Hegel 1991: §259). When Hegel describes the state as 'the actuality of the ethical Idea', he is referring to the state from the standpoint of universality and as also having its own particularity and singularity (§257).[21] If in his rendition of the idea of the person Hegel's position in relation to Kant becomes

[21] My claim is that Hegel uses the same *principles* of universality, particularity and singularity to reflect on both persons and states and not, as in debates on the so-called domestic analogy, that he extrapolates the substantive properties of states from those of individuals (see note 22 in Chapter 4). Hegel acknowledges that states 'exist' to some extent 'in a state of nature in relation to one another' (Hegel 1991: §333) and contends that both individuals and states come to understand who they are only when in 'a relationship' with other individuals or states (§331). Yet Hegel also argues that 'the welfare of a state has quite different justification from the welfare of the individual' (§337) and equally that, in contradistinction to individuals, '[t]he relationship between states is a relationship between independent units which make mutual stipulations but at the same time stand above these stipulations' (§330).

more nuanced, something similar takes place now in relation to Hobbes. Hegel put forward a very strong idea of the state indeed:

> [w]hether human beings know it or not, this essence realizes itself as a self-sufficient power of which single individuals are only moments ... The state consists in the march of God in the world, and its basis is the power of reason actualizing itself as will. In considering the Idea of the state, we must not have any particular states or particular institutions in mind; instead, we should consider the Idea, this actual God, in its own right. (Hegel 1991: §258A)

Hegel immediately counterbalances this claim, however. He again takes Hobbes as his reference point and now rejects what we saw was an equally central Hobbesian insight. The state is not artificial *vis-à-vis* human nature, its role is not to modify or improve on individual human nature:

> The state is not a work of art; it exists in the world, and hence in the sphere of arbitrariness, contingency, and error, and bad behaviour may disfigure it in many respects. But the ugliest of men, the criminal, the invalid, or the cripple is still a living human being; the affirmative aspect – life – survives in spite of such deficiencies, and *it is with this affirmative aspect that we are here concerned.* (Hegel 1991: §258A, my italics)

Even when the state is defined as an early god its purpose is to secure and enhance the life of its citizens – also and in particular of those who may be in danger of losing their fundamental human status and be seen as disposable. Hegel systematically tries to actualise what Kant thought were regulative ideas whose normative power would lie precisely in the fact they were not actualised. This becomes apparent again in the realm of civil society, the fundamentally modern domain where 'each individual is his own end and all else means nothing to him', where others are 'means to the end of the particular person'. Yet precisely through its unilateral amplification, 'the particular end takes on the form of universality' (Hegel 1991 §182A). The individual will is left to indulge itself in 'contingent arbitrariness and subjective caprice' only for this 'right to subjectivity' to contribute to the universality of 'ethical unity' because of its 'Christian' heritage (§185).[22] In turn, a major institution of civil society, the modern judiciary, can only begin to function on the basis of the most fundamental universalistic intuitions: '[a] *human being counts as such because he is a human being*, not because he is a Jew, Catholic, Protestant, German, Italian, etc. This consciousness ... is of infinite importance, and it is inadequate only if it adopts a fixed

[22] See Löwith (1967: 13, 32–3, 46, 240, 323–30) on the role of Christianity in Hegel's thought.

position – for example, as *cosmopolitanism* – in opposition to the concrete life of the state' (§209). Universalism is the only standpoint from which justice as equality before the law can be offered. Yet we ought to avoid falling below universalism's own critical threshold by turning it into an absolute that is merely *opposed* to the particularity and singularity of states and individuals. Instead of rejecting cosmopolitan universalism, Hegel opposes its reification as the apex of history.[23]

Similarly, in the *Natural Law* essays Hegel (1975: 115) defines the nation as 'the absolutely ethical' within which 'movement and vitality in the common being and doing of everyone is absolutely identical as both universal and particular'. But he immediately rejects crude identification of the universal with the nation's customs because that 'obviates *what is often the case*, namely that the laws of a nation *fail* to reveal what in that nation is right and realized. A lack of skill in formulating the true ethical principles as laws, and *the fear of thinking these principles ... is the sign of barbarism*' (116, my italics). In turn, in *Philosophy of Right*, this fear of barbarism is another key motif in the section on the state: '[h]atred on *law*, of *legally* determined *right*, is the shibboleth whereby fanaticism, imbecility, and hypocritical good intentions manifestly and infallibly reveal themselves for what they are, no matter what disguise they may adopt' (Hegel 1991: §258, note). And yet towards the end of the section on state, and of the book as a whole, we find countless comments about the nation-state being 'the spirit in its substantial rationality and immediate actuality ... the absolute power on *earth*' (§331), world history moving from one 'world-historical nation' to the next as a '*natural* principle' (§347) and, eventually that 'national spirits have their truth and destiny in the concrete Idea as *absolute universality*' (§352).

A final theme we need to address because of its importance for the rise of social theory, and which carries similar implications to those we have discussed so far, is Hegel's concept of alienation. In *Philosophy of Right*, the argument takes place in the rather specific context of the alienation of property: 'true alienation is a declaration by the will that I no longer wish to regard the thing as mine' (Hegel 1991: §65). Hegel devotes a special section to modern labour as a form of alienating one's time, the product of one's activity although *not* one's whole self (§67). But the phenomenon of alienation is not restricted to property and work and Hegel immediately connects it to 'the universal essence of my self-consciousness' (§66). A personality exists '*only through itself* and as

[23] See Robert Fine (2001: 132–50, 2003, 2012) for the full implications of Hegel's engagement with cosmopolitanism. See also Acton's (1975: 41) introduction to Hegel's *Natural Law* essays for the narrow statist interpretation.

infinite return to itself', its existence as a personality can only be realised in the interaction with the natural and social worlds, and this involves the permanent risk of external factors preventing the infinite return of the personality to itself. One may be made prisoner and be treated as an object, as in 'slavery' and 'serfdom', or one's particularity may be prevented from full expression, as 'in the disqualification from owning property, restrictions on freedom of ownership, etc' (§66). It is also possible for the personality to surrender its intellectual autonomy in 'morality, ethical life and religion ... when power and authority are granted to others to prescribe what actions I should perform' (§66). These types of heteronomy are a form of alienation because they treat the personality's essential determinants – freedom, autonomy, self-consciousness – as *objects* that it possesses. But they are not objects, they are fundamentally 'inalienable' and 'imprescriptible' (§66). Hegel's notion of alienation is therefore modern, as it presupposes modern civil society, but is also transhistorical in the sense that it describes a fundamental human tension between interiority and exteriority, between autonomy and heteronomy, between contingency and necessity, between possessions and essential determinants. Alienation refers to the mediations between immanence and transcendence in human history; it is a universal human phenomenon that makes apparent the real drama of ideal intuitions. Alienation will then reappear in Marx as the question of how social institutions systematically impede the development of our human potential.[24]

Hegel criticised earlier natural law in Hobbes, Rousseau and Kant for its inability to account for the transcendental presuppositions upon which it was constituted – the fixed essences of Hobbes and Rousseau were a necessary result of a fragmented and atomist starting point, the false sense of majesty of Kant a result of an ahistorical conception of the universal and its concomitant deficiency in thinking about the particular. Yet we witness a real tension in Hegel's argument: he upholds a

[24] In *Phenomenology of Spirit* the argument on alienation is 'cosmological' insofar as the internal struggles in the realm of culture – self, spirit, substance, absolute, particular, etc. – mirror the internal differentiation of nature into air, water, fire and earth (Hegel 1977: 300). But on this basis the argument on alienation focuses also and more directly on modern times. Hegel argues that in the struggle between master and servant the latter gains his freedom and self-awareness only thanks to his negative domination over the former. Legal equality tries to solve this but achieves it only in form (292–4). Modern culture (i.e. the Renaissance), which was centrally determined by the idea of equality, then finds its opposites in both power and wealth (the absolutist state and early capitalism), whose opposite is rational religion (the Reformation), whose opposite is the Enlightenment (modern science), whose opposite is the Terror (the French Revolution, 297–363).

universalistic orientation, criticises it for being too formal and abstract, finds concrete socio-historical expressions that are exalted to the point where the original reference to the universalistic orientation is nearly lost, only for universalism to be reinstated through the discovery of the rational content that has actually permeated into real human history. We may question whether his attempt to ground ideas of the absolute or the universal more firmly in actual social relations leads Hegel back to the thick conception of ethical life that Hobbes had already found difficult to justify. More positively, in terms of mediations Hegel's project is best seen as an attempt to rebalance the relative weight of form and content, immanence and transcendence, ideals and historical reality, within his wider definition of the ethical as 'the mover of all things human'.

Closing remarks

This chapter has explicitly emphasised what separates Kant and Hegel but its underlying claim is that, on the basis of their universalistic commitments, they belong equally to the tradition of natural law. Kant's 'formalism' mirrors Hegel's 'substantialism', Hegel's explicit concern with mediations is a result of Kant's formulations that left the connections between the universal and the particular undertheorised. Their centrality in relation to both natural law and modern social theory can then hardly be exaggerated. They both spell out the limitations of state of nature theories with particular sharpness. They question their asocial starting point and whether social relations can emerge out of the sublation of human nature. Kant and Hegel are slowly beginning to feel the need to incorporate the empirical in modern science, although the balance of power is yet to change in favour of science. The more decided integration of empirical developments into the conceptualisation of modern social relations will of course be a major development in the rise of modern social theory.

More substantively, there is the question of how to conceptualise the transcendental inside the immanence of social relations. Kant's categorical imperative represents a radical step forward in this context because of the way in which its open-ended proceduralism and internalism bring home the egalitarian orientation that is built into universalistic arguments. The justification of a universalistic standpoint remains a central concern in the attempt to think of ourselves as human beings. In order to work as a meta-norm, the categorical imperative needs to be able to do three things at once: to justify its importance as a universal procedure, to offer guidance for deciding between competing courses of action, and to motivate individuals to follow normative intuitions that may carry universal support. Hegel does not disown these insights and seeks to enhance them by looking at both their logical mediations and socio-historical realisation. At the same time, and regardless of the problems of the categorical imperative, Hegel sets the tone well for what will be a major challenge of social theory: '[t]here must be a supreme positive point from which compulsion according to the concept of universal freedom starts' (Hegel 1975: 85). What the principle is, where it resides, and how we get to know about it are all philosophical questions for which modern social theory does not need to provide explicit answers but which do not merely go away.

I should very briefly like to bring the three chapters of this part to a close by systematising some of the key themes that have occupied us: (1) the relationships between universalism and socio-historical change and normative variation; (2) the relationships between philosophical (normative) and scientific (descriptive) claims; (3) the relationships between our 'innate' human attributes and their social 'constitution'; (4) the relationships between immanence and transcendence for understanding the normative in social life; and (5) the relationships between form and content in modern proceduralism.

(1) Traditional natural law universalism is not immune to the charges of reification, essentialism and homogenisation. In more than one way, these criticisms are also present in modern universalistic orientations. We reviewed how questions of historical change, socio-cultural variation and normative disagreement have always been present when thinking in universalistic terms and argued that the very possibility of thinking about cultural differences requires that we accept that there are human beings who, on the basis of similar attributes, do things differently. Even if in spite of itself, the intellectual rationale behind cultural relativism, with its emphasis on historical and cultural particularity, actually depends on the respect of other human beings as human beings in so far as this 'presumes that there is a morally relevant common humanity' that *can* enter into inter-cultural dialogue (Selznick 1961: 93).

(2) While for the natural law tradition philosophical arguments systematically remain in a position of primacy, we witness the increasing importance of scientifically grounded propositions. There is no easy solution to this question, however, because although scientific knowledge is to achieve cognitive primacy in modernity, a key aspect of modern social theory is that answers to normative questions cannot be offered only in empirical terms. To the extent that normative reflections remain central to how we address ourselves as human beings, the scientific and philosophical strands of modern social theory must learn to talk

to one another while respecting each other's autonomy. As we shall explore in detail in Part III, modern social theory cohered on the combination rather than the opposition or fusion of philosophical and scientific arguments.

(3) Arguments on the state of nature figured centrally in Chapter 4. On the one hand, there is the question of how the transition from the state of nature to civil life was supposed to have taken place. But on the other hand there is the arguably more consequential issue of whether our fundamental human attributes are innate or whether they rather emerge as the sublated result of the rise of social life. At stake here is nothing short of the relationship between a philosophical anthropology and an ontology of the social: does social life take the form it does because it accommodates human attributes that are thus pre-social or, conversely, are those human attributes the result of social life itself and thus do we only become fully human because and to the extent that our social institutions take particular shapes? As we shall see in Chapter 6, the distinction between community and society in social theory became a critically modern rendition of this key concern in modern natural law.

(4) Although Strauss defines natural law as a rational attempt at understanding the immanent foundations of human morality, questions about the transcendental remain central to it. Is transcendence still necessary in increasingly empirical accounts of social life? How can the transcendental be justified beyond religion? Can moral norms be binding on purely immanent grounds or do we have to work out a sense of 'transcendental immanence' that will allow norms whose origins are knowingly social to become normatively binding? These are the vexing questions that classical social theory has also had to face and which, on the basis of presupposing our shared humanity, have allowed it to reflect on the location of the normative in modern social life.

(5) Proceduralism is a central feature of modern natural law but at least in such attributes as logical consistency and reasonableness were already part of traditional natural law as well. Arguably best represented in Kant's categorical imperative, modern natural law now adds to these attributes open-endedness, internalism and reflexive justification. The universalistic orientation of proceduralism, arguably best captured in the idea of impartiality, has thus become an essential normative component of all kinds of modern institutional settings: from scientific methodologies to democratic politics, from a healthy public sphere to an independent judiciary. What kinds of presuppositions are required by this proceduralism, and whether it can be actualised in real socio-historical instances, remain, however, major issues for us to consider in Part III.

Part III

Classical social theory

6 Classical social theory I: Marx, Tönnies and Durkheim on alienation, community and society

Marx

A sharp writer and a philosophical erudite, Marx must have been perfectly aware that his criticism of Hegel's philosophy echoed Hegel's own critique of the natural law tradition that we discussed in the previous Chapter. Marx acknowledged that in Hegel's philosophy 'criticism is genuine and often well ahead of its time', but in the same stroke he condemned Hegel's philosophy as a combination of 'uncritical positivism and equally uncritical idealism' in which 'the philosophical dissolution and restoration of the empirical world is already to be found in latent form, in embryo, as a potentiality and a secret' (Marx 1975: 384–5). In Hegel, Marx contends, positivism and idealism are ultimately two sides of the same problem (Colletti 1975: 20–2): while Hegel's 'positivism' expresses his tendency to reify the real – the state and Christianity are unduly elevated to the position of the universal – his 'idealism' is a result of the inversion of subject and predicate whereby ideas of the state, religion and private property take precedence over actual socio-historical practices and institutions. It is as though Marx intended his criticism to read as the old adage the more it changes, the more it remains the same, because in seeking to move radically beyond natural law he effectively reproduced Hegel's own critique of Hobbes's and Rousseau's 'positivism', on the one hand, and Kant's 'idealism', on the other. The argument always works through the same two steps: as soon as the rational core of previous thinking is identified and then integrated, what is presented as its apparently universal content is demystified as mere historical particularity which is then reified in a positivistic manner.[1] Marx is effectively repeating what by now were

[1] In his reconstruction of Marx's critique of modern natural law, which he calls classical jurisprudence, Robert Fine (2002: 20–1) argues thus: 'classical jurisprudence was the agent of the abolition of the form of natural law and for presenting law as what it was: a human product in its entirety . . . The problem with classical jurisprudence was not that it broke from traditional natural law theory, but rather that it failed to complete the break,

the conventional rules of engagement of philosophical criticism; his indictment closely resembles, in form as well as in content, the way in which Hobbes separated himself from traditional natural law, Rousseau sought to distance himself from Hobbes, Kant departed from both Hobbes and Rousseau and Hegel critically assessed Hobbes, Rousseau and Kant.[2]

We should of course critically assess whether Marx misinterpreted or exaggerated his own sense of rupture *vis-à-vis* previous natural law. Indeed, this very sense of rupture may in fact be taken as an expression of how effectively embedded Marx still was in natural law thinking. Following a main argument of this book, I expect to find neither radical rupture nor complete continuity in assessing Marx's intellectual debts. Rather, in what follows I should like to suggest that Marx's fundamental role in the rise of modern social theory is based on how his early philosophical writings represent the *Aufhebung*, the conservation and carrying forward, of modern natural law.

There are, it seems to me, two aspects of Marx's thought that appear radical and novel enough and which would therefore prevent the ironic reiteration of his criticisms of natural law being turned on himself. The first is what, in *The German Ideology*, Marx and Engels (1974: 42) explicate as the 'first' premise of the 'materialist method': namely, the fact that real human history depends on 'the existence of living human individuals'. To be sure, it was Feuerbach's innovation '[t]o have founded *true materialism* and *real science* by making the social relations of "man to man" the basic principle of his theory' (Marx 1975: 381). But it is only after we have grasped fully the consequences of the fact that 'men must be in a position to live in order to be able to "make history"' that we realise that '[t]he first historical act is thus the production of the means to satisfy these needs, the production of material life itself' (Marx and Engels 1974: 48). Read as ontological statements about how our existence is constituted on the basis of how human life actually reproduces itself, at least the first of these propositions is arguably compatible with Hobbes's and Rousseau's general claims. Even though neither writer made the sphere of production central to his intellectual concerns, a central tenet of their philosophy is that we need to understand what is primary in human beings and human institutions because only if we

it abolished natural law theory in its traditional [religious, transcendental] form, only to resurrect it in a modern form [capitalist and individualistic private property]'.

2 We shall see below in this chapter that Durkheim also made use of a claim to novelty as central to his attempt to establish sociology in terms of ever 'newer' rules of the sociological method.

comprehend how they actually are shall we be able to reflect on how they ought to be. Yet it is only Marx who unpacked the implications of these propositions: making real human beings the subject matter of philosophical reflection, on the one hand, and the reproduction of material life the most important sphere of human action, on the other. Conceptually, the task was now to define what were the practices, institutions and indeed the general human capacities through which human beings reproduced themselves as they transformed nature. Reflections on moral and political life ought now to leave space for a deeper and indeed more empirical understanding of human labour, the division of labour, the rise of private property, etc. Methodologically, Marx seeks to find a way to grasp what takes place in 'real living individuals themselves ... We set out from real, active men, and on the basis of their real life-process' (Marx and Engels 1974: 47). It is from here that Marx will move on to argue that relations of production are central to our understanding of the development of social relations:

In the whole conception of history up to the present this real basis of history has either been totally neglected or else considered as a minor matter quite irrelevant to the course of history. History must, therefore, always be written according to an extraneous standard: the real production of life seems to be primeval history, while the truly historical appears to be separated from ordinary life, something extra-superterrestrial. (Marx and Engels 1974: 59)

These are of course well-trodden arguments and we need not enter here into the debate on whether they represent Marx's 'definitive' position. But they allow us to reflect on Marx's engagement with natural law as we now introduce the second, surely more radical though arguably less successful, of Marx's innovations. Building on Feuerbach, Marx expected that the new materialistic premises would involve a radical redefinition of what counted as true human knowledge. A wholly materialistic method ought to centre on the idea of praxis, social life as it actually is (Feuerbach 1986: 23, 53). This partly continues within the tradition of natural law in the sense that the task was to combine the best insights of modern science and modern philosophy. Socially produced knowledge about social life can only emerge as the two are willing to engage with and learn from one another, even if at present '[t]heir momentary union was only a *fantastic illusion*' (Marx 1975: 355). But this is a process that will only be achieved if and when modern natural science and modern philosophy become fully integrated so that:

Natural science will lose its abstractly material, or rather idealist, orientation and become the basis of *human* science ... Natural science will in time subsume the science of man just as the science of man will subsume natural science: there will be *one* science . . . The *social* reality of nature and the *human* natural science or the *natural science of man* are identical expressions. (Marx 1975: 355)[3]

Because there is no such thing as pure cognition, human knowledge needs to be conceptualised as a form of social praxis that is expressed in social life itself. Just as the real sublation of religious and metaphysical thinking is only possible thanks to the combined heft of modern science and modern philosophy, praxis becomes for Marx the real sublation of modern science and philosophy. Marx still remains within conventional Feuerbachean territory, as the problem with Hegelian philosophy, which is indeed 'the culmination of modern philosophy' (Feuerbach 1986: 31), is that it is not philosophical enough. Hegelian philosophy is rather a form of 'rational theology' that is still unable to look at socio-historical reality for what it is:

Speculative philosophy as the realization of God is at the same time the positing and the cancellation or negation of God, at the same time theism and atheism; for God, in the theological sense . . . it is conceived as being distinguished from and independent of the being of man and nature. (Feuerbach 1986: 19)[4]

But Marx also departs from Feuerbach as he criticises his idea of a *philosophy* of the future because, even though it focused on real praxis, it remains only a form of philosophy. Thus, in *Manuscripts,* the claim is that '[i]n order to supersede the *idea* of private property, the *idea* of communism is enough. In order to supersede private property as it actually exists, *real* communist activity is necessary' (Marx 1975: 365). Marx's own trajectory and massive scientific and philosophical *œuvre* points against an anti-intellectualist interpretation of this preference for praxis, however: theoretical investigation is a form of praxis. And even if against Marx's own self-understanding we do not emphasise the revolutionary side of his idea of practice, I would argue that his claim of having moved beyond the philosophical tradition *is* original. To be sure, he argued that one 'cannot transcend philosophy without realizing' (250), but this is only one part of the problem because the more decisive proposition comes, towards the end of his *Introduction to the Critique of Hegel's Philosophy of Right*, in the realisation that this must have a concrete practical-political component: '[p]hilosophy cannot realize itself without the transcendence of the proletariat, and the proletariat cannot transcend itself without the realization of philosophy' (257). For Marx,

[3] In so reading Marx, it is not really necessary to separate out his 'philosophical' from 'sociological' work (Bottomore and Rubel 1978).

[4] On Feuerbach, see Löwith (1967: 69–80); on the relationship between Feuerbach and Marx, Löwith (1967: 410).

therefore, the true realisation of philosophy lies not only outside philosophy – a claim, incidentally, that is already radical enough *vis-à-vis* natural law. The true realisation of philosophy consists in the very transformation of the social conditions of existence that philosophy seeks to understand.[5]

I should then like to contend that Marx's definitive integration into the canon of modern social theory depends on the nuanced reception of these two arguments: first, a materialist position whereby the spiritual world can only be understood in relation to concrete socio-historical life; secondly, that intellectual work is to be realised outside and beyond itself, not in the world of ideas but in the transformation of concrete socio-historical life. Even though Marx's own position remains the subject of debate, the fact remains that his insights are key to the terms within which contemporary discussions are carried out. Marx's pride of place in modern social theory has been *definitively* gained by his proposition that we ought to understand real socio-historical practices in order to account for all aspects of human existence. His status as a classic of modern social science obtains from his view of real human beings needing to stay alive for society to exist, that in accounting for people's ideas, values and even emotions we need to connect them to their basic historical and socio-economic coordinates and that, for better and worse, our intellectual work does carry political implications.[6]

In a formulation that below we will see was echoed by Durkheim, Marx argued for the centrality of society without making individuality pay the price: '[i]t is above all necessary to avoid once more establishing "society" as an abstraction over against the individual. The individual *is* the *social being* ... Man's individual and species-life are not two *distinct things*' (Marx 1975: 350). This is something Marx addressed also in the *Theses on Feuerbach*, when he refers to society as 'social humanity', and similarly, in the *Grundrisse* an older Marx also argued that '[s]ociety does not consist of individuals, but expresses the sum of interrelations,

[5] Thus Habermas's (1996: 46) claim that Marx 'still held to a classical concept whose influence extends from Aristotle to Hegel, that of society as totality' is only partially accurate. The difference not to be missed is that while traditional conceptions involved a direct actualisation of philosophical knowledge in social and political institutions – arguably best represented in Plato's figure of the philosopher becoming a king – the key for Marx is that philosophy ought to be active in the transformation of those institutions that it tries to comprehend.

[6] Pierre Manent (1998: 52) is thus right when he argues that sociology, in so far as it has incorporated Marx's insights, 'penetrates and dominates all modern political thought'. And yet, at the same time, Marx went beyond social science (and remained connected to natural law) in his search for primary causes (65). We will come back to this question in Chapter 8.

the relations within which these individuals stand' (Marx 1973: 265). Society can only be adequately understood as the dialectical relationship of man with himself, with others and with nature: therein lies its fundamental universality. Axel Honneth and Hans Joas (1988: 18–25) have reconstructed this as a tension between an anthropological and a sociological moment in Marx's work, wherein young Marx's anthropological insights increasingly gave way to old Marx's sociological interests in *Capital*. While I remain agnostic on this argument as an internal interpretation of Marx's thought, the substantive claim is of critical importance for us here: whether a universalistic conception of humanity can remain stable *vis-à-vis* a theory of society that understands social life as truly emergent and autonomous. An explicit focus on social relations requires as its transcendental presupposition an implicit idea of human nature.

Marx avoids recourse to the state of nature and in fact explicitly criticises it as an intellectual resource. Kant and Hegel had of course already advanced such a critique, but Marx now discussed the state of nature in the tradition of political economy, even though the argument remains familiar: '[w]e must avoid repeating the mistake of the political economist, who bases his explanations on some imaginary primordial condition. Such a primordial condition explains nothing' (Marx 1975: 323).[7] The reasons for rejecting the state of nature as a methodological resource have not really changed, its main problem being that it 'assumes as facts and events what it is supposed to deduce' (323). Marx's critique of the state of nature is very much the same as Hegel's, Kant's and Rousseau's before him.

Yet the state of nature does play a role in one of Marx's most fundamental concepts, the idea of alienation. Understood as estrangement, mystified thought, inversion of subject and predicate, primacy of objects (or nature) over subjects (humanity), alienation describes the way in which actual human beings find themselves living under socially

[7] In *The Wealth of Nations*, Adam Smith justified the importance of the division of labour and private property by contrasting them with the state of nature: 'this original state of things, in which the labourer enjoyed the whole produce of his own labour, could not last beyond the first introduction of the appropriation of land and the accumulation of stock' (Smith 1985: 168, also 371). Smith sees the division of labour as a wholly universalistic development because it is based on the 'faculties of reason and speech ... [that are]... common to all men' (118). The division of labour is a social trend that is simultaneously inscribed in human nature: '[t]he division of labour, from which so many advantages are derived, is not originally the effect of any human wisdom ... It is the necessary, though very slow and gradual consequence of a certain propensity in human nature which has ... the propensity to truck, barter, and exchange one thing for another' (117). In other words, while social life is based on and reproduces itself through social inequality, it equally presupposes a universalistic conception of humanity as members of the same species.

produced institutions that stand in the way of the realisation of their human potential. It is thus highly illustrative that here Marx draws a contrast between a type of poverty that is natural and one that is artificial, very much along the lines of Hobbes's and Rousseau's arguments: 'the proletariat is not formed by *natural* poverty but by *artificially produced* poverty' (Marx 1975: 256). For us here the interest of Marx's theory of alienation resides in how it illustrates his engagement with natural law. Marx's idea of alienation is simultaneously a departure from and a continuation of previous natural law: whether, and to what extent, the same social relations that make our human existence possible also undermine our ability to develop our most fundamental human features. Alienated life is human life because it is human made and because it takes place under social conditions, but it is also not fully human life because we lose certain attributes which, as Hegel contends, are fundamentally 'inalienable' and 'imprescriptible'. It is human life in so far as it is the result of human interaction over time and to the extent that real human beings are able to reproduce themselves under such circumstances. Yet it is non-human life because that reproduction is self-contradictory: as human labour becomes a commodity, it reproduces itself 'as a mentally and physically *dehumanized* being' (336). Alienation represents the impossibility of living a life in which our common humanity is simultaneously realised in our various relations with nature, fellow human beings and our own individuality. In addition to the Rousseaunian motif of blaming civilisation for society's current ills, Marx reintroduces the state of nature in his argument on the alienated conditions of existence of modern capitalism. A new artificial state of nature emerges in modern society; we witness the rise of a human-made, socially produced, state of nature in which:

> [e]strangement partly manifests itself in the fact that the refinement of needs and of the means of fulfilling them gives rise to a bestial degeneration and a complete crude and abstract simplicity of need ... Man reverts once more to living in a cave, but the cave is now polluted by the mephitic and pestilential breath of civilization ... Universal *unnatural* neglect, putrefied nature, becomes an *element of life* for him. (Marx 1975: 359–60)

Marx's arguments also engage with what we will see in the two sections below is a major aspect of natural law thinking that has remained in modern social theory: the distinction between community and society. Throughout his early writings, Marx constructs the relationship between capitalism and communism, or between the state and civil society, as a sublated form of the opposition between the state of nature and the civil condition. To be sure, Marx's construction differs from natural law in that both sides of the opposition are a real form of social life within which real human beings pursue their life in society. But Marx returns to natural law as he argues that the same social bases that made capitalism possible are responsible for the increasing annihilation of our shared humanity. In *The German Ideology*, the argument centres explicitly on the communal basis of communism because '[o]nly in community ... is personal freedom possible ... In a real community the individuals obtain their freedom in and through their association' (Marx and Engels 1974: 83). The libertarian side of communism's *community* is thus opposed to instrumental intercourse as constitutive of *civil society*; the former's solidarity and cooperation are opposed to the latter's egoism and alienation. In *Manuscripts*, in fact, Marx had already elaborated further on the idea of communism, but there from the point of view of the reconciliation of the 'human' and the 'natural' components of human nature:

> *Communism* is the *positive* suppression of *private property* as *human self-estrangement*, and hence the true *appropriation* of the *human* essence through and for man; it is the complete restoration of man to himself as a *social*, i.e. human, being, a restoration which has become conscious ... This communism, as fully developed naturalism, equals humanism, and as fully developed humanism equals naturalism; it is the *genuine* resolution of the conflict between man and nature. (Marx 1975: 348)

Marx is not of course merely re-rendering the standard natural law opposition between the state of nature and the civil condition now in terms of politics against the economy, or the individual against communal life, because for Marx neither side allows our shared humanity to become fully realised. Marx's innovation, following the materialist premises we discussed above, is to explicate why certain social institutions, most notably, though not exclusively, private property, appear in a way that effectively hides their actual societal function:

> Man in his immediate reality, in civil society, is a profane being. Here, where he regards himself and is regarded by others as a real individual, he is an illusory phenomenon. In the state, on the other hand, where he is considered to be a species being, he is the imaginary member of a fictitious sovereignty, he is divested of his real individual life and filled with an unreal universality. (Marx 1975: 220)

Under modern capitalism, neither the state nor civil society is able to give full expression to our shared humanity, which is simultaneously natural, individual and social. Civil society openly undermines our sense of species being and, because it is ruled by alienated labour, it also undermines the full expression of individuality that it ought to have promoted.[8] Likewise, the state as the primary locus of modern political life ought to centre on collective self-determination, yet under its restrictive conditions of democratic participation, and because of its ultimate dependence on private property, it effectively makes impossible the emergence of a true sense of commonality. As they actually exist, both the state and civil society favour only the egoistic aspect of individuality. They not only downplay the social, species-being aspect of our shared humanity. They even undermine the full realisation of its individual side, because within civil society itself our species-being is being reduced to the 'sphere of egoism and of *bellum omnium contra omnes*', civil society 'is no longer the essence of *community* but the essence of *difference*. It has become the expression of the separation of man from his community, from himself and from other men, which is what it was *originally*' (Marx 1975: 221). Even political economy, the most advanced of empirical sciences of Marx's time, is able to see the worker only as a worker and thus fails to see that he and she are integral human beings: 'political economy knows the worker only as a beast of burden, as an animal reduced to the minimum bodily needs' (290).[9] The worker is denied his very humanity not only because he is described only in his functional role as a worker but also because the material reproduction of his life is observed only from the side of his natural needs: 'labour in which man alienates himself, is a labour of self-sacrifice, of mortification ... man (the worker) feels that he is acting freely only in his animal functions – eating, drinking and procreating ... – while in his human functions he is nothing more than an animal' (326–7). This comparison with animals is taken further in relation to the centrality of our humanity's sense of universality. While animals 'produce only for their own immediate needs or those of their young ... man produces *universally*' (329). Universal human production takes place 'in freedom' and when human beings are in effect able to produce 'the whole nature' (329).

The key question for Marx in this context, and here he is again dealing with the same challenges that are central to modern natural law, is that in order to understand how human life can be enhanced we must grasp the interconnections between the world of nature, social life and individuality itself. His argument on the universality of the human species is based on how human beings are able to bring these three spheres together: '[e]very self-estrangement of man from himself and nature is

[8] Later, in *Capital*, this is the argument of the fetishism of the commodity form (Marx 1976: 163–77).

[9] On Marx's appreciation on the role of the female labour force in the development of capitalism, see Marx (1975: 291–5).

manifested in the relationship he sets up between other men and himself and nature' (Marx 1975: 331). In so constructing their interrelationships, moreover, Marx argues that the universality of the human species 'makes the whole of nature his *inorganic* body', the whole of nature, that is, which is not the human body itself (328). In one and the same movement, man is part of nature, gives social meaning to nature and transforms nature.

The kind of inversion that is apparent in the reproduction of material life is then matched by a similar inversion in how material life is *represented*. We have seen that here Marx takes up Feuerbach's mode of criticism and connects the misrepresentations of the modern economy and modern politics with the critique of religion. But while traditional or pre-modern forms of alienation may have become more apparent in the sphere of religion, in its specifically modern form alienation is the result of the rise and eventual domination of private property. Marx's goal is to that extent not altogether different from what we have reconstructed as the central motif of modern natural law; namely, to make apparent the radically human origins of social institutions. What Hobbes made clear in relation to the modern state, Rousseau in relation to the people, Kant in relation to morality and Hegel in relation to the differentiation between the individual, the state and civil society, Marx will now do in relation to economic life. They all took what appeared as natural forms of organising social life and uncovered their human origins. In Marx's case, the importance of private property in capitalism lies in the fact that it makes apparent the universality of the modern form of alienation:

> [t]he emancipation of society from private property, etc., from servitude, is expressed in the *political* form of the *emancipation of the workers*. This is not because it is only a question of their emancipation, but because in their emancipation is contained universal human emancipation. The reason for this universality is that the whole human servitude is involved in the relation of the worker to production, and all relations of servitude are nothing but modifications and consequences of this relation. (Marx 1975: 333)[10]

[10] The argument turns eventually to the distance between what a current political struggle may achieve within the modern state, based as it is on restrictive notions of nationality or ethnicity, and human emancipation as such; '[*p*]*olitical* emancipation is certainly a big step forward. It may not be the last form of general human emancipation, but it is the last form of human emancipation *within* the prevailing scheme of things' (Marx 1975: 221). The universalistic orientation of Marx's argument is apparent in his constant references to the world-historical aspect of modern capitalism (Marx and Engels 1974: 55–78, Marx 1973: 225–8). I have discussed this in Chernilo (2007: 39–47).

Whether, in spite of himself, Marx reifies human nature in the form of praxis or labour, or whether his radical defence of social relations allows him to avoid that essentialism, remains an open question. Either way, his effort to explicate the relationships between the human and the social, on the one hand, and between nature, society and the individual, on the other hand, must be read as the sublated continuation of natural law. We can see that there is tension in Marx's conception of human nature: human beings are cooperative and communal in general but under current socio-historical conditions they are estranged, so conflict and competition prevail. In turn, Marx's ontology of the social also becomes dual, cooperative and communal in general and conflictive and estranged under capitalism. Marx's natural law moment, as it were, is that there is no true development of our species-being beyond society and yet social relations themselves are responsible for humanity's current self-estrangement. The whole purpose of producing knowledge about social life is only realised if intellectual practices contribute to the transformation of social life itself.

Tönnies

In *Dialectic of Nihilism*, Gillian Rose offers one of the few attempts to address the relationships between sociology's founding dichotomy of *community* and *society* and the tradition of natural law. Her argument is that the distinction between society and community was first suggested by Otto von Gierke and that it is through his indirect influence that it made its way into nascent sociology. The 'opposition of community and society', she argues,

> [p]its 'community', the fiction of Germanic law, against 'society', the fiction of Roman law, avoiding both the pitfall of socialism, which erects the fiction of Germanic 'community' in place of the fiction of capitalist 'society', and the weakness of sociology, which fails to distinguish adequately between 'society' meaning *socialitas*, with its economic, Roman, private law connotations, and 'society' meaning *consocialitas* with its moral or ethical connotations, developed by the Stoics. (Rose 1984: 47)

A key theme running through Part II above was the centrality of the distinction between the state of nature and the civil state in modern natural law, and its influence on the rise of modern social theory is arguably nowhere more apparent than in Tönnies's (2001) classic *Gemeinschaft und Gesellschaft*. First published in 1887, the text was a re-elaboration of Tönnies's second doctoral thesis of 1881 (Harris 2001: xiv–xv). The book was slow to attract attention but eventually underwent eight reprints before Tönnies's death in 1936, with a major new edition revised by the author coming out in 1912 (Adair-Totef 2005b, Bond 2010).

I should like to start with Tönnies's general reflections on sociology as they were introduced in his speech at the first conference of the German Society for Sociology in 1910. This short lecture provides a concise account of his vision on the development of the new discipline of sociology which, although it has faced much opposition and even 'hostility', has by the turn of the century succeeded in becoming a 'global . . . carrier of thoughts worldwide' (Tönnies 2005: 72). Sociology, claims Tönnies, is fundamentally 'a philosophical discipline'. This original connection between sociology and philosophy was already apparent in the ways in which early sociology was truly a kind of 'social philosophy', which in turn was inseparable 'from the history of legal philosophy' and its questions about the 'ethical and good conduct of life and forms of life' (57). Tönnies explicitly uses the idea of philosophical sociology to delimit a type of enquiry that concentrates on 'the structure of concepts': on the one hand, by contributing to clearer conceptual definitions inside sociology, on the other, by helping to establish 'the connections between the social and other sciences' (63).[11]

Tönnies dismisses the relativistic implications of the nineteenth-century Romantic reaction and argues that we ought to recover the earlier enlightened belief in the possibility of human improvement; sociology retains an idea of 'social good' as a fundamental 'human ideal' (Tönnies 2005: 58, Bond 2009). He argues that questions of 'whether there is absolute evil or absolute good for humanity' are no mere residue from earlier metaphysical ways of thinking; rather, they are essential to sociological enquiry as such. Natural law becomes relevant in this context because its sociological substance 'amounts to a doctrine of the possible, real (and necessary) *ethical* and *legal* connections, relations and associations of men'; natural law thus becomes a hugely 'important' part of 'theoretical sociology' (Tönnies 2005: 58). However much sociology has advanced and must continue to progress as a scientific project devoted to empirical study of contemporary life, its tradition and key concerns are indeed philosophical. Sociology retains a deep interest in normative issues and yet its intellectual worth depends equally on its scientific purchase: sociology must learn to approach normative questions in a non-normative way. It should study social reality empirically, mostly through such scientific procedures as statistics and historical evidence

[11] We will discuss Simmel's use of the idea of philosophical sociology in Chapter 7.

(68–71). In a language that has since become strongly associated with Max Weber's idea of value-free sociology, Tönnies describes the task of sociology as the attempt to understand what is rather than what should be. The sociologist must remain connected to political problems as urgent social issues, help clarify their implications and contribute to a more rational debate about different available options. But as a sociologist she is not in favour of or against particular political causes (62–4). Tönnies then concludes his lecture with the following interpretation of the call that is inscribed in the Oracle of Delphi. In a way that resembles Rousseau's rendition of the maxim 'know thyself!', as a commandment this is:

> [v]alid for *humanity,* for scientific man who, in the name of humanity, is called upon to think and to speak about being and becoming. Sociology is the impartial attempt to do justice to this commandment. Through it and in it will humanity know itself and there is the implicit hope that through self-knowledge, humanity will learn to master itself . . . Neither as man, nor as citizen of the state, nor as world citizen, nor as contemporary citizen, can anyone be indifferent to this hope. (Tönnies 2005: 72–3)

Tönnies's conception of sociology is thus philosophical as well as scientific, normative as well as descriptive. This outlook also transpires in the opening statement of *Community and Society,* whose focus is on providing a 'new analysis of the fundamental problems of social life' (Tönnies 2001: 3). Tönnies's argument on the tensional relationships between science and philosophy in contemporary intellectual enquiry sounds familiar *vis-à-vis* natural law: while precision and attention to detail were on the side of science, depth and meaningfulness remained philosophy's contribution to human knowledge. Indeed, while only '[m]athematics is the prototype of all real science, which in its inmost nature is artificial', true knowledge of human affairs can only emerge as a result of combining science and philosophy (172). In a view that, as we shall see, could have been endorsed by all the writers of this generation of social theorists whom we will revisit in this and the next chapter, he contends that '[t]he more that science becomes on the one hand universal, while on the other extending its methods to the organic world, the more it must become in this sense philosophical' (9). In the study of human affairs it is therefore possible to distinguish between formal knowledge about how human beings interact with one another, which Tönnies calls 'pure jurisprudence (or natural law)' and an understanding of the material content of such relationships, which is the subject matter of 'political economy' (11). In terms of intellectual sources, while in the preface to the first edition of

Community and Society Tönnies will also pay homage to such writers as Comte, Spencer and Gierke, this distinction between pure jurisprudence and political economy readily indicates his two major intellectual inspirations: Hobbes and Marx.[12]

Tönnies speaks of mutual affirmation as a universal human need which, as it necessarily involves social relations, must take one of two forms: it can either be conceived 'as having real organic life, and that is the essence of *Community*; or else as a purely mechanical construction ... and that is what we think of as *Society*' (Tönnies 2001: 17). The grounds for this distinction are analytical rather than historical as it aims to depict all possible types of human association. Indeed, the sociological relevance of this distinction for the understanding of social relations allows us to contrast not only forms of association but also types of social order, legal and moral systems and even historical epochs themselves (247–57).[13] If we now try to organise the main aspects of social reality that are then depicted through this distinction throughout Tönnies's book, the following can be mentioned:

- *Gemeinschaft* is a living being, *Gesellschaft* a mechanical artefact (17);
- *Gemeinschaft* has a metaphysical will of its own, *Gesellschaft* is an instrumental alliance of wills (187);
- *Gemeinschaft* is inclusive and collective, *Gesellschaft* is exclusionary and individualistic (18–19);
- *Gemeinschaft* is old, genuine and enduring, *Gesellschaft* is new, superficial and transient (19);
- *Gemeinschaft* is language, custom and belief; *Gesellschaft* is business, travel and science (18);
- *Gemeinschaft* is a 'warm' familial environment, *Gesellschaft* is the 'cold' public space (142);
- the natural law of *Gemeinschaft* is marriage, the natural law of *Gesellschaft* is contract (58–65, 187–9, 222);

[12] Not least because Hobbes and Marx are the two authors to whom he devoted more attention and even wrote their intellectual biographies (Tönnies 1932, 1974). Niall Bond put it thus in relation to Hobbes: 'the foundations of Tönnies' sociological and political thought were Hobbesian, i.e. strictly rationalist ... Tönnies' *Gemeinschaft und Gesellschaft* can be read as a reasoned response to Hobbes' presentation of the foundation of Commonwealth and human sociability as a set of norms laid down by an accepted authority to constrain human beings in their latent mutual hostility' (Bond 2011a: 1176). See also Bond (2010).

[13] Bond even argues that, in terms of the epistemology of the social sciences, the distinction also offered Tönnies a way to mediate between rival scientific schools: German historicism was best suited to the study of *Gemeinschaft* and modern rationalism to understand *Gesellschaft* (Bond 2011b: 38–41).

- *Gemeinschaft* is female, child-like and uneducated, *Gesellschaft* is male, adult and well instructed (152–71);[14]
- *Gemeinschaft* represents a natural will, *Gesellschaft* an artificial will (165);
- *Gemeinschaft* is home, village and town; *Gesellschaft* is metropolitan, national and international (173);
- *Gemeinschaft* is honest and simple-minded, *Gesellschaft* 'is glib and double-tongued' (173);
- *Gemeinschaft* is based on natural equality, *Gesellschaft* on artificial hierarchy (186);
- *Gemeinschaft* is oriented to the past, *Gesellschaft* focuses on the future (96);
- *Gemeinschaft* is mutual possession and enjoyment, *Gesellschaft* is private property and profit (36);
- *Gemeinschaft* is based on status, *Gesellschaft* on contract (201–3);
- *Gemeinschaft* is ruled by customs, *Gesellschaft* by social policy (251);
- *Gemeinschaft* centres on distributive justice, *Gesellschaft* on commutative justice (196–7);
- *Gemeinschaft* is the space of the worker, *Gesellschaft* that of the trader (173, 190);
- *Gemeinschaft* is best represented by the nation, *Gesellschaft* by the state (249);
- *Gemeinschaft* is directed by religion, *Gesellschaft* by public opinion (248–50);
- in *Gemeinschaft*, means and ends are prescribed, in *Gesellschaft* they change according to the individual will (206–7);
- *Gemeinschaft* is 'family-based communism' whereas *Gesellschaft* is 'state-based and international socialism' (260).[15]

Tönnies's normative preferences for *Gemeinschaft* being unmistakable, he fully realises that both forms of association are equally real and, even more importantly, that historical trends make it clear that *Gesellschaft* is on the rise (Outhwaite 2006: 9). The distinction is introduced and justified in analytical terms; we are warned that there is no such thing as a pure *Gemeinschaft* or *Gesellschaft*, but we do have to accept that

[14] To this extent, gender inequality is integral to Tönnies's argument in a way that is not the case in any of the other classical sociologists I am discussing in part III. See, in particular, Tönnies (2001: 152–71).

[15] In this case, though, the polarity includes an intermediate state of 'absolutely detached *cosmopolitan and universalist individualism*' (Tönnies 2001: 260). See Inglis (2009) on Tönnies's cosmopolitanism and Bond (2011b) for further discussion on Tönnies's changing views on socialism as a political programme *vis-à-vis* his theoretical arguments in *Community and Society*.

their relationships are taking the form of a teleological movement in which '[s]ooner or later the tragic conflict will unfold itself as inevitable in the evolution of Community into Society' (Tönnies 2001: 165). The explicit Rousseaunian connection is soon to emerge: 'the theory of *Gemeinschaft* is based on the idea that in the original or natural state there is a complete unity of human wills' (22). Tönnies refuses to get drawn into the issue of whether human nature is essentially competitive or cooperative, aggressive or considerate: '[p]ure and all-embracing evil-mindedness is ... just as rare ... as pure and universal "goodness of heart"'(126). And yet for all the subtlety with which he seeks to avoid essentialising human dispositions, the logic of the typology is fundamentally marked by its references to the state of nature:

> The theory of *Gesellschaft* takes as its starting point a group of people who, as in *Gemeinschaft*, live peacefully alongside one another, but in this case without being essentially united – indeed, on the contrary, they are here essentially detached. In *Gemeinschaft* they stay together in spite of everything that separates them; in *Gesellschaft* they remain separate in spite of everything that unites them. (Tönnies 2001: 52)

While Tönnies's inspiration for the idea of *Gemeinschaft* is taken from Gierke – the radically pluralistic forms of the local life as they spring from real small communities – it is to *Gesellschaft* that more attention is actually devoted. The conceptual and historical representations of *Gesellschaft* are then built on a combination of insights taken from Hobbes and Marx. The 'Hobbesian' notion of isolated, egoistic individuals is thus matched by the 'Marxian' proposition that economic exchanges are the archetypal form of social interaction in modern society. *Gesellschaft* becomes increasingly driven by the logic of markets, where the value of commodities is calculated in relation to the quantity of labour needed in their production. Money is the universal commodity which, in the form of capital, becomes the ultimate embodiment of *Gesellschaft*: 'money as a form of obligation, and obligation as form of money' (Tönnies 2001: 191). All economic profit that is generated in modern *Gesellschaft* goes to a single class, the commercial bourgeoisie, which in turns makes the modern state an instrument for the further and worldwide enhancement of capitalist relations. Tönnies then spells out the universalistic implications that are built into *Gesellschaft*. The substantive inequality that is created by class power and differences in wealth requires an increasingly egalitarian conception of human beings. *Gesellschaft* cannot avoid becoming a 'universal, all-embracing human society' because, according to its

> [o]wn conception of natural law all people, as reasonable beings and free agents, are a priori equal ... The recognition of these universal and inescapable qualities

as inherent in every adult human makes legal slavery an absurdity and leads to its abolition. (Tönnies 2001: 71–2).

Slavery, however, remains in modern society and Tönnies, following Marx (1975: 325–38), accepts that artificially created poverty creates conditions of substantive inequality that then undermine the very principles of natural equality on which *Gesellschaft* is supposed to be organised:

> [o]ut-and-out slavery is by no means *legally* incompatible with a *Gesellschaft* system, for it is an entirely artificial, man-made institution, while the premise that all adult humans are equal through their capacity for free will is implicit in nature and thus in the simplest and most basic scientific knowledge. (Tönnies 2001: 194)

Tönnies's conceptualisation of the distinction between community and society is then heavily inspired by modern natural law. Yet it would be wrong to depict his attempt as a mere restoration of natural law. First, because for Tönnies neither moment is conceived as asocial in the way that the state of nature is: community as well as society represents a specific and equally real kind of truly *social* relations. Secondly, because the transition from one to the other does not imply the full realisation or sublation of human nature (or, as in Marx, an opposite transition to a condition of generalised alienation also thanks to the rise of specific social institutions). For modern natural law, the appearance of social relations is the key aspect that makes the difference between the state of nature and the civil condition. It is only through the social that human beings eventually recognise each other as members of the same species and begin to develop their human powers. While for Tönnies, and indeed for social theory more generally, the social is central to both sides of the dichotomy between community and society (and to that extent he departs from modern natural law), his work also presupposes that the social as an autonomous domain is the condition of possibility of the realisation of our common humanity. Indeed, Tönnies also claims that certain forms of association lend themselves to the further enhancement of certain aspects of our humanity and are thus normatively more important than others. That is the case in his analysis of *Gemeinschaft* even though actual historical trends seemed to be moving in the opposite direction. Tönnies has thus sublated the most fundamental of insights of modern natural law: social relations are necessary for the full extent of our humanity to express itself.[16]

[16] While his overall depiction of modernity is more optimistic, Durkheim (1984) offered arguably the same claim with the distinction between mechanical and organic solidarity in *Division of Labour*. See below.

The final issue we need to clarify in Tönnies's work is introduced in the third part of *Community and Society*, which concentrates explicitly on the sociological significance of natural law. The key tenets of Tönnies's understanding of natural law were introduced above in Chapter 3: a universalistic sense of common humanity as a useful fiction for thinking about ourselves as human beings; notions of equality, freedom and rationality that were triggered by the increase in economic exchanges in the ancient world (*Gesellschaft* does find its most developed expression in capitalism but is a transhistorical analytical type); a general legal framework for the institutionalisation of early international economic exchanges that came as a result and sought to restrict the legal particularism of different regions; an enhanced proceduralism in logical reasoning and jurisprudence; and the prevalence of universalistic ideas of justice. Now in relation to the role of natural law arguments *within* his social theory, Tönnies depicts his own intellectual challenge as similar to those of the 'ancient philosophy of law', namely 'whether law was a product of nature (*physei*) or of artifice (*thesei* or *nomô*)' (Tönnies 2001: 211). The modern specificity of that ancient dilemma lies in how for the moderns 'everything originating from the human mind or formed by it is both natural and artificial'. The increasing importance of *Gesellschaft* in relation to *Gemeinschaft* has, however, the consequence that now 'the artificial overtakes the natural, and the more specifically human ... gains in scope and importance, until in the end it attains at least relative autonomy from its natural base and may even come into conflict with it' (211). The artificial is now suffocating the natural; excessive rationalism, formalism and legal positivism are the kind of dangers that derive from the current imbalance between what is natural and what is artificial in social life. In fact, we listed above that both *Gemeinschaft* and *Gesellschaft* have their own kind of natural law. In the case of *Gemeinschaft*, the substance of common life lies in organic relations. Close personal contact is its crucial dimension and Tönnies depicts this natural law as 'essentially a union of natural wills', which he then connects with the stable relationship of a heterosexual couple: marriage becomes the most developed representation of this first type of natural law (202). In the case of *Gesellschaft*, the substance of its common spirit is the rationality objectified 'in the transfer of property and exchange of goods' (202). Best expressed in the legal institution of the contract, 'its purest form' is found 'in the law of trade or commerce' (217).

As a result of the typological orientation of his argument, Tönnies does not prescribe that the two types of natural law will work in harmony. Tönnies criticises the flat kind of universalism that underpins the

Gesellschaft-type of natural law as it does not allow for a radical difference between our ability to recognise each other as members of the same species and that of animals to do likewise. What does make our humanity unique *vis-à-vis* all other animal species are those aspects of our lives that are fundamentally social and remain closer to *Gemeinschaft*. The difficulty lies in that this universality, however artificial in its origins, is ultimately as real as the thicker, more organic cultural markers that characterise communal life; universality develops socio-historically and can be grasped only through our real particularities. The reconstruction of the ways in which both types of natural law relate to one another, he contends, must proceed by looking at

> [t]he basic characteristics of mankind, not as an abstraction but as the concrete embodiment of the human race, and as effectively the most universal of species. We then move on through the basic characteristics of race, people, tribe and smaller groups to arrive in the end at the single individual. (Tönnies 2001: 181)

As a general analytical device, therefore, there is a fundamental transhistorical component in Tönnies's idea of natural law. And although modern capitalism certainly constitutes the most advanced representation of societal life, *Gesellschaft* natural law emerged not as a result of capitalism but of much earlier forms of economic exchange:

> The more people of diverse kinds come together and recognise each other as rational human beings or as equals, the more probable and ultimately necessary it becomes that a universal order and system of Society be established among them ... The rule of Rome over the *orbis terrarum*, which has its material foundation in commerce, brings all cities closer to the one city, and gathers together all the shrewd, bargaining, prosperous individuals, the entire ruling elite of this boundless empire, all haggling together in the Forum. It erases their differences and inequalities, gives them all the same outward appearance, the same language and form of expression, the same currency, the same culture, the same covetousness and the same curiosity. The abstract human being, that most artificial, 'routinised' and sophisticated of all machines, has been conjured up and constructed, and can be observed – like an apparition – in the bright unglamorous light of day. (Tönnies 2001: 217)

Gesellschaft natural law is, by definition, global and favours universalism over all forms of particularity. But then the only way in which human beings become who they are and develop the skills that will allow them to be a part of this global society has to do with their communal life – as we put it in relation to Hegel, the universality of the person lies also in its particularity and its singularity. There is, Tönnies contends, a 'natural' sense of solidarity towards those with whom we share features that appear essential. The possibility of universal human solidarity depends on the sublation of our particularity without either ever losing its specificity: '*Gemeinschaft* law is an end in itself... It takes for granted a certain solidarity among human beings as a natural and necessary mode of existence' (Tönnies 2001: 211). 'Our' community is always and necessarily ours – it cannot be universally shared. But precisely because of that Tönnies claims that the 'highest' form of human fellowship 'would ultimately be a commonwealth which must be imagined as including the whole of mankind' (234). Partly natural and partly artificial, partly unrealisable and partly already accomplished, partly a precondition of our moral thinking and partly the outcome of the need to regulate economic exchange, partly economic and partly cultural, '[t]his notion of a higher commonwealth may be thought of as an original and suggestive idea that can exist only through the medium of the creative visionary imagination found in myth' (232). A universal *society* may then have to be seen as the unintended result of actually existing *communities*, its artificial sense of universality emerging and developing only and to the extent that it is rooted in those more natural similarities that bond people closely together.

Durkheim

The main text for exploring Durkheim's explicit engagement with the tradition of natural law is his short book on *Montesquieu and Rousseau. Forerunners of Sociology* (1970). The text was put together as a single piece only posthumously in the 1950s, but its straightforward division into two parts does not make this decision particularly problematic. The first section is devoted to Montesquieu and is a translation of Durkheim's Latin thesis on *Montesquieu and his Contribution to the Rise of Social Science*. The dissertation was submitted in 1892 and was therefore written at the same time as Durkheim's French thesis on *The Division of Labour in Society*. The second part of the book is a study of Rousseau's work, mostly though not exclusively on the *Discourse on Inequality* and *Social Contract*. Although it was originally written in 1901–2, the piece appeared only in 1918 (Lukes 1973: 279).

The general thesis of both studies is well captured in the book's title. As he unpacks a tensional assessment of how much modern social science depends upon, but also needs to depart from, these writers' natural law theories, Durkheim reads Montesquieu and Rousseau as *true* forerunners of sociology. The two texts share the main thesis that both philosophers grasped and helped give form to the most fundamental of sociological insights: the autonomy of the social as a domain of reality that is as available for truly scientific study as any other aspect of natural and individual reality. Montesquieu's commitment to the thesis on the autonomy of the social is first demonstrated when he is able to distinguish between state and society – 'the kinds of society should not be confused with the different types of state' (Durkheim 1970: 9) – or, similarly, that the form of government does not determine the nature of a society (33). Montesquieu is also credited with having anticipated another dimension that became central to Durkheim's own sociological programme – the distinction between individual and social reality: 'Montesquieu's science is really social science' because '[i]t deals with social phenomena and not with the mind of the individual' (17). The autonomy of political institutions *vis-à-vis* the social, on the one hand, and the separation between the individual and society, on the other, are of course among the most precious aspects of Durkheim's sociological programme. Yet he does not hesitate to acknowledge that both principles were already well formed in the writings of Montesquieu.

Montesquieu is also praised for arguing that descriptive and explanatory claims ought to take precedence over normative ones. Social science would only emerge if it tried to grasp the laws of society as they really were and not as they ought to be. For a science of society to exist, society itself has to be subject to scientific laws. The general cosmology that made natural science possible needed to be applied to the social sciences as well: 'since the principle that all the phenomena of the universe are closely interrelated has been tested in the other domains of nature and has never proved to be false, it is also valid, in all likelihood, for human societies, which are part of nature' (Durkheim 1970: 10). Yet social phenomena are difficult to observe, as they are not readily apparent to immediate or untrained observation. Unlike natural ones, sociological observations require a sense of 'completeness'; scientific observations become useful in sociology if and when they are able to transcend partial accounts and aim for the description of society as a whole: '[i]n pointing to the interrelatedness of social phenomena, Montesquieu foreshadowed the unity of our science' (57). Methodologically, Montesquieu acknowledged the importance of induction and the limitations of deduction for the development of a truly scientific attitude (although, as we will see below, Durkheim criticised Montesquieu for not consistently applying this insight). Experiments are crucial for the development of science but they can hardly be carried out in social science and Durkheim praises Montesquieu again for having made the comparative method central to the scientific attitude of the sociologist: '[i]n order to discover the laws of nature, one need only make a sufficient number of comparisons between the various forms of a given thing' (51).

The autonomy of the social, the complexity of finding visible symbols to account for underlying social causes, the unity of social and natural science, the importance of the empirical for sociology are all claims that Durkheim made systematically throughout his career. We ought never to exaggerate the importance of any individual thinker, Durkheim contends, but on the basis of all these observations Montesquieu is for him truly the first to have 'laid down the fundamental principles of social science' (61).[17]

If we now turn our attention explicitly to natural law, Montesquieu had already understood that social science did not have to *recreate* natural law. The laws of nature were for Montesquieu the laws of human nature and these were the task of psychology and not of social science (Durkheim 1970: 12–13). Montesquieu's laws of nature are similar to Hobbes's as they include the preservation of one's life and the right to peaceful coexistence, but more importantly he distinguishes between the natural laws of human psychology and laws that, because they regulate society proper, 'cannot be inferred from the nature of man' (19). Political laws, civil laws, the laws of nations, in effect 'all the major social institutions' that regulate life in society, are not in this sense part of the laws of nature because they are social. The picture is, however, not so simple and Durkheim warns us that:

> [w]e must be careful in interpreting Montesquieu's terminology. It is true that he does not apply the term *natural* to these various forms of [social] law, but *this does not mean that he regards them as foreign to nature.* To his mind they are based on reality, but not in the same way as the natural laws, *since they result from the nature not of man, but of societies.* Their causes are to be sought in social conditions ... If Montesquieu applied the word 'natural' only to the laws of individual life – as though the other laws did not deserve to be so called – this must be ascribed to the habits of his age. For the philosophers of the time a 'state of nature' was the state of man living without society, and 'natural laws' were those to which man conformed in such a state. Montesquieu accepted this current use of the term despite the ambiguity it involved. (Durkheim 1970: 19–20, my italics)

Durkheim argues that Montesquieu did not stay within the traditional conception of natural law as belonging exclusively to the asocial aspect of

[17] It should be pointed out that this not the ultimate claim of Durkheim on the subject. In an article on sociology in France in the nineteenth century, pride of place in the setting up of sociology is attributed, more conventionally, primarily to Comte and secondarily to Saint-Simon (Durkheim 1973). Although this is also how the sociological mainstream has read Durkheim (Giddens 1978, Gouldner 1959 and Zeitlin 1968), Rousseau, Kant and French socialist Charles Renouvier have also been suggested for the role of the prime influence in Durkheim's works. See, respectively, Cladis (1992), Layne (1973) and Jones (2001).

human life as experienced in the state of nature. Montesquieu sought instead to establish social life as a domain that was equally fundamentally susceptible to its own laws of nature. Montesquieu is after a different type of laws of nature, ones that can be derived 'from the "nature" not of man but of the social organism. He understood with a wonderful lucidity that '*the nature of societies is no less stable and consistent than that of man* and that it is no easier to modify the type of a society than the species of an animal' (Durkheim 1970: 21, my italics). The tone of the discussion echoes the one we reconstructed from Hobbes to Hegel in the previous two chapters: the same modernisation of natural law that Durkheim finds in Montesquieu, Montesquieu himself thought he had achieved *vis-à-vis* 'Grotius and his disciples' (21). Even as attention turns to the variation to be found in different types of society we are bound to realise that there are general laws that apply to social life as such. The object of social science is to grasp this variation as much as it is to come to terms with the ultimate nature of the social. Conceptualising the social also requires us to reflect on its universalistic underpinnings and here the foundations of Montesquieu's distinction between laws of nature that focus on human psychology and laws that concentrate social life becomes problematic:

> Just as all societies, even those that are most dissimilar, have something in common, so certain laws are to be found in all societies. These are the laws that Montesquieu considers suitable to society in general. Present wherever society exists, they are implied in the very notion of society and can be explicated by it ... Montesquieu calls these laws *law* in the absolute and universal sense, and declares that they are none other than human reason considered as the power governing all societies ... Perhaps it is because they are to be found in all nations and are conceived in a sense as anterior to the establishment of societies that he does not clearly distinguish them from the laws of nature. (Durkheim 1970: 22)[18]

Durkheim reads Montesquieu in very much the same way as we have seen writers in the natural law tradition attempted these engagements before: the social is an autonomous domain which although it is to be conceptualised as independent from human nature must ultimately be thought as compatible with it; a scientific approach is the way to advance modern knowledge forward but the complexity of social issues requires us to address them also with a philosophical attitude. Durkheim

[18] In this sense, I depart from Lukes's (1973: 282) interpretation that Durkheim praised 'Montesquieu's relativism' and that Durkheim 'rightly discerned in Montesquieu a residual belief in natural law'. Natural law was integral to instead of residual in Montesquieu and therein lies precisely its interest for Durkheim.

reads Montesquieu as a way of clarifying his own thinking; when he discusses Montesquieu, Durkheim is talking about himself.[19]

Written a decade later than the Latin dissertation on Montesquieu, and arguably exempt from the constraints of a text that was devised for examination, Durkheim assesses Rousseau equally thoroughly but more critically. Again in this case, Rousseau's continuous commitment to natural law is as essential as it is problematic. Durkheim describes Rousseau's conception of the state of nature as wholly unhistorical and emphasises how for Rousseau the state of nature is no more than a 'methodological device' (Durkheim 1970: 69). An important step forward over previous conceptions of the state of nature, the substantive results are not radically different from those at which Montesquieu arrived; namely, the distinction: 'between the social elements of human nature and those inherent in the psychological makeup of the individual' (66).

Durkheim finds Rousseau's state of nature problematic because it cannot explain how and why individuals leave – voluntarily or otherwise – the state of nature. Men, argues Rousseau, 'emerge naturally from the state of nature' as they are challenged by their physical surroundings: '[s]ociety comes into being because men need each other. This mutual assistance is not *naturally* necessary. Each individual can be self-sufficient. Thus, in order for society to arise, external circumstances must increase man's need and consequently modify his nature' (Durkheim 1970: 81). The problem with Rousseau's argument is that either both human nature and society are equally real, in which case social life cannot logically emerge out of the state of nature, or society is truly an offshoot of human nature, in which case there is no ground to argue that social life can represent an improvement over life in the state of nature. At stake here is a key postulate in all state of nature theories: namely, that while society is not inscribed in nature, this does not automatically mean that it is against nature. 'The more perfectly the collective realm reflects (though in an entirely new form) the essential characteristics of the natural realm, the more perfect will be the social order' (126). As an autonomous field of scientific enquiry, there is no doubt in Durkheim's mind that for Rousseau society has 'the impersonal character of natural forces'; society is a new kind of 'corporate body' that

[19] Durkheim none the less criticised Montesquieu for being unable to apply this autonomous notion of society consistently and thus falling back on an individualistic conception of natural law. He also challenged Montesquieu's insufficient attention to historical and empirical detail and argue that, because of this, he was unable to grasp how the pathological is itself an expression of deeper social trends. Above all, as he confounded the rational with the real, Montesquieu failed to realise the importance of the pathological when looking at modern society (Durkheim 1970: 54–5).

is '*sui generis*' (99). But as in his critique of Montesquieu, the need to establish firmly the social as an autonomous domain led Rousseau to conflate what was natural with what was rational: '[i]t may seem surprising at first to find Rousseau, for whom society is not in the domain of nature, saying that the force on which society is based must be natural, that is, grounded in nature. But *natural* is here synonymous with *rational*' (95).

Durkheim then reflects on the truly dramatic consequences that are triggered by the transition from the state of nature to a civil state. Not only do human beings move from a '*de facto* order to a *de jure* order' but morality itself is born: '[m]orality could come into being only with society' (Durkheim 1970: 75). The rise of the social effectively transforms human nature, but the challenge now is to form a type of society which, although it is autonomous from human nature, itself becomes a form of nature that does not contravene or cause injury to human nature. Once again, the more Durkheim appears to be reflecting on Rousseau's argument the more he is effectively trying to come to a satisfactory solution for himself. The social is definitively independent of human nature; it must radically transform human nature, but it cannot be against human nature. To the extent that a new form of social order can be logically devised and then put into practice, freedom and equality, which are fundamental values in the state of nature, must now be sublated:

> Man must change completely if he is to survive in the environment he himself has created. This means that *the characteristic attributes of the state of nature must be transformed and, at the same time, maintained* ... They must assume a new form without ceasing to be. This they can do only if social man, though differing profoundly from natural man, maintains the same relation to society as natural man to physical nature. (Durkheim 1970: 93, my italics)

Sociology thus emerges as a new form of natural law: first, it sublates human nature in order to accommodate artificial, socially created, nature; secondly, it argues that this new nature of man is as strongly dependent on society as individual human nature was on the state of nature.

Durkheim is critical of Rousseau on at least three issues that are fundamental to his understanding of modern society. First, Rousseau's conception of the division of labour is deficient as it misses the point of its capacity to create new forms of social solidarity (Durkheim 1970: 112). Secondly, Rousseau's scepticism towards secondary groups is wholly misplaced as they are key to the mediations between the individual and the state in modern society (107, 131). Thirdly, the wholly individualistic conception of the state of nature is replaced by a wholly collectivist conception of the civil condition, but neither monistic approach really works (99). In a more positive tone, Durkheim's body metaphors are inspired by Rousseau's even though his 'vitalism' is severely criticised (83, 112). Likewise, and as we will have the occasion to review in some detail below, Durkheim endorses Rousseau's argument on the quasi-religious elements of all forms of thinking (119). But after all subtleties have been put to one side, the most dramatic aspect of Durkheim's reading of Rousseau is how the idea of the general will becomes fundamentally compatible with his own idea of society:

> If there is no justice among individuals, there must be something outside them, a being sui generis, which acts as arbiter and determines the law. This something is society, which owes its moral primacy, not to its physical supremacy, but to its nature ... the moral order transcends the individual ... it requires a foundation in some being, and since there is no being in nature that satisfies the necessary conditions, such a being must be created. This being is the social body. (Durkheim 1970: 103)

The general will is moral because it is social; there is no such thing as natural morality but all morality rather derives from social life itself. The general will is based on the same attributes of equality and freedom that are constitutive of the state of nature, which can now only reappear fully in their sublated social/moral form. Nowhere is this better expressed than in an idea of democracy which, although it is truly 'humanly unattainable', remains however 'the ideal form of government' (Durkheim 1970: 126). Once again, this was not only Rousseau's view, but also Durkheim's. Conceptually as well as normatively, universalism is central to his conceptualisation of social life.[20]

The emphasis on continuity that comes from a detailed reading of one's intellectual precursors can now be counterbalanced as we discuss some of Durkheim's claims to scientific autonomy and intellectual originality. The opening pages of Durkheim's *The Rules of the Sociological Method* (1982) offer a good insight into what he considered was its ground-breaking contribution to the establishment of sociology. Its general orientation can be explicated in four steps: (a) methodological self-clarification is urgent though up to now relatively rare in sociology; (b) because of this insufficient self-clarification, sociology remains in a state of relative underdevelopment or immaturity *vis-à-vis* natural science and individual psychology; (c) strictly methodological reflections are thus essential to establish sociology on a firm scientific basis; (d) it is only on the basis of methodological self-clarification that

[20] See Durkheim (1992: 65–109) on the universalistic orientation of his ideas of national and world patriotism or cosmopolitanism (also Chernilo 2007: 61–73 and Inglis and Robertson 2008 for further discussion). A similar argument, though focused on religion, is found in the conclusions of *Elementary Forms of the Religious Life* (Durkheim 1965: 472–4, 493–4).

the substantive definition of society as sociology's object matter can be meaningfully attempted (Durkheim 1982: 35–49). A great irony of Durkheim's book is that its claim to originality inaugurated what has since become a rather conventional sociological genre – from Parsons (1968) to Giddens (1993) and Luhmann (1995). An even greater irony, however, is that this sociological genre, Durkheim's contribution included, shows a severe lack of appreciation of the extent to which these claims on inadequate self-clarification and insufficient maturity and scientificism already replicate the rather canonical way of handling justificatory claims in modern natural law (Chapters 4 and 5). Understood as a reality *sui generis* that is external to and exercises coercion on individuals, society is an extremely complex web of collective representations that can only be studied through its visible symbols. Society is an autonomous ontological domain that is part of the natural world and exists alongside the natural and individual worlds. Positivism is not a good way of describing Durkheim's project because he understands far too well that the insistence on the scientific validity of his invitation to sociology is itself philosophical. It implies justificatory claims about the ontological continuity between nature and society, the validity of the scientific method for both the natural and social sciences, and the multilayered constitution of social reality, among the most salient.[21]

The decade between 1892 and 1902 that encompasses the preparation of the two pieces on Montesquieu and Rousseau includes the publication of three of Durkheim's major works: *The Division of Labour in Society* in 1893, *The Rules of the Sociological Method* in 1895 and *Suicide* in 1898. Indeed, the central argument in *Division of Labour* (1984), the distinction between two types of social solidarity, organic and mechanical that correspond to underlying changes in collective consciousness, is arguably based on the natural law dichotomy between the state of nature and the civil state. Durkheim shares with Tönnies the analytical and typological orientation of the dichotomy, and the fact that he developed his argument in independence from Tönnies's speaks in favour of the idea that they both were engaging with similar problems in modern natural law (Aldous, Durkheim and Tönnies 1972). To be sure, Durkheim proceeds less through an explicit discussion of philosophical sources than Tönnies and prefers to engage with a variety of ethnographic, comparative and even statistical materials. Durkheim is also

[21] In *Rules*, Durkheim (1982: 33) rejects the label positivism and argues that rationalism, which is of course an equally problematic term, be used. I thus concur with Hans Joas' (2004: xii) claim that Durkheim's sociology is a 'philosophical project'. For a friendly yet critical interpretation of Durkheim's *Rules*, see Gane (1988).

more optimistic than Tönnies on the development and future prospects of modern society; his normative preferences lie with society rather community. But in relation to natural law both writers share the fundamental insight that either side of the typology represents different though equally universal forms of social relations: while organic solidarity proceeds through similarity and the high intensity of collective feelings, mechanical solidarity works through the functional differentiation that results from the division of labour.

First published in 1912, *Elementary Forms of Religious Life* offers a highly instructive reading *vis-à-vis* the tradition of natural law. Although the question of religion is of course the book's central theme, natural law does not figure highly in the text. As Durkheim concentrates on early or 'primitive' forms of religion, mostly from Australian aborigines, the aspects of Christianity that are more closely related to natural law are absent from the discussion. Furthermore, Durkheim's assessment of these early religious rites, beliefs and practices remains silent on the kind of universalistic beliefs that I have characterised as constitutive of natural law. In fact, one of the book's main arguments, the fundamentally social core of all kinds of religious experiences, seems to point to a kind of cultural relativism that would stand in stark contrast to any such connection with universalism and natural law.[22] Yet there are more than just traces of universalism in the book and I should now like to finalise this section by reconstructing some of these main arguments.

Partly historical and partly analytical, Durkheim's methodological justification for looking at what is truly 'elementary' in religious life is deeply immersed in a central tenet of modern natural law. Early in the text, Durkheim explains the reasons that led him to focus on primitive religions in a manner that brings him again very close to arguments in the state of nature: '*[e]very time that we undertake to explain something human*, taken at a given moment in history – be it a religious belief, a moral precept, a legal principle, an aesthetic style or an economic system – *it is necessary to commence by going back to its most primitive and simple form*' (Durkheim 1965: 15, my italics). Capturing what is fundamentally human requires us to grasp it at its purest. Durkheim's commitment to this procedure is substantiated further in the context of his explanation of totemic beliefs. As he reiterates the proposition that the simplicity of totemic beliefs makes them somewhat paradigmatic of religion in general, Durkheim emphasises again that it is through this exploration of elementary religions that we will be able to account for the

[22] Durkheim's claims in *Elementary Forms* have thus lent themselves to constructivist or postmodern interpretations (Seidman 1998, Mestrovic 1992).

universality of religious sentiments. This is the best way to grasp the fact that religion is a fundamentally human form of experience: '[i]f we succeed in discovering the origins of the belief which we have just analysed, we shall very probably discover at the same time the causes leading to *the rise of the religious sentiment in humanity*' (195 my italics). Indeed, Durkheim opens the book's conclusion by arguing that, as a general procedure, this recourse now even has proven *scientific* validity. Methodologically, this is an adequate way of gaining access to the basic components of social life; analytically, this simplification allows us to distinguish the social from human nature; normatively, it allows us to delineate the fundamentals of our shared humanity (462–3).

The main argument in *Elementary Forms* is of course that the centrality of religion in human life expresses its fundamentally social nature. Society is the ultimate cause by which all aspects of our human life can be explicated, it is central to our individuality, to our ability for logical thinking, to our responsiveness to morality as well as to our religious feelings. In an argument that resembles Simmel's idea of society to be discussed in Chapter 7, Durkheim's conception of society can be referred to as a *universal mediator* because everything human has to go through society. On the one hand, as a reality *sui generis* society 'has a nature which is peculiar to itself and different from our individual nature' (Durkheim 1965: 237). On the other hand, and equally importantly, 'society cannot exist except in and through individual consciousness' (240). The duality that is central to society's nature – being autonomous *vis-à-vis* the individual while at the same time existing only in and through individuals – is equally found in human nature itself:

> [m]an is double. There are two beings in him: an individual being which has its foundation in the organism and the circle of whose activities is therefore strictly limited, and a social being which represents the highest reality in the intellectual and moral order that we can know by observation – I mean society. (Durkheim 1965: 29)

All human beings are able to make and remake society and while the discovery of society is a modern phenomenon that only goes back to the first part of the eighteenth century with Montesquieu, its reality as an autonomous domain is transhistorical and transcultural.

Religious ideas, to the extent that they represent social forces, are therefore 'physical as well as human, moral as well as material' (Durkheim 1965: 254). As a universal mediator, moreover, Durkheim also refers to 'the social origin of the categories' as the only possibility for rationally understanding how it is that human beings started to represent the natural world in the ways that they have. The distinction between right and left, or the separation of animals and plants into classes and hierarchies, are ultimately 'the product of representations which are religious and therefore collective' (25). At the same time, however, social life is part of nature, so even if society is central to the constitution of our world, it is not the only domain of reality and 'differs from the others only by greater complexity' (31). This greater complexity of society makes it more difficult to observe its events and thus social facts only become visible through symbols: 'social life, in all its aspects and in every period of its history, is made possible only by a vast symbolism' (264). The methodological handling of the relationship between complexity and symbolism in society is a central feature of Durkheim's sociological project as a whole. In *Rules*, he argues that it is essential to 'indicate how, by outward signs, it is possible to identify the facts that the science must deal with, so that the social scientist may learn how to pick out their location and not to confuse them [social facts] with other things' (Durkheim 1982: 43). This approach had already been applied to the observation of crimes, customs and above all the law, in *The Division of Labour in Society* (Durkheim 1984: 24–9). An empirical understanding of the law allows the sociologist to conceptualise how different societies assess different institutions and also what values and beliefs are held by particular groups. Durkheim's sociological understanding of the law emphasises its positive character and socio-historical roots. At any moment in time the law is what it is, and changes in the way it does, because social relations themselves have changed: not only is 'the law is pre-eminently a social matter' but also, and more importantly, 'all law is public because all law is social' (70, 81).

But there is also a more philosophical justification for Durkheim's sociological interest in the law and here we are touching again on a fundamental problem of modern natural law or, as I have called it, the location of the normative in social life: how are we to explain the binding character of moral norms after we have accepted that their origins are immanent rather than transcendental? Durkheim (1965: 30) argues that while there is no actual identity between 'logical necessity and moral obligation' their interrelationship can be thought of analogically. We need a notion of moral or normative authority which, although it is external is, however, the result of human interaction and human interaction alone. A sense of transcendence whose origins are exclusively social: 'we ordinarily think of it under the form of a moral power which, though immanent in us, represents within us something not ourselves: this is the moral conscience, of which, by the way, men have never made even a slightly distinct representation except by the aid of religious symbols' (242). Religious, that is, in the sense of the transcendental representation of social life itself.[23]

At the same time as it makes social relations the ultimate source of morality, Durkheim's sociology explicitly rejects relativism (LaCapra 2001: 232–79). He rather unpacks the fundamentally universalistic qualities of social relations: 'saying that concepts express the manner in which society represents things is also saying that conceptual thought is coeval with humanity itself' (Durkheim 1965: 486–7). This argument, Durkheim contends, applies to all forms of thinking – traditional as well as modern, religious as well as scientific. And underlying what makes religious beliefs *seem* irrational, there is an intrinsic rationality that is brought about by the sociological point of view:

> [l]aw, morals and even scientific thought itself were born of religion, were for a long time confounded with it, and have remained penetrated with its spirit ... Surely *it ought to be a principle of the science of religions that religion expresses nothing which does not exist in nature* ... The only question is to learn *from what part of nature these realities come* and what has been able to make men represent them under this singular form which is peculiar to religious thought. (Durkheim 1965: 87, my italics)

Although religious representations can portray the physical world, their main task is to depict the social order as external as well as internal, natural as well as artificial, individual as well as collective, immanent as well as transcendental. Not only are our categories social in origin and grounded in nature, their religious roots also express a fundamental moment of thinking in general. It is in the nature of religious beliefs to go beyond first appearances and offer a narrative that can connect events that seem separated at first; there is, quite simply, 'no abyss ... between the logic of religious thought and that of scientific thought' (Durkheim 1965: 271). A commonality between religion, philosophy and science becomes visible on the basis of their shared social roots. All three participate in the general human need to relate events in order to orient social life: 'from the moment when men have an idea that there are internal connections between things, science and philosophy become possible. Religion opened up the way for them. But if it has been able to play a part, it is only because it is a social affair' (270). There is even a built-in proceduralism in early religious practices in terms of a strictly defined formula or rite that needed to be closely followed to

[23] Thus, for instance: '[t]his aptitude of society for setting itself up as a god or for creating gods was never more apparent than during the first years of the French Revolution. At this time ... things purely laïcal by nature were transformed by public opinion into sacred things: these were the Fatherland, Liberty, Reason' (Durkheim 1965: 244–5).

regulate the transition between the sacred and the profane, and indeed religious formalism was 'very probably the first form of legal formalism' (50). Transcendental immanence, therefore, is the last expression of Durkheim's *Aufhebung* of natural law.

Closing remarks

The works of Marx, Tönnies and Durkheim are of course all very different and there is no single thread running through them. I have sought to demonstrate, however, that these writers were very much aware of the importance of and even their debt to natural law, on the one hand, and that they remained committed to its key universalistic orientation, on the other.

Marx takes up Hegel's mediations of the dichotomies of natural law and makes them his own in the realm of praxis: an unintended result of human interaction, society makes possible the full expansion of human potential at the same time as it undermines it. Marx makes apparent the Janus face of society, its ability to enrich and enliven but also to damage and undercut human life. Marx had little time for imaginary questions about the state of nature but as he came back to it he did so characterising it in the form of a fundamentally social condition whose poverty and misery were explicitly human made. For their part, Tönnies and Durkheim make apparent the extent to which the rise of sociology, as expressed in the distinction between community and society, resulted from a direct and even explicit engagement with the distinction between the state of nature and the civil condition that is core to modern natural law. Their arguments differ of course in the way in which they justify its importance, as Tönnies offers a more philosophical and speculative analysis while Durkheim opts for one that centres on comparing ethnographic materials. As they offer contrasting views on which side is to be preferred normatively – *Gemeinschaft* for Tönnies and organic solidarity for Durkheim – they share the socio-historical diagnosis that communal forms were on the wane and that contractual and indeed global trends were expanding.

In its sublated sociological version, community and society are both equally real forms of social relations. They represent forms of social coordination in the strict sense that neither side of the distinction is conceived as asocial in the way that Hobbes and Rousseau spoke about it. The importance of this transformation should not be underestimated: society is now at least as primordial as human nature itself and, in fact, explicit attention is now devoted almost exclusively to conceptualising the nature of society rather than human nature as such. As Durkheim's analysis of elementary religious practices makes clear, even though we want to explicate our human attributes in their most basic form, this needs to be done by looking at what takes place in society and by taking into consideration how fundamentally social those attributes ultimately are.

As the sociological distinction departs from natural law in this crucial way, it none the less retains some of its original normative orientation: society is introduced as artificial *vis-à-vis* the individual and there is always one side of the dichotomy, and thus certain types of social relations, which enhance human nature and allow it to grow and expand. Community and society, mechanical and organic solidarity, possess the same conceptual status but do not carry the same normative weight. The dichotomy always operates at both philosophical (or normative) and scientific (or empirical/conceptual) levels.

7 Classical social theory II: Simmel and Weber on the universality of sociability and reasonableness

Simmel

Simmel opens his major *The Philosophy of Money*, first published in 1900, with a distinction that reflects the neo-Kantian mainstream of his time. There he contrasts the domain of nature, where *equality* reigns because all things have at least in principle the same worth, and that of values, where subjective preferences make *hierarchical* decisions necessary. The natural and human sciences are thus devoted to separate spheres of knowledge that are endowed with their own specific ontological properties. Yet Simmel does not want to reify that separation and argues that social life offers the possibility of mediation in so far as its empirical study can only be adequately apprehended by looking at both realms simultaneously. A social scientific approach to social relations must establish the differences as well as the interconnections between the human world that is full of value judgements and the inert natural world that is ruled by the laws of causality: '[v]aluation as a real psychological occurrence is part of the natural world; but what we mean by valuation, its conceptual meaning, is something independent of this world; is not part of it' (Simmel 2005: 57).

The specificity of the social sciences lies in their having to study phenomena whose existence can be credited in a similar fashion to natural phenomena – social life *is* real. But the social is simultaneously different from the natural because values, which are central to society, are incomprehensible in their normative specificity within a naturalistic framework: the yet-to-be fully established disciplines devoted to the study of social life must be able to handle nature and values at the same time. It is then not wholly surprising that Simmel is sceptical about the role of natural law in this process: '[t]he existence of real life is not necessary in terms of any law; it would not contradict any logical or natural law if nothing existed. It is also not "necessary" that natural laws exist ... There can be no natural law that natural laws must exist' (Simmel 2005: 107). A first explicit rejection of natural law is then based on Simmel's argument about the ontological difference between nature and society. But there is also a second side to Simmel's argument that is more epistemological in kind. Although here Simmel does not withdraw his first critique, he now concedes that the universalistic presuppositions of natural law may in fact be useful – indeed necessary – for an adequate understanding of human sociality. On the one hand, he reinstates the claim that '[i]t would be to move in a circle to assume that there is a natural law that entails natural laws'. Yet on the other hand he now grants that something may be gained by thinking in these terms: 'I leave it open, however, as to whether this circle is nevertheless legitimate because it is part of the fundamental processes of thought to return to their origin or to aim at an end that lies in infinity' (119). Simmel exemplifies these fundamental processes of thought with the familiar names of the Stoics, Kant and Hegel and concludes that there are general ideas that are needed in order to capture the historically changing nature of the objects to which they are directed. We will discuss Simmel's notion of society below, but before we do this I should like to clarify further his argument on natural law.[1]

Simmel rejects the idea that nature can be studied in terms of the teleological fulfilment of an immanent goal that can then be used to orient the study of social life. It is only on the basis of a misconstrued idea of *purposeful nature* that the concomitant notion that 'natural laws exert an inescapable coercion upon things' can be said to make sense (Simmel 2005: 488). Rather the opposite, he argues, 'natural laws do not *act* at all since they are only formulae for the activity of specific materials and energies' (488). It worthy of note, Simmel continues, that those who believe that 'natural laws direct reality as real forces' are in fact replicating the religious natural law argument of 'God's direct control over our earthly life' (488). When it comes to understanding social life, there is little to be gained by replacing god's transcendence with a new form of transcendental nature. Religious and naturalistic grounds are equally problematic because normative arguments derive their obligatory force from a tension between freedom and coercion which is strictly immanent and exists only in human spheres of action: '[n]atural events as such are not subject to the alternatives of freedom and coercion, and the "must" injects a dualism into the simple existence of things that only makes sense to the conscious mind' (488). Simmel

1 These claims are of course consistent with the sociological 'Kantianism' that inspires Simmel's philosophy and sociology, as famously expressed in his excursus on 'How is society possible?' (Simmel 1909) or in his opening remarks on the problems of the philosophy of history (Simmel 1977). See Adorno (2000), Frisby (2002) and Outhwaite (2006) for further discussion.

decidedly objects to this naturalistic idea of natural law as a viable path for the social sciences. We will never move forward in understanding social life if we remain committed to explaining it through a teleological idea of nature that depends on non-human factors; if we treat human life as normatively dependent on inert or transcendental factors. As we have discussed throughout this book, the fact that natural laws are to be discovered through strictly immanent means still says nothing about the need to have recourse to transcendental sources of authority in order to make them normatively obligatory.

But at the same time as he rejects a role for this kind of natural law in the social sciences, Simmel recognises the need to retain a universalistic orientation whose immanent core – the fact that value decisions are inevitably changeable and made by people – retains a sense of *internal* transcendence. He understands that normative justifications are necessarily challenging under modern conditions because they need to find exclusively immanent sources by which to uphold a sense of normative obligation. But as well as being problematic, normative challenges are inevitable and central to social life. Simmel is here arguing for the kind of transcendental immanence that we have also encountered in previous chapters as a key aspect in the quest for locating the normative in social life: 'throughout the modern era', he contends, the individual has been on a permanent quest

> [f]or a fixed and unambiguous point of reference. He needs such a fixed point more and more urgently in view of the unprecedented expansion of theoretical and practical perspectives and the complication of life, and the related fact that he can no longer find it anywhere outside himself. (Simmel 1971: 223)

We shall discuss below how Simmel makes the 'democratic structure of all sociability' the key aspect of this social normativity, but for now his argument remains focused on how to make plausible connections between the ontological and epistemological specificity of the social sciences, on the one hand, and their normative justifications, on the other. Universalism is a condition of possibility for thinking about binding normative obligations but as traditional transcendental grounds like nature and religion are no longer available to uphold universalistic claims, the question is whether and how they can be reinstated on purely immanent grounds:

> The evolution of the modern naturalistic spirit tends to dethrone universal concepts, and to emphasize singular instances as the only legitimate content of conceptions. In theory and in practice, the universal is treated as something purely abstract which acquires meaning only in its material embodiment, that is in tangible instances. In rising above these concrete instances one seems to enter

a void. *Yet the sense of the significance of universals, which reached its climax with Plato, has not altogether disappeared*; and we should attain a completely satisfying relation to the world only if every aspect of our worldview reconciled *the material reality of singular instances with the depth and scope of a formal universality.* (Simmel 2005: 202, my italics)

Simmel's argument is particularly important for us: explicit rejections of the idea of universality and the denial of its significance say in his view nothing in terms of the presuppositions that are actually in place in sociological arguments. To the extent that they study human action and cultural developments they do need the kind of universalistic orientation that is otherwise being explicitly criticised. Attempts to provide a meaningful understanding of our human experiences of the social world require us to engage with the universalistic presuppositions of social scientific thinking and, quite crucially, therein lies also the specificity of the modern social sciences as distinct from both the natural sciences *and* philosophy. It is surely worthy of note that Simmel mentions Plato as representing the 'climax' of a sense of universality that 'has not altogether disappeared'. But for our purposes the most fundamental claim is Simmel's contraposition between the 'material embodiment' of universalistic ideas, with their risk of reification, and the appearance of 'formal universability' that he will eventually explicate through an original rendition of Kant's proceduralism. This interest in formality should not, however, translate into formalism; the disciplines devoted to the study of social life

[a]re attempts to confirm universality and yet to deny its abstractness, to transcend the singular instance, to derive the singular from the general without sacrificing its material reality; for *society is universal but not abstract.* The valuation of functions as distinct from content has its place here. (Simmel 2005: 202, my italics)

This tension between formal abstraction and material reality is in fact central to Simmel's explanation of the conflict between the claim to universality of ideas, ideals and values of modern institutions and their always contingent and problematic actualisation in real life.

In relation to the historical evolution of modern ideas of universalism, Simmel claims that notions of individual freedom and equality contrast badly with the 'inadequacy of the socially sanctioned forms of life in the eighteenth century' that through traditional values and social rank were still fundamentally embedded in practices that contravened this normative orientation (Simmel 1971: 218). The tension between unfulfilled universal ideals and actual social practices that effectively restrict, undermine or even contravene them – in effect Simmel's theory of alienation – is central to the functioning of modern society: newly established conceptions of universal equality 'never did exist in reality as accomplished fact, and at the instant individuals received unlimited freedom, unmistakable inequality would generate a new repression' (221). The key here is that these universalistic ideals are as real a part of social life as inequality and repression. It is in this context that Simmel comes back to the question of the history of natural law; he traces modern natural law back to the Renaissance and explains thus its modern development:

> [f]reedom and equality can be seen to belong together by right from the very outset. For if universal humanity – natural-law man, as it were – exists as the essential core of every man, who is individualized by empirical traits, social position, and accidental configuration, all one need to do is free him from all these historical influences and diversions that ravage his deepest essence, and then what is common to all, man as such, can emerge in him as this essence. (Simmel 1971: 219–20)

Freedom and equality are fundamental for the development of both modern ideas and modern institutions because they constitute the core of the modern idea of universality. What Simmel finds truly radical in these values is that they simultaneously express what is unique in the individual as an individual and what is it that he shares with the rest of humanity as a fully fledged member of a single human species:

> [t]he worth of each individual's configuration is based, to be sure, on him alone, on his personal responsibility, but along with that it is based on what the individual has in common with all others. The deepest point of individuality is the point of universal equality. (Simmel 1971: 220)

Simmel is aware that this resembles natural law arguments on the state of nature as this rather naturalistic conception of universal humanity depends 'on the fiction of isolated and identical individuals'. Abstract ideals are surely not enough for a sociological account of modern society but they are none the less highly consequential as these naturalistic foundations of modern individualism have 'obviously' turned

> [i]nto laissez faire, laissez aller. If in all men, ever identical 'man in general', exists what is essential to them, and if the full, unhampered development of this core is assumed, there is naturally no need for special regulating intervention into human relations. (Simmel 1971: 221)

Simmel thus distinguishes between three different sources of eighteenth century universalism: '[w]hether it is *nature*, *reason*, or *man*, it is always something shared with others in which the individual discovers himself when he has discovered his own freedom, his own selfhood' (Simmel 1971: 221, my italics).[2] Nature, reason and humanity as possible sources of universalistic ideals seem to cover the main options we have already encountered in this book. This 'liberal', 'Enlightenment' and ultimately flat form of universalism is, to be sure, only part of the story and by the nineteenth century a change had now taken place. As the new sense of individuality was now 'sufficiently strengthened by the feeling of equality and universality', inequality was 'sought once again ... but this time an inequality determined only from within ... What mattered now was no longer that one was a free individual as such, but that one was a particular and irreplaceable individual' (222). This different form of individualism counterbalances what was culturally and historically invisible in previous universalistic arguments. The enhanced awareness of the diversity and uniqueness of the Romantic reaction is not for Simmel an automatic move against universalism. A fundamental dynamic of modern social life now emerges between 'uniqueness', eighteenth-century Enlightenment individualism and 'singleness', nineteenth-century Romantic individualism. Modern social life depends upon the two forms of individualism working together: 'the doctrine of freedom and equality is the basis for free competition; and the doctrine of differentiated personality is the basis for the division of labor' (225). For all the sociological insights of his reflections on the rise and development of modern ideas and institutions, the words with which Simmel concludes his essay of modern individualism are those of the philosopher. Although economic forms of individualism are the ones that have become more strongly institutionalised in modern society, there may still be:

> [a] higher form that constitutes the hidden ideal of our culture. I would prefer to believe that the idea of free personality as such and the idea of the unique personality as such are not the last words of individualism – that, rather, the unforeseeable work of mankind will produce ever more numerous and varied forms with which the human personality will affirm itself and prove the worth of its existence. (Simmel 1971: 226)

As I intimated above, Simmel offers the idea of philosophical sociology as a fundamental part of his intellectual project. Philosophical sociology is neither a rejection of empirical sociology nor the sublation of sociology and philosophy into a more refined form of knowledge. Rather, its first task is to explicate the epistemological preconditions that make sociological

[2] Differently put, natural law universalism can but does not have to be based on our shared human nature. Reason, and above all *a purposefully created sense of common humanity*, are equally or even potentially more fruitful ways of making sense of our universal commonality as members of the same species.

thinking possible. It focuses on the clarification of sociology's concepts, methods and postulates, on the elucidation of those fundamental presuppositions without which sociology would be impossible. But Simmel contends that there is also a second 'metaphysical' dimension to philosophical sociology, which for my purposes is arguably more important. Simmel claims that, in order to move forward, all sciences need to overcome the restrictions that emerge from the slow pace at which their scientific contributions actually evolve; in order to fulfil their cultural meaning, they need to be willing to close the gaps in empirical knowledge, which is necessarily incomplete and fragmentary. It is only through this work of anticipation, indeed of truly philosophical speculation, that we can endow the 'totality' of social phenomena 'with significance' (Simmel 1950: 24). The most pressing questions that make sociology a relevant discipline are precisely those for which exclusively empirical answers are largely inadequate:

> Is society the purpose of human existence, or is it a means for the individual? Does the ultimate value of social development lie in the unfolding of personality or of association? Do meaning and purpose inhere in social phenomena at all, or exclusively in individuals? Do the typical stages of the development of societies show an analogy with cosmic evolutions so that there might be a general formula or rhythm of development in general ... which applies to social and material data alike? Are social movements guided by the principle of the conservation of energy? Are they directed by material or by ideological motives? (Simmel 1950: 24–5)

The centrality he gave to the task of reflecting on sociology's key idea of society reflects at least to some extent the importance Simmel gave to this task of philosophical speculation with a sociological focus. He arrived at a positive definition of society only after an exercise of elimination of contemporary alternatives and started by rejecting a methodologically individualistic definition of society as reduced to individuals' subjective representations. He was equally opposed to metaphysical notions of the mystical kind that were found in German *Völkerspsychologie*:

> [i]t is no longer possible to explain ... the contents of culture, the types of industry, the norms of morality, by reference solely to the individual, his understanding, and his interests. Still less is it possible, if this sort of explanation fails, to find recourse in metaphysical or magical causes. (Simmel 1909: 292)

As an idea, society is always in danger of being wrongly treated as 'a collective name arising from our inability to treat single separate phenomena ... we do not make the required distinction between that which takes place merely *within* society, as within a frame, and that which comes to pass *through* society' (Simmel 1994: 34). Simmel thus contrasts *society as a frame* with *society as an active force* and only the latter comes close to an acceptable definition of society. The influence that individuals exercise upon one another leads to the creation of emergent forces which they can neither anticipate nor control, but which at the same time are essential for their individuality. Simmel then introduces the idea of society as 'types of reciprocal influencing' and argues that if 'there is to be a science, the object of which is to be "society" and nothing else, it can investigate only these reciprocal influences, these kinds and forms of socialization' (Simmel 1909: 297–8). Simmel's conception of society as reciprocal influences, his notion of sociation, represents the most abstract forms of human interaction. Crucially, in modernity these reciprocal influences refer to the universality of both social interaction and commodity exchanges (Simmel 2005: 99).[3] Having arrived at a universalistic concept of society understood as a principle of reciprocal influencing, Simmel also seeks to elucidate the methodological difficulties that arise as we avoid 'treating society either as a "real product" or as a "purely transcendental presupposition of sociological experience"' (Frisby and Sayer 1986: 63). As the active principle of reciprocal interaction, society is both a general framework that makes social scientific analysis possible and a real result of human interaction. The best methodological possibility is for Simmel phenomenological: positive knowledge of society arises from the actual ways in which people experience this reciprocal influencing in their own life. The fact that society cannot be known beyond how it appears in everyday experiences means, from a methodological viewpoint, that society is the most abstract way of accessing the *objective nature of intersubjectivity as it is experienced by the individual.*

Simmel is a reluctant sociologist. He is a philosophical sociologist whose interest in sociology is truly philosophical: in whether sociology can actually contribute, conceptually and methodologically, to grasping what is truly social in modern social life. Sociology studies the most general forms of sociation, indeed its universal forms: authority, subordination, competition, secrecy, cooperation, imitation, opposition, differentiation. The actual content of these forms of sociation (i.e. religious, political, military, artistic and so on) is crucial for sociological observation but does not constitute its prime object of study (Simmel 1896a, 1896b, 1902a, 1902b, 1906). Sociology is interested less in the discovery of new facts and more in the presentation of ascertained facts from a new point of view:

3 Simmel would have agreed with Marx's idea of society as 'the product of human reciprocal action' (Schrader-Klebert 1968: 99). See also Deflem (2003) for further discussion.

the separation of content and form (Simmel 1909: 296–7). The study of sociability as 'pure' social relations offers him the chance to test his methodological and conceptual universalism. Simmel chose the subject of social gatherings – *soirées*, reading groups, dinner parties, public lectures and all similar meetings where the flows of interaction are essential to the success of the meeting – for his speech at the first conference of German Sociological Society. He explains why the separation of form and content is crucial for the emergence of a truly sociological point of view that is fundamentally universalistic:

> [e]veryone should guarantee to the other that maximum of sociable values (joy, relief, vivacity) which is consonant with the maximum of values he himself receives. As *justice upon the Kantian basis is thoroughly democratic*, so likewise this principle shows *the democratic structure of all sociability* ... Sociability creates, if one will, an *ideal* sociological world, for in it ... the pleasure of the individual is always contingent upon the joy of others; here, by definition, *no one can have his satisfaction at the cost of contrary experiences on the part of others.* (Simmel 1949: 257, my italics)

There is no fully developed normative programme in Simmel's sociology, but his depiction of the social does carry normative commitments.[4] The deployment of conceptual and methodological universalism in this notion of sociability brings with it normative implications that remind us of the proceduralist and internalist innovations that are central to Kant's categorical imperative. Simmel's image of the good society is that of a free-flowing sociality that is intrinsically democratic; a type of social interaction that has no end beyond itself and is oriented fully to the enhancement of the personalities taking part in it: 'the personalities must not emphasise themselves too individually' (Simmel 1949: 255). These webs of social relations are fundamental for our individual development as it is only through them that we gain in moral autonomy, political freedom, economic liberty, aesthetic innovation or erotic fulfilment. Even as these increments in individual freedom come with a price in terms of loneliness and indifference in all kinds of social settings, for Simmel the question is how to balance sociation and individualisation. A normatively universalistic conception of humanity is now an integral part of the argument:

> If we now have the conception that we enter into sociability purely as 'human beings,' as that which we really are, lacking all the burdens, the agitation, the inequalities with which real life disturbs the purity of our picture, it is because

[4] On the normative implications of Simmel's sociology, see Gangas (2004), Honneth (2004) and Schlecker (2011). On Simmel's importance for the development of Parsonian sociology, see Levine (1980, 1991). On his politics, see Harrington (2004).

modern life is overburdened with objective content and material demands. Ridding ourselves of this burden in sociable circles, we believe we return to our natural personal being and overlook the fact that this personal aspect also does not consist in its full uniqueness and natural completeness, but only in a certain reserve and stylizing of the sociable man. (Simmel 1949: 257)

As individuals, our inner core is shaped in society even though at no point can we or should we fully disclose our individuality. Normatively, Simmel's thesis is not only that with the rise of modern society all individuals will in due course take part in those social trends that will help in the development of a fully emancipated individuality. Equally importantly, he argues that our very humanity as modern individuals is crucially attached to our belonging to modern society. In other words, while the *society* of the modern society becomes apparent in the increasing intensity these processes of reciprocal influencing, its *modernity* lies in the fact that more and more aspects of social life become fundamentally reshaped by these processes. Natural law does not figure centrally in Simmel's work and yet the question of universalism is one of the defining features of his sociology as a condition of possibility of thinking about social life, on the one hand, and about the relationships between the social and the individual, on the other hand. In his engagement with universalism, in the idea of philosophical sociology, and indeed with his emphasis on the separation between form and content, Simmel's project bears the mark of the foundational themes of modern natural law.

Weber

Simmel's engagement with the question of universalism is far from systematic and yet his intellectual project can hardly be understood without universalism. In Weber, as we shall now discuss, the picture is at one level similar: universalism is far from an unproblematic orientation. But if in Simmel philosophical and conceptual arguments tend to have primacy, in Weber we shall see that there are methodological insights that will offer a complex picture in relation to the problem of universalism (see Chapter 2).

Weber's reflections on the problems of reification and essentialism as he found them within German academic circles at the turn of the twentieth century are not dissimilar to Simmel's (Outhwaite 1975: 45). For instance, the core of his long critique of economic historians Wilhelm Roscher and Karl Knies focused on how these two writers sought to found legitimate scientific knowledge upon traditional organicist arguments, mostly in the form of intuitionism and chauvinism. Weber (1975: 73) criticised Roscher's understanding of a people as a 'single organism' of a 'closed type' and rejected the view that a 'national legal peculiarity can be derived from any differences in the operation of the [allegedly endogenous] "sense of justice"' (Weber 1968b: 760). He disapproved of all attempts at conceptualising the nation as a cultural individual, which would find expression not only in such spheres as arts, language and politics but 'even attempted to taste the character of a Volk in its wine' (Weber 1975: 74). In these conceptions, argues Weber (61–2), the traditional idea of the *Volksgeist* develops a wholly unacceptable 'metaphysical status' whereby it is equated with both 'the life of an individual human being and the development of a culture . . . it is an *intuitable* totality, the cultural bearer of a *meaningful* total essence'.[5] As we will see below, Weber is sceptical of the contemporary relevance of natural law but that does not prevent him from acknowledging that it has a key positive function in this context. Natural law allows us to realise the fallacies that are involved in:

> [a]ll those half historical and half naturalistic theories of Romanticism which regard the *Volksgeist* as the only natural, and thus the only legitimate, source from which law and culture can emanate, and accordingly to which all 'genuine' law must have grown up 'organically' . . . The irrationalism of such axioms stands in sharp contrast to the *natural law* axioms of *legal rationalism* which *alone* were able to create norms of a *formal type*. (Weber 1968b: 867, my italics)

As part of these writings against intuitionism and ideas of empathy based on 'common blood' or 'shared culture' Weber offered his own suggestions about how to carry out sociological research, which I suggest can be reconstructed as a form of methodological universalism. In *Science as a Vocation*, Weber (1970a) put forward his now well-known views on value-freedom and the thesis that science is in no position to grant, justify or indeed establish ultimate values. As he explicates the debate generated by Weber's lecture, Wolfgang Schluchter (1996: 39–45; 273) argues that Weber received attacks from different, indeed, at times opposite, flanks; but most of them concentrated on Weber's refusal to justify philosophically some general hierarchy of ultimate values – whether in the form of a nationalistic worldview, some notion of progress or a proletarian revolution.[6] Value orientations do exist in the world, of course, and

[5] I have discussed the wider theoretical implications of Weber's political, though not methodological, nationalism in Chernilo (2007: 49–60).

[6] The debate includes contributions, among others, by Ernst Troeltsch, Max Scheler and Heinrich Rickert (Lassman, Velody and Martins 1989). Weber was not alone in pushing for this agenda, of course, as the principle of scholarly independence figured centrally at

they are of the highest importance not only in political life and ethical action but in scientific enquiry as well. Decisions on what constitute significant areas of research will always be based on the scientist's value orientations, so they are better explicitly justified. Weber's methodological reflections are particularly challenging because, as discussed in Chapter 2, they try to combine two ontological claims that do not sit comfortably together: the polytheism of values that in modernity makes ultimate normative decisions highly problematic if not outright impossible, and the claim to transhistorical and transcultural validity of modern scientific procedures that depends on a universalistic orientation. In other words, a tension between description and normativity can be said to lie at the centre of Weber's project. While the descriptive side of scientific validity is based on empirical or causal adequacy, in relation to normative relevance our research depends on its cultural significance within particular socio-historical contexts. This is more than a clash between the universal orientation of science and the particular orientation of culture. As Gary Abraham (1992) has correctly pointed out, Weber's idea of universal history effectively requires both moments: to assess the world-historical significance of a certain cultural development is independent from our ability to explicate it through a causal hypothesis.[7]

Universalism is a defining feature of Weber's social scientific programme, as it underlines the development of ideal types as the preferred methodological procedure for the nascent social sciences. Weber's aim was to construe sociological explanations of individual historical cases that could successfully pass a 'test of universality'. He introduced two clauses to ensure this. First, what we may call the principle of the 'Chinese researcher': if properly applied and explained, methodological rules should allow a researcher from any socio-cultural background to arrive at similar results. Weber (1949: 59) acknowledges that this may not be totally achievable in practice, but he certainly expects that this methodological universalism will work as a regulative idea – a type of regulative universalism. Secondly, his claim that 'one need not be Caesar in order to understand Caesar' works as a critique of the idea

the first meeting of the German Sociological Society in 1910 (Adair-Toteff 2005a, 2005c). See also a more personal account of Weber's involvement in organising this conference in M. S. Weber (1975: 420–5).

[7] Abraham's (1992: 127–73) general discussion of Weber's idea of universal history clearly explicates the two dimensions that are involved in Weber's idea of universalism: 'the [cultural] connection we construct between ourselves and the Greeks is distinct from the actual connections between Greek life and our life' (Abraham 1992: 163). But I disagree with his misconstruction of universalism as the mere refraining from passing judgement on cultural difference and with his reading of Weber's universalism as 'essentially ... parochial' (Abraham 1992: 170).

that social science must be based on, or can be reduced to, empathy (Weber 1968a: 5). Weber chose means–end rationality as the preferred form of causal imputation – and decided to model ideal types on the basis of this imputation of rationality – because means–end rationality provided him with clear procedures and standards to reconstruct and then assess different possible causal explanations (6–7). It was this kind of universalistically oriented procedure that would help transcend the relativism that Weber thought came with all other forms of empathetic understanding and cultural essentialism. Problematic as it is in strictly explicative terms, Weber's reliance on means–end rationality does not bear the implication that individuals, or collective actors such as classes or the state, ought to behave or do in fact behave in this way in their everyday practices. Ideal types grant any researcher the possibility to set out clear explanations so that any fellow investigator (who may come from a distant land and never have ruled over an empire) is able to reassess independently these explanations and come to an understanding of the actor's choices in their context (Weber 1949: 27).[8]

This methodological rule is consistent with the way in which Weber established his enquiry right at the very beginning of his comparative sociology of world religions. I will not discuss this in any real detail, but his claim is that the world-historical relevance of modernity must be first disentangled and only then reassociated with what is particularly Western in it: 'to what combination of circumstances the fact should be attributed that in Western civilization, and in Western civilization only, cultural phenomena have appeared which (as we like to think) lie in a line of development having *universal* significance and value' (Weber 2001: xxviii). Even though no unified normative outlook can be derived from Weber's social theory, there are at least two arguments that are compatible with normative universalism. First, it can be argued that universalism is a prerequisite of Weber's comparative sociology of world religions. Based as it is in cognitive and emotional dispositions that are universally human, Weber's argument is that the need for transcendental beliefs in the meaning of life is a universal dimension of our shared humanity. As for the recognition of historical specificity – the West's particular combination of circumstances that gave rise to capitalism as a world-historical event – Weber's proposed research is significant precisely because, while it speaks to Weber's own cultural and socio-political context, it simultaneously points beyond

[8] Despite recent arguments to the contrary (Swedberg 2003), this is also a reason why I contend that Weber's preference for means–end rationality is methodological rather than ontological and indeed normative.

this particular context. Indeed, the variety of empirical materials from different historical contexts and periods that Weber uses throughout his *œuvre* also makes apparent the built-in methodological universalism of his work: all materials are equally subject to the same conceptual framework and the same kind of critical scrutiny. Ideal types work only because their goal is to help us make sense of social, historical and cultural variation. Secondly, there is Weber's depiction of the normative condition of modern social life as a radical polytheism of ultimate values that he describes as the tragedy of modern culture (Weber 1970b, 1970c). He argues that even inside the West there are many value orientations that emerge from the actual structural differentiation between value spheres: politicians, workers, artists, scientists and the clergy are required to act differently in order to fulfil their roles competently. In turn, increasingly incompatible normative demands emerge from this differentiation – the impossibility of serving different 'gods' faithfully. While modern society is populated by too many value orientations, all of which claim general validity for themselves, this is not a claim on the irrationality of modern culture: ultimate values are undergoing no process of definitive dissolution and surely they *can* be rationally understood. Weber's social world is not one without normativity but one in which there are too many rationalities. The impossibility of a single or definitive resolution of normative conflicts, an argument that has accompanied us throughout this book, remains a long way away from the claim that we live in an essentially irrational world where no rational normative engagement is possible. As modern society expands throughout the world and increasingly encompasses the whole of humanity, we begin to face *similar* kinds of structural and normative pressure: a claim to universalism becomes more challenging but also inevitable.[9]

Let me now turn to Weber's explicit discussion of natural law, which appears in a small section at the end of the chapter on the sociology of

[9] Heavily inspired by Weber, this is precisely the kind of universalistic orientation that is central in twentieth-century historical sociology. As they seek to grasp the long-term historical development of human societies while simultaneously using the most contemporaneous scientific means available to them, Weber's studies of comparative religions, Norbert Elias's (2000) explanation of the civilization process, Barrington Moore's (1967) enquiry into forms of human violence, injustice and harm, Reinhard Bendix's (1964, 1978) studies on the transformation of political authority or Michael Mann's (1986, 1993) research into power relations throughout human history are only comprehensible if we accept that transhistorical research is possible – not least because modern scientific procedures are deemed adequate to account for the permanent features of social life before the rise of modernity. Furthermore, and even though these reflections tend to remain implicit, whatever is presupposed as the constitutive features of human nature has to be found equally plausible to human beings in the past as well as in the present.

law in *Economy and Society*. As in his writings on world religions, Weber admits that his treatment of the subject is restricted to explaining its connections with 'the economic order' (Weber 1968b: 868). The choice of this economic standpoint when looking at religion and natural law exemplifies further Weber's insight that our own cultural contexts are the ones that give significance to our scientific decisions – in Karl Löwith's words, 'what it is that makes man "human" within the capitalistic world' (Chapter 2). And it also highlights Weber's insight that in order to understand social reality we need to understand 'ideal' contents as much as 'material' factors. In this case, while the intellectual significance of natural law depends upon its ideal or normative force, its sociological relevance is to be determined by looking at whether it effectively shapes actors' views or institutional practices. A sociological understating of natural law requires paying attention to both its normative content and substantive appeal:

> [c]onceptions of the 'rightness of the law' ... become sociologically relevant only when practical legal life is materially affected by the conviction of the particular 'legitimacy' of certain legal maxims, and of the directly binding force of certain principles which are not to be disrupted by any concessions to positive law imposed by mere power. (Weber 1968b: 866)[10]

Historically, this belief in the importance of the rightness of the law has taken the name of *lex naturae* and, as in our discussion in Chapter 3 above, Weber claims that natural law was a fundamentally Stoic creation which was then taken over by Christianity 'for the purpose of constructing a *bridge* between its own ethics and the norms of the world' (Weber 1968b: 866, my italics). Medieval natural law being arguably its most advanced expression (Honnefelder 1995), natural law did not automatically decline with the rise of modernity. Rather the opposite: it can be found 'at the beginning of modern times and during the Revolutionary period, and in America it still exists' (Weber 1968b: 866). But in addition to its historical origins and sociological relevance, Weber argues that the original function of natural law is to bridge the gap between divine and positive law. Natural law has a mediatory role between immutable and ultimately uncognoscible divine law and contingent positive law which, although it is enforced only through state power, carries no normative authority of its own. Weber then defines natural law as 'the sum total of all those norms which are valid independently of, and superior to, any positive law and which owe their dignity not to arbitrary

[10] More generally, Habermas (1996: 66) argues that these two dimensions constitute the core of Weber's 'dualistic anthropology', which in turn would also account for the tensions between description and normativity in Weber's work.

enactment but, on the contrary, provide the very legitimation for the binding force of positive law' (867). Natural law thus becomes a necessary though not sufficient condition for actual social and legal institutions to exist. It is not an extreme and wholly unrealistic conception of the good, justice or rightness, but a form of conceiving the middle ground that mediates between the two poles of absolute and transcendental law, on the one hand, and state-enacted historically contingent positive law, on the other. Natural law is then independent of positive law but must at the same time be able to provide legitimacy for it. Weber explicates this further as he expands on the implications of his definition:

Natural law has thus been the collective term for those norms which owe their legitimacy not to their origin from a legitimate lawgiver, but to their *immanent and teleological qualities*. It is the *specific and only consistent type of legitimacy of a legal order which can remain* once religious revelation and the authoritarian sacredness of a tradition and its bearers have lost their force. Natural law has thus been the specific form of legitimacy of a revolutionarily created order. The invocation of natural law has repeatedly been the method by which classes in revolt against the existing order have legitimated their aspirations. (Weber 1968b: 867, my italics)[11]

This formulation is remarkable: natural law is to be identified by the sense of rightness with which it endows the law in general and at the same time it is immanent because it is human made. Natural law's teleological quality refers to its ability to non-coercively motivate actions in the direction of their own rational fulfilment: to provide legal orders that are legitimate as well as enforceable. Or, differently put, only human beings who are free to act feel the non-coercive normative pressure that is built into the law. Natural law embodies the kind of 'legal rationalism' that, increasingly in modern society, is alone 'able to create norms of a formal type'; legal norms whose *ultimate* acceptability depends on being found legitimate by individuals themselves, whose formalism is central to the open-ended nature of modern proceduralism and which can count on state support. Weber then emphasises that it is precisely because of these qualities that natural law has in fact

[s]trengthened the tendency towards logically abstract law, especially *the power of logic in legal thinking* ... The codifications of the pre-revolutionary rationalistic modern state, as well as the revolutionary codifications, were influenced by the

[11] We have encountered the argument on natural law's revolutionary potential above in Chapters 1 and 3. It is worth pointing out however that Weber (1968b: 867) immediately notes that natural law has also proved to be useful for conservative causes and the maintenance of the status quo.

dogmas of natural law, and they ultimately *derived the legitimacy of the law which they created from its 'reasonableness'*. (Weber 1968b: 873, my italics)

Natural law offers modern society a critical sense of rational legitimacy which, however contentious, weakened or problematic it may have become, remains essential in providing a sense of reasonableness in a postmetaphysical world. Combining again ideal and material factors, as a way of expressing the tension between facts and norms, the argument is that natural law rationalism comprises them both: as a normative *body of doctrine* natural law has proved *causally effective* in the ways in which actual modern legal systems have evolved. The importance Weber gives to natural law for the rise of legal and political modernity cannot be overlooked: reasonable acceptability, procedural impartiality and a self-propelling search for universalistic justifications are all essential components in modernity's foundational act of normative self-justification. None of them comes down to substantive notions of the good life, nor are they justified on the basis of anthropological conceptions of human nature. As a general conception of rightness of the law, the argument can be made that natural law is the infrastructure, the layout, the underlying grammar of modern legal thought and practices.

Even though they portray a somewhat different Weber in terms of his general view of modern normative orders, the terms under which he has discussed natural law so far cover relatively familiar territory. As we now concentrate on Weber's distinction between formal and substantive natural law, a new argument emerges. To be sure, the idea of separating formal and substantive conceptions of natural law is not particularly controversial – the more so as he immediately acknowledges that 'there simply cannot be a completely formal natural law' (Weber 1968b: 868). But the trajectory Weber now offers is unusual, because while the reconstruction in this book has emphasised the tendency to abandon substantive arguments and embrace procedural formalisation, Weber's proposition is that a historical transition has taken place in the opposite direction, from formal to substantive natural law. Weber defines formal natural law as a 'concept which arose in the seventeenth and eighteenth centuries ... in the form of the "contract theory," and more particularly the individualistic aspects of that theory. All legitimate law rests upon enactment, and all enactment, in turn, rests upon rational agreement' (868). Ideas of freedom of competition and of contracts are thus central to this individualistic or bourgeois conception of natural law that Weber characterises as formal. We have seen Weber's positive assessment of formal natural law in terms of its degree of formalisation and proceduralisation. But he does not miss the fact that formal natural law was instrumental for eighteenth-century liberal economics to evolve from a mere 'technique' into a real *Weltanschauung*. The synergy between liberal economics and formal natural law has then also had 'an important consequence insofar as it obstructed the discovery of the problematic character of that standpoint which had been assumed as self-evident' (Weber 1949: 85). The shared individualistic foundations of both bourgeois economic and modern natural law have worked towards blocking the possibility of their critical scrutiny.

But more recent socio-economic changes in the second part of the nineteenth century led to the transformation of the sources of legitimacy of natural law, which now 'came to be tied up with the substantive economic rather than with the formal modes of acquisition' (Weber 1968b: 870). More precisely, Weber concentrates on the revolutionary tradition of the late nineteenth and early twentieth centuries to explicate this transition from formal to substantive natural law. He argues that the recent 'turn towards substantive natural law is connected primarily with socialist theories of the exclusive legitimacy of the acquisition of wealth by one's own labor' (871). Weber's notion of substantive natural law does not remain restricted to socialist thinking, and we just saw how his critique of historicism is similarly predicated on the view that formal principles were being subordinated to substantive considerations – in that case on the basis of culture and nationality rather than class. Arguably, Weber did not include historicism here because he had already discussed its limitations in his other methodological essays. And this is also justified because of the analytical angle from which his reconstruction of natural law proceeds: in looking at natural law from the point of view of conceptions of economic order, it was mostly the implications of socialist thinking that needed further clarification.

But while he has so far left us in little doubt about its salience in modernity, towards the end of his discussion of natural law Weber eventually addresses the question of its contemporary relevance. The case that we have somehow been expecting right from the start, the decline of natural law in modernity, is now made with full force:

> [*t*]*he axioms of natural law have lost all capacity to provide the fundamental basis of a legal system*. Compared with firm beliefs in the positive religiously revealed character of a legal norm or the inviolable sacredness of an age-old tradition, even the most convincing norms arrived at by abstraction seem to be too subtle to serve as the bases of a legal system. Consequently, legal positivism has, at least for the time being, advanced irresistibly. *The disappearance of the old natural law conceptions has destroyed all possibility of providing the law with a metaphysical dignity by virtue of its immanent qualities* . . . this extinction of the metajuristic implications of the law is one of those ideological developments which, while they have increased scepticism towards the dignity of the particular rules of a concrete

legal order, have also effectively promoted the actual obedience to the power, now viewed solely from an instrumentalist standpoint, of the authorities who claim legitimacy at the moment. (Weber 1968b: 874–5, my italics)

As a coherent body of legal doctrine with the ability to legitimate positive legal orders, natural law is much weakened in contemporary society. Weber's position here is very much that of the sociologist who no longer trusts metaphysical systems with the task of resolving societal normative disputes, the sociologist who wants to understand how conformity to positive law works; above all, the sociologist for whom normative compliance is increasingly attached to one single institution: state-enacted positive law. Weber is sceptical of what natural law can do in modern society, but we have seen that he offers other, equally fundamental, reasons to be sceptical about what positivism means for the development of modern law. At the same time as it unmasks the dogmatics behind natural law, positivist legal thinking fixates natural law's sense of justice, reasonableness and proceduralism into substantive entities that eventually cannot but undermine their own case: the nation, the state, culture, progress, god, the proletariat. Yet positivism itself contains its own natural law moment, as the continuous expansion of positive law in modern society follows the path of formalisation and reasonableness that is central to natural law. The process of positivisation of law

[l]eads to a reorganization of legal validity, in that it *simultaneously* transposes the basic concepts of morality and law to a postconventional level . . . the positivity of postmetaphysical law also means that legal orders can be constructed and can continue to develop only in the light of rationally justified, hence universal, principles. (Habermas 1996: 71–2)

On their own, neither natural law nor positive law is adequate in modern society: the former is too feeble and formal while the latter is too dogmatic and substantive. Yet Weber's broader discussion of natural law has shown that a major strength of natural law, one that is crucially lost in positive law, is its mediatory role: dogmatically, as a bridge between divine and positive law; historically, as the repository of reasonableness in jurisprudence; normatively, in terms of the need for legitimacy that is built into modern law; methodologically, in highlighting the operation of ideal factors alongside material ones.

I should then like to bring this section to a close by going back to the question of universalism in Weber's thought. The two main strands of his work on which we have concentrated here, scientific rationality and immanent legal reasoning, share the kind of universalistic features that have accompanied us throughout this book; both strands of his thinking share the same regulative principle of 'immanent reasonability'.

The empirical or descriptive aspect of his universalistic orientation is independent of his assessment of the role of natural law in normative thinking. Quite rightly, Weber does not seek substantive normative answers for what can prove to be transhistorically and transculturally valid in terms of the results of empirical research. Even though no definitive normative programme emerges out of Weber's intellectual commitments, it is above all the methodological universalism that is central to such ideas as value freedom, scientific neutrality, legal rationality and individual autonomy that ultimately become central to his normative outlook (Schluchter 1996: 69–101). Because the modern world thinks of itself as ethically irrational – evil deeds can result from good intentions – normatively sound decisions are only those that emerge from the application of reflexive principles that take some kind of procedural form. As substantive answers become not only more difficult to justify but also less fit for the purpose under modern conditions, Weber turns, even in spite of himself, to the view that the justification of moral decisions needs to be formal in character, based on an internally driven commitment, to remain open to criticism and to take into account the action's foreseeable consequences. It is eventually only the individual himself who takes responsibility for the principles and consequences of his actions – that, not least, is also the main thrust of his *Politics as a Vocation* (Weber 1994). Positive legal regimes certainly simplify normative decisions but this does not exonerate us from the burden of moral responsibility. In order to be effective, positive law not only needs to appear enforceable; equally importantly, it must carry with it the 'reasonableness', that general sense of the 'rightness of the law', that is built into natural law universalism.

Closing remarks

The broad and indeed only partial account of Simmel's and Weber's works in this chapter offers the somewhat conventional view that their sociologies are to a large extent compatible – indeed, their mutual sympathy and respect is well documented (Radkau 2009: 430–3; M. S. Weber 1975: 358, 370, 468). I have concentrated on how they engage with questions about universalism and natural law, which are aspects that do not figure prominently in their contributions to the establishment of modern social science. Following what is a constant thread running through this book, my argument has in fact been twofold: I have tried to reconstruct their understanding of the tradition of natural law, on the one hand, and to reassess the role of universalism in their own works, on the other.

We have looked at Simmel's interest in the forms of social interaction, individuality, the relationships between science and philosophy and the democratic structure of sociality. On Weber, we concentrated on methodological universalism, his critique of historicism and positivism and his analysis of legal rationalism. Both writers thought that the traditional body of natural law doctrines was becoming increasingly exhausted in modern society. Their critique of natural law is mostly related to the kind of unified cosmology for which there is little room in modernity – not least in terms of the need to differentiate more clearly between normative and descriptive claims, between legal and moral responsibility, between substantive and formal arguments. It is then particularly interesting that the universalistic orientation that remains central to Weber's and Simmel's works functions in a differentiated manner: while neither writer has a clear normative agenda to offer – indeed, they did not see offering one as their principal task – their conceptual and methodological commitments lead the way to propositions that only make full sense within a universalistic framework. The fact that they consciously refrained from offering decisive normative statements cannot be interpreted as lack of normative sensibility. This may help explain at least partly some of the reasons why their programmes have been mistakenly read as a reaction against universalism. Rather the opposite: it has been my contention that their engagement with normative questions is a prime expression of the fact that, in modernity, we never approach normative questions on their own but always in relation to wider conceptual, methodological and indeed socio-historical considerations. Normative principles do not work as first principles from which descriptive statements are simply derived; rather, they tension and correct one another.

8 Social theory as the natural law of 'artificial' social relations

The previous two chapters reconstructed the engagement of classical social theorists with the tradition of natural law. I searched for their explicit treatment of natural law and their interest in universalism. More generally, I sought to reflect further on some key themes that emerged in Part II: the internal differentiation of universalism between normative, conceptual and methodological planes, the modern renditions of the dichotomy between the state of nature and the civil condition, the role of social life in the expansion or obstruction of our human features, the tension between scientific and philosophical knowledge, the relevance of proceduralism in modernity. None of these issues is particularly original, to be sure, yet they have not been at the centre of twentieth-century debates on the rise and main features of modern social theory. In this last chapter, which is also partly a general conclusion to the book as a whole, my goal is to use the insights we have gained about the connections between the two traditions to reassess our understanding of the rise and main features of modern social theory.

Writing in the early 1970s, Robert Nisbet opens his important *The Social Philosophers* with a statement that marks quite a contrast with the situation of the previous generation that was writing in the 1950s (see Chapter 2), as well as with our own intellectual panorama. He argues that, quite rightly, social scientists were at the time highly interested in the historical and philosophical foundations of classical social theory: '[n]o single trend in recent years has been more vivid in the social sciences than the reawakening of interest in the sources and channels of the ideas, perspectives, and values that lie beneath the varied theories and methodologies of the social sciences' (Nisbet 1976: 9). Retrospectively, we now see that this claim was made right in the middle of a twenty-year period, between the early 1960s and the early 1980s, in which sociologists engaged extensively with their discipline's past.[1] I will not try to survey the main arguments of this

[1] If we concentrate only on those works with an explicit sociological interest, the following works can be mentioned in alphabetical order (and several of them will be discussed at

generation in what follows, but a key aspect that they share, and that I am convinced we ought to retain, is that they approached their reconstructions in the realisation that while sociology's scientific component was crucial for the rise of social theory, equal attention needed to be paid to philosophical and normative considerations. To echo another of Nisbet's (1967: 18) propositions, a main insight that transpires from these reconstructions is that all key ideas in the social sciences:

> [i]nvariably have roots in moral aspirations. However abstract the ideas may eventually become, however neutral they may come to seem to scientists and theorists, they do not ever really divest themselves of their moral origins . . . The great sociologists never ceased to be moral philosophers.

I favour a vision of social theory in which historical, normative as well as scientific concerns are all allowed in as a way of trying to make social theory relevant for wider socio-cultural and normative debates. I shall proceed in four steps. First, I explicate what is specifically modern in classical social theory by reference to its constitution as a novel intellectual genre. I then come back to the question of universalism as social theory's most fundamental regulative ideal and argue that this universalism operates at three relatively autonomous levels: the normative, conceptual and methodological. As a consequence of this universalistic orientation, in the third section I suggest that we need to revisit social theory's alleged as well as real modernist bias – whether social theory's modern origins make modernity its necessary focal point (but also inevitable blind spot). I conclude with an argument on understanding social theory as the natural law of an artificial realm – emergent social relations.

some point below in this chapter): J. H. Abraham (1973), Raymond Aron (1965, 1967), Ted Benton (1977), Richard Bernstein (1976), Simon Clarke (1991 [1982]), Lewis Coser (1977 [1971]), Robert Fine (2002 [1984]), Anthony Giddens (2003 [1973]), Johan Goudsblom (1977), Alvin Gouldner (1965, 1970, 1975), Jürgen Habermas (1974), Geoffrey Hawthorn (1976), Wolf Lepenies (1988 [1985]), Robert Nisbet (1967, 1976, 1977), Gillian Rose (2009 [1981]), Steven Seidman (1983), Edward Shils (1980), Werner Stark (1963), Hermann Strasser (1976), Irving Zeitlin (1968). To this list, one should also add at least works by Alex Callinicos (2007), Johan Heilbron (1995 [1990]), H. S. Hughes (1974 [1958]), Donald Levine (1995), Herbert Marcuse (1973 [1940]), John Rundell (1987), Piet Strydom (2000) and Peter Wagner (2001, 2006) even though chronologically they fall outside the period I have just demarcated. Here, I am explicitly excluding what is arguably a different genre in contemporary sociological theory – the kind of works that reassess its constitutive theoretical debates and its more strictly conceptual operations. See, for instance, in Patrick Baert (2001), Barry Barnes (1995), Hans Joas and Wolfgang Knöbl (2009 [2004]), Richard Kiliminster (1998), Derek Layder (1994), Nicos Mouzelis (1995, 2008), George Ritzer (2001), John Scott (1995).

Social theory as a modern intellectual genre

The thesis of modern social theory being the *Aufhebung* of natural law has required us to place equal emphasis on the continuities and discontinuities of both traditions: they take the question of universalism seriously, but social theory needs a more differentiated argument about how its universalism will work at different levels; both traditions are able to grasp the importance of socio-historical change and normative diversity but social theory faces this much more intensely as an intellectual challenge; both traditions seek to establish the relationships between the individual and society but only social theory offers an explicit argument on the *nature* of social life; both traditions seek to understand the meaning of our life in common but social theory has a primary concern with how this takes place under modern conditions. Over the past two centuries, social theory has evolved as a modern intellectual genre that, as it has tried to articulate philosophical and scientific concerns has, however, fallen somewhere in between the two. It is neither empirical enough in relation to modern social science nor philosophical enough in relation to natural law; it is neither classical enough in relation to moral and political philosophy nor novel enough in relation to media, cultural, gender or subaltern studies. We can see that as a fundamental hindrance or, alternatively, as a major asset. In Robert Nisbet's view, social theory cohered around a specific intellectual style that goes beyond the individual preferences of particular writers. His argument is that social theory's originality ultimately lies in it being a genre that successfully brings out the best of scientific and artistic commitments:

> Scientists Marx, Weber, Durkheim and Simmel were without question. But they were also artists, and had they not been artists, and they contented themselves with demonstrating solely what had been arrived at through aseptic problem design, through meticulous verification, and through constructions of theory which would pass muster in a graduate course in methodology of sociology today, the entire world of thought would be much poorer. (Nisbet 1977: 7)

As a new intellectual genre, then, modern social theory constituted itself by drawing variously from a wide range of available sources and traditions. This constitutive heterogeneity was one of its trademarks right from its inception: '[t]he very fact that Voltaire was a writer, Montesquieu a jurist and Condorcet a mathematician indicates how futile it would be to even try and understand these social theorists without scrutinizing the structure of the intellectual regime and its transformations' (Heilbron 1995: 14). A similar eclecticism is also visible in the transition from traditional to modern natural law (Hochstrasser 2000: 23–30) and indeed the centrality of the claims to originality that we have reconstructed throughout may well be based on both traditions' ability to recombine the intellectual resources that are available to them at particular junctures. The claim that social theory has always 'absorbed its points of view from philosophy, its materials from history and its cognitive model from natural science' (Levine 1995: 26) is possibly best known through the thesis that sociology is truly a 'third culture' that arose in between the sciences and the humanities:

> The problem of sociology is that, although it may imitate the natural sciences, it can never become a natural science of society: but if it abandons its scientific orientation it draws perilously close to literature ... sociology's precarious situation as a kind of 'third culture' between the natural sciences on the one hand and literature and the humanities on the other was exacerbated by the fact that the intellectual traditions of the Enlightenment and the counter-Enlightenment struggled with one another over its destiny. (Lepenies 1988: 7)

If we take into account the worldwide institutionalisation of academic sociology during the twentieth century, the third culture argument can be said to apply better to a broader idea of social theory than to sociology as such. A more general proposition can then be made that modern social theory evolved as an intellectual genre which, though at times internally inconsistent and at odds with contemporary disciplinary practices, has attracted and can continue to attract attention precisely because it is able to combine older and newer concepts, philosophical presuppositions, intellectual traditions and areas of empirical research creatively. Starting from its commitment to universalism, one key aspect that this intellectual genre has found challenging and rewarding in equal measure is the need to handle the tension between the normative considerations and insights that are needed in order to reflect meaningfully on social life, and the descriptive and explanatory tasks that are needed for empirical accounts to be found adequate. Modern social theory is bound to remain immersed in normative questions but can do so by simultaneously acknowledging that it possesses no privileged access to their potential resolution. Because of its built-in universalistic orientation, its cognitive operations carry forward normative presuppositions and implications that can only be accounted for from within social theory itself: there are actually existing social practices that we need to understand, but at the same time we can always think about new or better social institutions, regulations and indeed principles that may improve social conditions.

We have seen how classical, twentieth-century and contemporary social theory has had a permanent interest in normative questions.

It enquires as to the location of the normative in social life as a space of transcendental immanence – where do normative obligations come from? – and, as it explicates that their origins are always and necessarily social, it seeks to grapple with how these socially produced normative commitments can simultaneously be deemed binding. This is an idea of social theory which, although it is deeply interested in normative questions, differs from critical theory in so far as it does not presuppose that there is a definitive normative stance waiting to be discovered and then deployed 'out there' in the real world. As a 'messy' intellectual genre, social theory addresses normative questions that are partly unanswerable because the scientific side of its commitments prevents it from going that far, and they are also partly unanswerable because social life itself is emergent, contingent and ultimately unpredictable. The socio-historical fact that normative questions do not find definitive answers, however, says nothing about an equally important social fact – that people imagine and create different ways of thinking about themselves as part of the same human species. Our normative difficulties and challenges do not necessarily boil down to a definitive sense of incommensurability. Arguably, quite the opposite may be said to be the case: they make sense as normative questions because they ultimately refer to the universally human struggle of trying to understand what happens to human beings as they live in society – how and why we (fail to) recognise one another as members of the same species.

A claim to universalism

My goal in this book has been to argue that a universalistic orientation is central to social theory's past, present and future. Social theory's debt to natural law is apparent in its presupposition of the universal humanity of human beings as competent agents in the social world. It is human beings who create and recreate society even as this takes place in prestructured settings that are not the result of current actors' making. But the quest to delineate human nature definitively is already part of the natural law baggage that social theory has systematically sought to leave behind; social theory 'presupposes the humanity of man without further inquiry into what constitutes his humanity' (Manent 1998: 64). In contradistinction to natural law, social theory does not want and indeed cannot offer a positive determination of this shared humanity. In relation to Durkheim, Pierre Manent has reflected on this challenge as follows:

> Sociology is constructed as a science comparable to and parallel with the sciences of nature in taking as its object something other than the nature of man and in

> deliberately refusing to take man's nature as its object. It seeks to and must abstract from this nature. Sociology as a science, or 'science of man' as it will soon be called, exists only by refusing to be a science of the nature of man. (Manent 1998: 54)

Social theory needs to secure the existence of the social; it creates the social as a legitimate realm of intellectual enquiry that it can then claim as a domain of its own. As the task of explicating the social proves extremely challenging, social theory just cannot be 'distracted' by a philosophical anthropology that enquires directly into what is human nature. The positive and definitive determination of our shared humanity becomes impossible in so far as social theory sees its own task as that of explicating how social relations have causal powers and create the conditions within which our human features emerge and develop. What social theory gains in terms of understanding the social it loses in terms of leaving unaddressed the humanity of human beings. An idea of humanity is social theory's condition of possibility but as such it is something that it cannot adequately account for with its own theories and methods. A 'sociological principle of humanity' is a contradiction in terms because whereas there is no society without acting human beings, social theory is more interested in social causation than in human nature as such – social facts rather than our shared humanity are what ultimately count. Social theory does not explicitly spell out its universalistic presuppositions about our shared humanity because that would effectively undermine its own intellectual case – the theoretical account and empirical description of *social* life. The problematic centrality of universalism lies here in that social theory requires the presupposition of the unity of the human species ultimately without, however, being able to found that argument. Somewhat paradoxically, the philosophical core of the sociologist:

> [c]onsists in not raising 'the question he should naturally raise.' He nonetheless cannot remain in complete indetermination. He is obliged to have recourse to a principle of the unity of human experience or at least to something resembling that. He will have to do what he forbids himself doing and speak as a philosopher ... of social conditioning, social stratification, social reproduction and above all of society. (Manent 1998: 67)

In what is a relatively rare account, Johan Heilbron (1995: 76–7) argues that there are four anthropological preconditions for the rise of social theory: (1) that human nature is stable but extremely complex to define positively; (2) that an increasingly immanent striving for this-worldly happiness replaces the beliefs in other-worldly salvation; (c) that passions, motives and interests are more important for understanding human action than obligations and duties; (d) that individual features are not innate but fundamentally shaped by society. Modern social science has moved forwards in terms of what it has explicitly set itself out to do – our empirical knowledge about the social world has clearly improved over time – but the price we pay for this is that we grow unable even to reflect on the difficulties that are involved in making universalistic claims either anthropologically – what is human nature – or normatively – about how we should organise our lives in common.

In Chapter 3 we reviewed how natural law emerged as a way of understanding the mediations between universalistic ideas of humanity and observations about socio-cultural variation, socio-historical change and normative disagreement. The standard answer within natural law was first to assert what constituted the universal in human nature only for 'the empirical' to be accommodated later into the larger cosmological scheme. In the case of social theory, this is reframed as a 'dialectic of natural unity and sociocultural diversity', whose central tenet is that human actions are partly uniform, because of human beings' natural properties, and partly diverse, because they take place within highly varied socio-cultural settings (Seidman 1983: 29). The argument can thus be made that the complicated relationships between natural law, the Enlightenment and social theory are to be explicated precisely through this dual sensibility towards universal human nature and socio-historical particularity. From a sociological point of view, this is of course more than just a philosophical debate:

> In the eighteenth century, the philosophes articulated their doctrine of individual liberty chiefly in *the idiom of natural rights*. It is at this *ideological* level that the *natural law pronouncements* of the *philosophes* must be understood . . . As is well known, the reaction to the Enlightenment took the form of a critique of natural law . . . [However]. . . *the actual historical departure from the Enlightenment in this regard was less analytical than ideological.* The natural law doctrine served the *philosophes* as, so to speak, the available idiom in which to articulate their liberal ideology. Accordingly, the critique of natural law by the Enlightenment critics represented an all-out assault on Enlightenment liberalism. (Seidman 1983: 50–1, my italics)

With the notion of the early Enlightenment, I argued that a different periodisation was needed to understand the relationships between natural law and social theory. And by emphasising that an idea of universalism is central to both traditional and modern natural law, I equally tried to escape from the admittedly important though also reductionist reconstruction of modern natural law as essentially liberal and bourgeois. Yet there are at least two issues that deserve attention here. On the one hand, there is an explicit argument about the transition from natural law to natural rights that took place during the Enlightenment: although it was highly critical of traditional natural *law*, the newly found individualistic language of natural *rights* still found those traditional terms useful. On the other hand, the main ideological function of this dual recourse to natural law/right was to offer justifications that could simultaneously appeal to the past, via the transcendental weight of tradition, and to the future, via the immanent strength of progress. Either way, natural law/right was regarded as valuable because it spoke in a universalistic language – the more so, as soon became apparent, because a liberal social order was to be established on normative premises that it could neither adequately justify nor practically fulfil. The normative basis of modern society 'presupposes a condition of sociocultural and political pluralism' while at the same time it encourages 'the realization of individual freedom' as a universal value (Seidman 1983: 15). Moreover, the socio-historical realisation of this normative project is based on economic conditions that preclude the realisation of this normative vision: 'in its mix of universalism and particularism, liberalism discloses, on the one hand (expressing its universalistic aspect) a tendency of transcendence, and, on the other hand (expressing its particularism) a tendency to function as a legitimation of class domination' (17). Geoffrey Hawthorn offers an arguably more nuanced argument as he focuses on the cognitive challenges, instead of on the ideological implications, that are involved in the transition from natural law to social theory:

> A distinction had to be drawn between criteria applicable to all men and their societies at all times and criteria applicable to each society by virtue of its unique constellation of circumstances. In one respect, it was a modern distinction ... But this is merely to say that we have since partly returned to the ancient view against which the more uncompromisingly rationalist philosophes were defining themselves, the view that a Persian or an Athenian or a Frenchman is to be understood as much as a Persian or an Athenian or a Frenchman as a man independent of any historical or cultural contingency. (Hawthorn 1976: 18)[2]

These historical reconstructions address the relationships between natural law, the Enlightenment and the rise of modern social theory. Indeed, they assert that the universalistic vocation of natural law played an important role in shaping the philosophical and normative foundations of nascent social theory. The question of universalism comes up as a challenge and a requirement, a difficulty and an aspiration, a

[2] Yet another compatible account is found in Irving Zeitlin's influential reconstruction of the tradition of social theory from a Marxist point of view: 'by studying nature – including the nature of man – one could learn not only about what *is*, but about what is *possible*; likewise, by studying society and history one could learn not only about the workings of the existing factual order, but about its inherent possibilities' (Zeitlin 1968: 9).

philosophical argument and an empirical necessity. But in order to understand how social theory sublates natural law, we still need to be more precise on the internal differentiation of social theory's claim to universalism. The approach to universalism that social theory adopts from natural law remains at one level philosophical but is also much more decidedly empirical. Social theory unpacks natural law universalism into three relatively autonomous levels: the conceptual, methodological and normative.

Conceptually, classical social theory attempted to grasp emerging forms of social relations in a universalistic fashion. Whether defined as labour, sociation or functional differentiation, all substantive conceptualisations of the social are built upon an implicit understanding of those universal human capabilities that allow us to make and remake society (though never at will and under conditions that to a large extent are given). The autonomy of the social being a modern discovery, its existence as an ontological realm is not. The social is conceived as a universal domain of reality whose existence is both historically real and transcendentally presupposed.

Methodologically, there does not seem to be much in common between, say, Weber's imputation of rational behaviour when constructing ideal types, Durkheim's naturalism in treating social facts 'as things' and Marx's critique of the ideological representation of social institutions. Yet as methodological rules they are the ones that actually made possible the empirical study of the universalistic definition of the social understood as an autonomous ontological domain. If the empirical vocation of classical social theory was expected to work as an antidote against reified versions of the universal, the claim to universalism of its concepts and methodological procedures represents an equivalent antidote against any sacred treatment of the particular.

Normatively, the differentiation between conceptual and methodological universalism prevents the unmediated translation of political preferences into explanatory stances. At the same time as classical social theory offers no unified ideological or political programme, the ultimate subject of its universalistic orientation is, however, an idea of humanity as an increasingly real socio-historical entity. Classical social theory tried explicitly to understand the extent to which a geographically particular set of historically circumscribed processes led to the rise of a number of tendencies that were having a general though differentiated impact all over the world. The implicit normative corollary of this empirical claim on the global impact of modernity is that, despite all differences, humankind is effectively one and needs to be theorised as such. For classical social theory, the emergence of modern society is understood as humanity beginning to forge its own destiny. Classical social theorists required and helped to give concrete meaning to a universalistic idea of humanity from which no one was in principle excluded; an idea of humanity that was built on a strong sense of the individual, on the one hand, and of socio-cultural particularity, on the other hand. The idea of humanity is a key normative intuition of classical social theory.

The crucial intellectual resource that was missing in natural law, and that social theory did develop, was a systematic interrogation of what constituted legitimate empirical knowledge. Methodological procedures and conceptual tools were predisposed to encounter variability in social life but, because of that, understood such variation as part of a universalistic conception of humanity. In turn, methodological disputes are always about methodology but never only about methodology – they are also conceptual, ideological and ontological (Archer 1995, Bernstein 1976, Habermas 1972). Social theory is not a conventional science but never cut itself off from the scientific outputs of its constitutive disciplines in the social sciences. It remains scientific in its commitment to understanding social life empirically while simultaneously not restricting its claim to knowledge only to what can be empirically ascertained. And to the extent that its substantive results and methodological justifications are always provisional, so are the bases on which universalistic normative claims are derived. Classical social theory's original universalistic orientation developed, and must continue to develop, as a regulative principle of intellectual enquiry. This is why I think it can be referred to as a *claim to universalism* – universalism remains its key regulative principle, a standard to strive for even as it remains ultimately unachievable (Emmet 1994).

The centrality of modernity

As we discussed in Chapter 2, Karl Löwith argued that Weber and Marx's sociology of capitalism was able to decouple, at least partly, the link between modernity and social theory. For Löwith, the question was not only to grasp what was specific in modern capitalism but also what it was to live a 'human' life under the particular conditions of capitalist modernity. Social theory comes then closer to natural law as both traditions seek to grasp fundamental human concerns about the nature of life in common. This can be seen as a logical consequence of the proposition that universalism is social theory's ultimate guiding principle. Social theory ought to come to terms with the most general aspects of human existence as they necessarily take place within particular socio-cultural and socio-historical contexts.

The question for us in this section is to reflect social theory's alleged as well as real modernist bias (Yack 1997). In his highly influential account, Anthony Giddens put the modernist argument thus:

> If Renaissance Europe gave rise to a concern with history, it was industrial Europe which provided the conditions for the emergence of sociology ... the conjunction of events linking the political climate of the French Revolution and the economic changes wrought by the Industrial Revolution provided the context from within which sociology was formed. (Giddens 2003 [1973]: xi–xii)[3]

Peter Wagner has put forward a particularly sophisticated version of this modernist argument. He asserts the centrality of the connection between modernity and social theory by explicitly reflecting on the challenges that are posed by their nearly incestuous relationships. The opening lines of his *A Sociology of Modernity* present the case as follows:

> To propose a sociology of modernity seems tautological at best. What else is sociology, if not the systematic attempt to come to an understanding of modern society? At worst, a sociology of modernity could seem an impossible project. If sociology grew with modernity, as its mode of self-monitoring, then it could never achieve the distance to the object that every analytical endeavour requires. (Wagner 1994: ix)

Wagner's continuous engagement with these problems coheres around the question of how social theory can achieve the critical distance that will allow it to reflect on our modern conditions in a way that is philosophically consistent, scientifically viable and socially relevant (Wagner 2001). Wagner has also suggested that the intellectual vitality of sociology is greatly dependent on its original connection with moral and political philosophy and has argued that its emergence can be understood as the rise of a new empirical political philosophy (Wagner 2006). As he elaborates further on this argument, he claims that there are three – political, epistemic and economic – *problématiques* that are key to understanding modernity. These constitutive *problématiques* are not, however, 'specific to modernity as such; they traverse all human societies. But the view that solutions to them are not given but need to be sought is that which the modern commitment to autonomy, the modern way of confronting these *problématiques*, entails' (Wagner 2008: 13). The lack of critical distance that Wagner first argued made the task of a sociology of

[3] More recently, and beyond sociology, the first line of Charles Taylor's (2004: 1) *Modern Social Imaginaries* simply states that: 'From the beginning, the number one problem of modern social science has been modernity itself'.

modernity tautological at best is now explicitly readdressed by making a stronger connection between social theory and universal concerns that traverse all human societies. Modernism remains, however, in the claim that it *is only in modernity* solutions in these three realms are 'not given but need to be sought'. There is now a greater sense of transhistorical continuity in terms of fundamental questions yet the rise of modern social theory is still depicted as a quest for autonomy – and that is a quest that is above all forward looking (the past is no source for legitimacy) and inward looking (external sources such as nature and religion can no longer provide legitimacy). I should like to contend that the materials we have discussed throughout this book offer a much more ambivalent picture, however.[4]

Robert Nisbet is possibly one of the most outspoken critics of social theory's modernist bias. He sees a fundamental continuity in the philosophical quest to understand our life in common and speaks of a long-standing tradition of 'social philosophy' which has run for over two millennia:

> Western philosophy is little more than a series of commentaries on Plato's fundamental ideas. Whether in the realm of philosophy as such, in theology, in the history of mathematics and the physical sciences – at least down into the early Renaissance – *or what we today call the social sciences.* (Nisbet 1976: 114, my italics)[5]

All the ideas of community that Nisbet reconstructs in *Social Philosophers* – the military, political, religious, revolutionary, ecological and pluralistic – are presented as having atemporal traits that make them relevant to grasping fundamental aspects of collective life. There is then a prima facie connection between Nisbet's atemporal idea of communal life and natural law because these different notions of community address questions about

[4] See Piet Strydom (2000: 1–22), for the argument that Karl Mannheim was the first to advance this unrelenting link between the rise of modernity and that of social theory.

[5] Or, in relation to Aristotle, Nisbet argues that he was 'the first real social scientist' because of his very 'attitude toward human behavior in society' (Nisbet 1976: 397). The opposite account is found, for instance, in Raymond Aron, for whom the project of sociology was 'grasping the social *as such*'. Aron makes the case as follows: 'Aristotle's *Politics* is a treatise on political sociology. But the central interest, the point of reference in Aristotle's *Politics*, is the political regime and not the social organization. Thus, to my way of thinking, sociology marks a moment in man's reflection on historical reality, the moment when the concept of the social, of society, becomes the centre of interest, replacing the concept of politics or of the regime of the state' (Aron 1965: 14–15). In what was arguably one of the most influential accounts of his generation, Alvin Gouldner's thoroughly modernist attitude towards the role of sociology is, somewhat paradoxically, intellectually justified by a strictly *sociological* rendition of Plato. See Gouldner (1965 and 1970: 412–46).

the nature of life in common throughout human history. Nisbet himself acknowledges that natural law plays a role in the way in which philosophical resources remain available in modernity. Speaking about the seventeenth century, he argues that '[i]t is not Roman law but natural law to which Hobbes appeals ... But natural law, as Hobbes and many of his contemporaries conceived it, is hardly more ... than a transmutation of Roman law' (Nisbet 1976: 143–4). Without an increasingly secular understanding of natural law it would be extremely 'difficult to imagine that very much of the actual political theory of the so-called natural law would ever have come into existence in the modern age' (144). But in conceiving of natural law in this way Nisbet unwillingly reintroduces the modernist bias he criticises. He conflates natural law with the rise of modern individualism and liberalism and thus misses the point by explicating the rise of modern social theory as a wholly conservative reaction against liberal contractualism:

> [t]he whole secular theory of natural law from 1500 to 1800 was engaged in working out little else but a theory of society. But behind the rationalist image of society in this period there was always the prior image of naturally free individuals who had rationally bound themselves into a specified and limited mode of association. Man was primary; relationships were secondary. Institutions were but the projections of fixed, atom-like sentiments innate in man. Volition, assent, and contract – these were the key terms in the natural-law view of society. (Nisbet 1967: 48)

There is too little in this argument on the differentiation between natural law and social science, on the one hand, and too narrow a depiction of natural law as just 'Enlightenment liberalism', on the other. Nisbet's approach makes it difficult to conceptualise the *relationships* between social theory and natural law and indeed misses a key point we discussed in Chapter 4: while it is true that social institutions appear after individual human nature in modern natural law, they were certainly not secondary or their mere projection. Social life sublates rather than simply accommodates human nature in Rousseau and Hobbes.

My argument in this section is not that the socio-structural transformations that we commonly describe as constitutive of modernity – the rise of the nation-state system, the emergence of capitalism, functional differentiation and so on – have left unchanged the ways in which human beings live and see themselves. But in order to understand what it is that makes them modern, we need also to reflect on what is universally human about living under such conditions. Modern social theory may be able to renew itself as we define its main task as the attempt to grasp universal human concerns as they take place in modernity. And it does so by combining long-standing ways of thinking, on the one hand, with the more empirical means of modern science, on the other. The relevance of studying modern socio-cultural processes lies more in that those are the historical conditions under which we now live in the present and less in their having a special status *vis-à-vis* other ages. At the same time as its intellectual scope is enlarged thanks to its intrinsic commitment to universalism, social theory's modernism is fundamentally undermined. Taking universalism seriously comes at a cost.

The natural law of an artificial realm: social relations

Let me briefly recapitulate the steps we have taken so far in this final chapter. We first explored the novelty of social theory as a modern intellectual genre; we then argued for the centrality of universalism as social theory's central regulative idea, which in turn made us question its relationships with modernity. In this final section, I should like to suggest that we see social theory as the natural law of an artificial or emergent realm: social relations.

We may start by discussing an argument that does not really belong to the body of scholarship on which we have focused so far. John Milbank's *Theology and Social Theory* is interesting because it offers a challenge to social theory's core contention that the social exists as an autonomous domain of reality. Arguing from a Christian standpoint, his critique of the idea of the social is offered as an indictment of the whole project of social theory; he seeks to advance a 'sceptical demolition of modern, secular social theory' because '"scientific" social theories are themselves theologies or anti-theologies in disguise' (Milbank 2006: 1–3). His criticism centres on the standard modernist view that sociology emerged with a view to giving an account of the truly 'social' forces that underpinned the rise of capitalism. The nascent social theory that was thus articulated became a renovated, though not necessarily new, 'attempt to resolve the great antinomy encountered by secular social science – do humans construct society, or does society construct humanity?' (51). In clearly polemical fashion, Milbank argues that social theory's complicated relationships with secularisation do not represent 'an emancipation *from* theology' but rather a much deeper 'shift *within* theology' (28). The more it criticises theology (i.e. Christian natural law), the more social theory's quest for the social proves itself to be a form of theology in disguise. Social theory suspends the enquiry into the historical emergence of the social right at the time when such an account would have been most needed. Social theory cannot answer the question about the rise of the social as an autonomous domain because it conceptualises the social ahistorically. The attempt to define the limits of human understanding', and so to go beyond metaphysics, which is of crucial importance for the rise of modern social theory, is only possible as a transcendental point of view. That is of course problematic because 'it is impossible to isolate the pre-given, categorical element (which for sociology is schematized as "society" – as fact or norm)' from the rest of the elements that make up human life:

> The 'critique of metaphysics' which sociology ... claims to carry forwards, thus turns out to be a new metaphysics which lays claim to a totalizing and once-for-all representation of finitude, and also a humanism which safeguards a free and ineffable subject that only 'has an apparent effect' within this finitude, yet always, in essence, transcends it. (Milbank 2006: 105–6)

Although sociology thinks of itself as having carried out a radical critique of both theology and metaphysics, the attempt was never radical enough and remained at best incomplete. The introduction of the social is an unwarranted metaphysical move because it reintroduces the same foundationalism for which social theory had criticised theology and natural law. This line of criticism is not altogether different from those we discussed in Chapter 2. Following Löwith, there is the challenge of social theory's incomplete secularisation and, following Voegelin, there is the question of whether social theory can grasp the transcendental (or the normative, as I rather put it) in a non-transcendental way.

If we now return to the sociological literature, not too dissimilar a critique of social theory, although it is completely different in intellectual orientation, is found in Gillian Rose's (2009) *Hegel Contra Sociology*. Rose criticises sociology's claim of having securely defined the social as an autonomous domain of reality and knowledge and argues that sociology has never really moved beyond natural law because it has systematically failed to account for the socio-historical conditions of its own emergence. This also explains why the operations of its central concepts are chronically problematic: the more they seek philosophical consistency the less they can deliver empirically. The aporia she seeks to unfold is that whereas in terms of ambitions social theory is surely at the forefront of modern intellectual enquiry, in terms of actual conceptual and methodological operations it has never got beyond what she considers is Hegel's *definitive* critique of Kant. Rose thus criticised both Weber and Durkheim for still inhabiting a pre-Hegelian universe that had not fully historicised the key categories with which they sought to give an adequate explanatory account, as well as a normative critique, of modern society. Sociology, argues Rose, is a discipline in which 'logic is separated from cognition, validity from representation'. This means that the substantive problem of the emergence of social relations as an autonomous domain has been systematically pushed aside by merely formal propositions that only take the form of a 'general logic' – a mere methodologism (Rose 2009: 9). She presents her charge thus:

> Durkheim granted the question of validity priority over the question of values, and made validity into the sociological foundation of values (moral facts). Weber granted the question of values priority over the question of validity and made values into the sociological foundation of validity (legitimacy) ... It was the ambition of sociology to substitute itself for traditional theoretical and practical philosophy, as well as to secure a sociological object-domain *sui generis*. (Rose 2009: 15)

As I see it, Rose's critique of Durkheim and Weber comprises two different issues and the problem with her critique is that she conflates both charges. The first claim requires a clear-cut separation between validity and values – the former being given priority in the scientific logic of sociology (i.e. in Durkheim's rules of the sociological method), the latter asserting the normative undecidability of modern social life (i.e. Weber's thesis on the polytheism of values). In so far as each sociologist favoured one particular side of that separation over and against the other, Durkheim and Weber ended up offering equally one-sided, rigid and ahistorical accounts of modern social life. Sociology's neo-Kantian heritage reinforces in Rose's view the dogmatic separation between the descriptive and normative planes of social theory – a separation that she claims works at the level of neither scientific procedures nor philosophical foundations. Rather than overcoming natural law's lack of historicity and insufficient attention to empirical knowledge, social theory ended up with a rather reified separation of both realms. Similar to Milbank's, though now from the perspective of critical social theory, the argument is that social theory dogmatically reproduced rather than overcame the unmediated connections between description and normativity in the natural law tradition.[6]

The second of Rose's charges has, however, to do with her negative comments on Durkheim and Weber resorting to *naturalistic* reductions in spite of themselves. Rose contends that it is only through these reductions that their more general sociological arguments

[6] Milbank (2006: 103) argues in similar terms: '[a]fter Durkheim's neo-Kantian[ism] ... the social becomes a name for the finite presence to us of the Kantian "kingdom of ends": it sanctifies and embodies the sublime freedom of every individual within the State. It is also the *a priori* schema which supplies the categorical universals under which are to be comprehended all empirical contents ... [for] Max Weber, by contrast ... the social is not the site of the *a priori*, rather, the social itself is to be known *a priori* in terms of the primacy of instrumental reason and economic relationship.'

appear to work. In the case of Durkheim, this naturalism is expressed as a conflation between social relations and the natural order. Best expressed in Durkheim's proposition of treating social moral facts as things, she suggests that Durkheim has no model for understanding social facts other than those of the natural world (Rose 2009: 19). In relation to Weber, her critique is that he smuggled in the key anthropological presupposition that human beings are cultural beings with an essential capacity for turning the world into a meaningful universe. Weber was only able to make this move because he wrongly presupposed that meanings could be unequivocally apprehended through naturalistic methodological procedures – his ideal types:

> But if reality is a value which is only properly knowable by means of ideal-types which are accentuated values themselves, then we can have no independent access to an empirical given which might be 'measured' or 'compared' by means of the ideal-type. We cannot make the judgments of validity implied by 'measuring' and 'comparing'. (Rose 2009: 20)[7]

If I rephrase this in relation to the connections between social theory and natural law, the problem now becomes the equation between first, 'human' nature and second 'social' nature – to what extent the properties of the former function as a model and are found in the latter. But as mentioned above there are two separate arguments in Rose's critique. They are independent because whereas the first argument focuses on a strict separation between validity and values (or between description and normativity) at the level of the cognitive operations within sociology, the second concentrates on the ontological properties that make up the social *vis-à-vis* the human – whether they are comparable if not directly the same. Rose's claim is that sociology is unable to go beyond the limitations of neo-Kantianism in terms of either proposition: how it conceives its cognitive operations (charge one, which is a logical one) and how it conceptualises the outside world (charge two, which is ontological). In her view, the problem with sociology is that it seeks to grasp the ultimate nature of social relations but this is a philosophical quest for which it is inadequately prepared. And this is also the reason why her solution comes in the form of a metacritique that takes

[7] Rose is not alone in thus reading Durkheim and Weber's arguments on the foundations of sociology's knowledge claims. Pierre Manent also suggests that when Durkheim speaks of social objects and Weber of values, they are in fact referring to something very similar because 'the two propositions judge things in the same neutral and egalitarian way' (Manent 1998: 71). What Rose does not mention, but Manent recognises, is that, in so doing, they equally rejected 'the classical idea of an objective hierarchy of ends and human goods inscribed in human nature' (71).

inspiration from Hegelian/Marxist dialectics. A metacritique, that is, which is able to expose 'the formation and deformation of both transcendental [my charge two] *and* methodological [my charge one] reason' (Rose 2009: 24). But the only justification that allows her to put the two charges together is that Rose had already made up her mind that sociology as a whole is at fault. The critique depends upon both Weber and Durkheim still naively believing in the desirability of modelling sociology from what takes place in the natural sciences in both logical and ontological planes. The alleged neo-Kantianism of sociology is, however, only an indictment of sociology's positivism: the scientific aspect of sociology (charge one) creates a discipline that is ontologically bland and normatively blind (charge two).

Needless to say, I do not share the results of Milbank's and Rose's critiques. In the previous two chapters I hope to have demonstrated convincingly that social theory developed with a far more ambivalent relationship to science and philosophy, to description and normativity and indeed to immanence and transcendence than these criticisms allow for. All classical social theorists engaged and sought to adopt elements from the natural sciences and therein surely lay a great deal of their novelty and appeal. But science was never a goal in itself and methodological procedures, however important, did not work as gold standards: methodological innovations did not automatically regress into methodologism. Social theory sought to ascertain the empirical cognoscibility of social relations even as philosophical justifications remained problematic. Conversely, it sought to ascertain the centrality of philosophical questions even as their insights could not be fully justified in empirical or scientific terms. Modern social theory is the natural law of an emergent and artificial realm – social relations – because: (1) it works under the presupposition that social relations do have a nature; (2) seeks to understand what is unique or 'artificial' in that nature; and (3) locates the normative in social relations as a strictly immanent realm whose transcendental limit lies in our universally shared humanity.

(1) Because of the centrality of universalism, social theory has a systematic preoccupation with securely establishing what is the constant element that makes up social relations – what it is that makes social relations *definitively* social. It may or may not try to answer this question explicitly, but it is never enough to offer an empirical account, however exhaustive, of socio-cultural, historical or indeed normative variation in the social world. Modern social theory presupposes that, while seeking to understand particular historical processes and events, there is something stable in the way in which

social relations are produced and reproduced in different contexts and epochs. Whether it sees social life as consisting of communication, power or the material reproduction of social life, one of modern social theory's permanent concerns is, and remains, that of grasping the ultimate nature of social relations in general. Modern social theory works under the fundamental presupposition that social relations have a nature of their own.

(2) The substantive definition of the nature of social relations has remained contentious. One thing we do know, however, is that it is different from physical and human nature. Social relations are emergent as they cannot be reduced to, or explicated by, the properties of its component elements which are of course none other than individual human beings. Actions always take place in previously structured socio-historical contexts and outcomes remain changeable and ultimately unpredictable. Social relations are artificial because human beings themselves see the social institutions and practices they create and help reproduce as things of a different nature. What takes place in society is artificial because its ultimate source is not our innate 'human nature': modern social theory seeks to understand the artificial nature of social relations.

(3) This conception of social relations as artificial nature locates the normative somewhere in between immanence and transcendence. Understanding the location of the normative in modernity involves a tension between immanent justifications that make arguments rationally acceptable and transcendental grounds that make them binding. Transcendental sources are not allowed to intervene in the affairs of human beings. While such elements as our genetic dispositions or technological devices are increasingly being integrated into conceptions of who we are as human beings, these elements become relevant and meaningful only through prior and systematic human intervention. Social relations are to be understood in strictly immanent terms, i.e. through human means and human means alone. But it is our universally shared humanity that constitutes the transcendental that inheres within fully immanent social relations. Our humanity lies outside society, and thence it is never the direct object of study for social theory. Yet it poses cognitive limits on how we can explain society as well as normative limits about what is acceptable in society.

Epilogue

My book on the idea of the nation-state in classical and contemporary social theory sought to offer an account of its rise and main features in modernity which, in the same move, rejected the mainstream argument of social theory's intrinsic methodological nationalism (Chernilo 2007). While most of the materials I discussed there had to do with explicit arguments on the relationships between the nation, the state and the global in social theory, a secondary line of reasoning emphasised the universalistic thrust that in my view is constitutive of modern social theory. On the one hand, the idea of society refers to the existence of an autonomous ontological domain; the discovery of society is a universal accomplishment in so far as it refers to the transhistorical and transcultural dimension that defines human interaction as intentional yet unpredictable, contingent yet patterned, socio-historically located yet universally understandable. The fact that an explicitly immanent science of society only emerged in modernity requires us to explain the conditions that made it visible only then but does not alter the fact that there is nothing intrinsically modern in social life as an ontological domain. On the other hand, the importance of universalism also became apparent as I started exploring the question of modernity's global orientation through an engagement with contemporary debates on cosmopolitanism: whether and to what extent ideas of modernity and cosmopolitanism depend on unacknowledged universalistic presuppositions on the ultimate unity of the human species. My *original* idea for a book on the natural law foundations of modern social theory thus began as an attempt to come to terms with the historical and philosophical roots of those universalistic arguments that were *actually* present in contemporary theories of modernity, the nation-state and cosmopolitanism.

As I started working on this project, the book I wanted to write, and for quite a while the one I thought I was actually writing, would make the case for the interconnections between universalism and natural law, rapidly survey traditional and modern natural law, and then be mostly devoted to exploring in detail the extent to which deep-seated universalistic presuppositions have remained and have proved inevitable in modern social theory – classical but mostly contemporary. The initial plan was then to have more Luhmann than Rousseau, more Latour than Hobbes, more Rorty than Kant. My intention was to demonstrate that many if not most of the best attributes of these contemporary writers are based on universalistic presuppositions and commitments that have to remain in place even as they work against their explicit intellectual orientations and best known theses. I wanted to help redress some of the scepticism against universalistic ideas in contemporary social and political thought. Although some of this original intention is still visible in Chapter 1, Habermas's case is different because of his explicit interest in universalism and natural law. As it actually developed, then, this book offers little in terms of contemporary critique mostly because the sheer wealth of the philosophical materials I started to review made that original plan untenable: the connections between universalism and natural law needed to be reconstructed and explicated more carefully; the differentiation between traditional and modern natural law proved to be more complicated and consequential, many of classical social theory's foundational themes mirrored, in both form and content, issues that had been central to modern natural law. What at first were mostly 'preparatory' materials *vis-à-vis* contemporary debates became central to, indeed the centre itself, of my research.

Natural law is surely not one of social theory's constitutive motifs, but I hope to have demonstrated that natural law has played a major role in the rise of social theory. Explicitly, as it appears as an important area of research in a variety of contexts: the history of social and political thought, legal sociology, the sociology of knowledge or the sociology of religion. Implicitly, as a number of key themes of the natural law tradition are sublated, *aufgehoben*, in modern social theory: the tensional relationships between scientific and philosophical knowledge claims, the challenges to and need for proceduralism in modernity, the coupling/decoupling between conceptions of the social and the human, immanence and transcendence, claims to intellectual originality and the need for a clean slate, *Gemeinschaft/Gesellschaft* as a modern rendition of the state of nature/civil condition. Similarly, modern social theory's self-identity, as it has developed over the past fifty or sixty years, still has much to gain if it confronts that much longer-term philosophical tradition which, at face value at least, it has sought to leave behind. Rich as social theory undoubtedly is in terms of conceptual, methodological and normative insights, some of its best intuitions have not, however, been brought to bear on the history, main features and normative implications of social theory itself. For all its theoretical sophistication and its several attempts at the constitution of general theories of society, our understanding of the philosophical foundations of modern social theory remains relatively unsatisfactory; for all its methodological sharpness, creativity and originality, claims on radical innovation, complete rupture and thoroughgoing novelty are in fact part of a long-standing heritage, repeat themselves far too often and are still being accepted far too readily; for all its sensibility towards socio-historical particularity and empirical detail, our reconstructions of the sociological tradition remain surprisingly self-centred on what social theorists say to themselves; for all its passion for political action, we still struggle to come to terms with social theory's normative implications and the challenge to locate the normative in society.

The epigraph that opens this book is Eric Voegelin's assertion that the idea of universality is central to our constitution as a single species because it is only through an idea of universality that we transcend our biological likeness and become able to recognise each other as human beings. Ideas of humanity, themselves a universal human accomplishment, have of course varied greatly and need to be reconstructed historically, contextualised socio-culturally, explicated philosophically and assessed normatively. In so far as the social sciences try to reflect on questions about social life in general, they enter a terrain where they can learn from the philosophical tradition of natural law. Without the idea of humanity as a general regulative intuition we are left with no foundations with which to recognise each other as fellow human beings. We still need to subject the universalistic underpinnings of key concepts and theories to greater scrutiny.

In the corollary to my ten theses in the introduction, and then in Chapters 2, 6 and 7, I briefly drew on the idea of philosophical sociology to try to capture what is at stake in this intellectual project: the relationships between conceptions of the social and conceptions of the human, existential human concerns under the particular socio-historical conditions of capitalism, the need to anticipate general philosophical arguments for our attempts to produce empirical knowledge about social life to be come meaningful, the fact that the best scientific questions are philosophical and the need to address them accordingly. For a science of the social to emerge, questions about human nature needed to be pushed to the background yet the fact that they have left centre stage does not mean that they have disappeared. They remain and are the condition of possibility of our social scientific thinking: epistemologically, conceptually, normatively. Philosophical sociology may thus become an umbrella term for a type of enquiry that, on the basis of social theory's *Aufhebung* of natural law, seeks to capture underlying conceptions of the human in socio-historical explanations – what Axel Honneth and Hans Joas (1988: 7) refer to as 'the unchanging preconditions of human changeableness'.

I should like to finish with three different though essentially intertwined questions, as I hope they will provide additional purchase for the idea of philosophical sociology. First, there is the issue of the location of the normative in social life. As a question rather than as a single answer, we have seen that this is a major problem for natural law and social theory alike. From Hobbes to Habermas, reflections on the location of the normative have simultaneously taken place on two different planes. On the one hand, they focus on questions about rational assent, acceptability, compliance; what makes individuals uphold certain values, norms and institutions beyond or at least in addition to fear and self-interest. A principle of acceptability that in the last instance needs to be granted by individuals themselves is central to understanding the location of the normative in modern social life. On the other hand, such questions as justice, fairness or legitimacy, however much they need to remain connected to positive regulations, are never only about positive law. Normative ideas and ideals only exist, can only be understood in their normative importance, because they retain a *halo of transcendence.* For them to work in society as normative ideas, they must be seen as human made as well as setting a normative limit to socially available options: victors' justice can be many things and carry many implications yet it is anything but justice.

Thus, secondly, a universalistic idea of humanity is the transcendental condition of possibility, and hence also the ultimate limit, for the immanent type of intellectual enquiry that is modern social theory. It is on the basis of the universality of the idea of humanity that we come to see and recognise each other as human beings. Even as we focus on material cultures, non-fully human 'actants' or biopolitical transformations, even as we redefine our ontologies in terms of communication or networks, from the point of view of social theory these matter on the basis of their impact on human life. At the same time, social theory's empirical purchase becomes possible only to the extent that this universality of the idea of humanity is suspended, say in the form of a phenomenological bracketing, so that the actual focus of research can remain on what we actually want to explicate empirically or socio-historically. In order to retain some normative purchase, conceptions of the human, human nature and humanity preserve this halo of transcendence. Yet it is this same halo of the idea of humanity that complicates social theory's ability to access the normative more reflexively.

Thirdly, there is the question of the anthropological capacities that make life in society possible. A key one that transpires from the materials we have discussed is the fundamental human capability to *imagine a different world*; our general ability to create and recreate our sense of unity on the basis of our differences and disagreements. Far from reintroducing a modernist bias in terms of a world that can be changed in full and at will, this is asserting that human beings have always tried to represent the world they live in by anticipating an ideal state of affairs that may or may not be realised. As we exercise this capacity we effectively learn about who we are and what we can actually accomplish. This is surely not all that is needed for society to exist but is an essential contribution of our humanity to social life. It is immanent as it can only be exercised in society but it is transcendental in so far as it is a condition of possibility of social action (and of our thinking about social action); it is natural to the extent that all human beings are in principle equally endowed with it yet it is realised only in the artificial environment we create as we try to live together.

Note on the original versions

All the materials contained in this book have been specially prepared for their publication here. However, some materials have appeared first as follows: Chapter 1 is a modified version of 'Jürgen Habermas' social theory as postmetaphysical natural law', *Journal of Classical Sociology* 13(2), in press. Chapter 2 expands on arguments originally developed in 'On the relationships between social theory and natural law: Lessons from Karl Löwith and Leo Strauss', *History of the Human Sciences* 23(5): 91–112, 2010. Chapters 6, 7 and 8 include some very short passages that are included in 'A quest for universalism: Re-assessing the nature of classical social theory's cosmopolitanism', *European Journal of Social Theory* 10(1): 17–35, 2007.

References

Abraham, G. (1992) *Max Weber and the Jewish Question: A Study of the Social Outlook of his Sociology*, Urbana and Chicago: University of Illinois Press.

Abraham, J. H. (1973) *Origins and Growth of Sociology*, London: Penguin.

Acton, H. (1975) 'Introduction', in G. W. F. Hegel, *Natural Law*, Philadelphia: University of Pennsylvania Press.

Adair-Toteff, C. (2005a) 'Ernst Troeltsch and the philosophical history of natural law', *British Journal for the History of Philosophy* 13(4): 733–44.

Adair-Toteff, C. (2005b) 'Introduction', in Adair-Toteff, C. (ed.) *Sociological Beginnings: The First Conference of the German Society for Sociology*, Liverpool University Press.

(ed.) (2005c) *Sociological Beginnings: The First Conference of the German Society for Sociology*, Liverpool University Press.

Adorno, T. (1994) *Hegel: Three Studies*, MIT Press.

(ed.) (2000) *Introduction to Sociology*, Cambridge: Polity Press.

(ed.) (1976) *The Positivist Dispute in German Sociology*, London: Heineman.

Aldous, J., Durkheim, E. and Tönnies, F. (1972) 'An exchange between Durkheim and Tönnies on the nature of social relations', *American Journal of Sociology* 77(6): 1191–200.

Apel, K.-O. (2004) 'Kant, Hegel, and the contemporary question concerning the normative foundations of morality and right', in Pippin, R. and Höffe, O. (eds.) *Hegel on Ethics and Politics*, Cambridge University Press.

Archer, M. S. (1995) *Realist Social Theory*, Cambridge University Press.

Arendt, H. (1958) *The Origins of Totalitarianism*, New York: Meridian Books.

(1965) *On Revolution*, New York: The Viking Press.

Aron, R. (1965) *Main Currents in Sociological Thought*, Vol. I, London: Weidenfeld and Nicolson.

(1967) *Main Currents in Sociological Thought*, Vol. II, London: Weidenfeld and Nicolson.

Baert, P. (2001) *Social Theory in the Twentieth Century*, Cambridge: Polity Press.

Barash, J. (1998) 'The sense of history: On the political implications of Karl Löwith's concept of secularization', *History and Theory* 37(1): 69–75.

Barnes, B. (1995) *The Elements of Social Theory*, London: Routledge.

Bauman, Z. (2009) 'Seeking in modern Athens an answer to the ancient Jerusalem question', *Theory, Culture and Society* 26(1): 71–91.

Behnegar, N. (1997) 'Leo Strauss' confrontation with Max Weber: a search for a genuine social science', *Review of Politics* 59: 97–124.

(2009) 'Strauss and social science', in Smith, S. (ed.) *The Cambridge Companion to Leo Strauss*, Cambridge University Press.
Bendix, R. (1964) *Nation-building and Citizenship: Studies of our Changing Social Order*, New York and London: John Wiley and Sons.
(1967) 'Tradition and modernity reconsidered', *Comparative Studies in Society and History* 9(3): 292–346.
(1978) *Kings or People*, University of California Press.
Benhabib, S. (2002) *The Claims of Culture: Equality and Diversity in the Global Era*, Princeton University Press.
Benton, T. (1977) *Philosophical Foundations of the Three Sociologies*, London: Routledge.
Bernstein, R. (1976) *The Reconstructing of Social and Political Theory*, Oxford: Basil Blackwell.
Bloch, E. (1996) *Natural Law and Human Dignity*, MIT Press.
Blumenberg, H. (1983) *The Legitimacy of the Modern Age*, MIT Press.
Bobbio, N. (1993) *Thomas Hobbes and the Natural Law Tradition*, University of Chicago Press.
Bond, N. (2009) 'Ferdinand Tönnies and Western European positivism', *Intellectual History Review* 9(3): 353–70.
(2010) 'Ferdinand Tönnies and Friedrich Paulsen: Conciliatory iconoclasts', *European Legacy* 15(1): 35–53.
(2011a) 'Rational natural law and German sociology: Hobbes, Locke and Tönnies', *British Journal for the History of Philosophy* 19(6): 1175–200.
(2011b) 'Ferdinand Tönnies and academic "socialism"', *History of the Human Sciences* 24(3): 23–45.
Bottici, C. (2003) 'The domestic analogy and the Kantian project of perpetual peace', *Journal of Political Philosophy* 11(4): 392–410.
Bottomore, T. and Rubel, M. (1978) 'Introduction', in Marx, K. *Selected Writings in Sociology and Social Philosophy*, London: Penguin.
Bull, H. (1977) *The Anarchical Society*, New York: Columbia University Press.
Burns, T. (1996) *Natural Law and Political Ideology in the Philosophy of Hegel*, Brookfield: Avebury.
Callinicos, A. (2007) *Social Theory: A Historical Introduction*, Cambridge: Polity Press.
Cassirer, E. (1977) *An Essay on Man*, New Haven: Yale University Press.
(1979) *The Philosophy of the Enlightenment*, Princeton University Press.
Chernilo, D. (2002) 'The theorization of social co-ordinations in differentiated societies: The theory of generalized symbolic media in Parsons, Luhmann and Habermas', *British Journal of Sociology* 53(3): 431–49.
(2007) *A Social Theory of the Nation-state: The Political Forms of Modernity beyond Methodological Nationalism*, London: Routledge.
(2010) 'Methodological nationalism and the domestic analogy: Classical resources for their critique', *Cambridge Review of International Affairs* 23(1): 87–106.
(2012) 'Cosmopolitanism and the question of universalism', in Delanty, G. (ed.) *The Routledge Handbook of Cosmopolitanism Studies*, London: Routledge.

Cladis, M. (1992) *A Communitarian Defense of Liberalism: Emile Durkheim and Contemporary Social Theory*, Stanford University Press.

Clarke, S. (1991) *Marx, Marginalism and Modern Sociology: From Adam Smith to Max Weber*, London: Macmillan.

Colletti, L. (1975) 'Introduction', in Marx, K. *Early Writings*, London: Penguin.

Connell, R. (2007) *Southern Theory: Social Science and the Global Dynamics of Knowledge*, Cambridge: Polity Press.

Coser, L. (1977) *Masters of the Sociological Tradition: Ideas in Historical and Social Contexts*, New York: Harcourt Brace Jovanovich.

Deflem, M. (2003) 'The sociology of the sociology of money: Simmel and the battle of the classics', *Journal of Classical Sociology* 3(1): 67–96.

d'Entrèves, A. P. (1970) *Natural Law*, London: Hutchinson

Donaggio, E. (2006) *Una Sobria Inquietud. Karl Löwith y la Filosofía*, Buenos Aires: Katz.

Douglass, B. (1976) 'The gospel and political order: Eric Voegelin on the political role of Christianity', *The Journal of Politics* 38(1): 25–45.

Douzinas, C. (2000) *The End of Human Rights*, Oxford: Hart.

Drury, S. (1985) 'The esoteric philosophy of Leo Strauss', *Political Theory* 13(3): 315–37.

(1987) 'Leo Strauss's classic natural right teaching', *Political Theory* 15(3): 299–315.

Durkheim, E. (1965) *The Elementary Forms of the Religious Life*, New York: The Free Press.

(1970) *Montesquieu and Rousseau: Forerunners of Sociology*, Michigan: Ann Arbor.

(1973) 'Sociology in France in the nineteenth century' in Bellah, R. (ed) *On Morality and Society*, University of Chicago Press.

(1982) *The Rules of Sociological Method*, New York: The Free Press.

(1984) *The Division of Labour in Society*, London: Macmillan.

(1992) *Professional Ethics and Civic Morals*, London and New York: Routledge and Kegan Paul.

Edelstein, D. (2009) *The Terror of Natural Law: Republicanism, the Cult of Nature and the French Revolution*, University of Chicago Presss.

Elias, N. (2000) *The Civilizing Process*, Oxford: Blackwell.

Emberley, P. and Cooper, B. (eds.) (2004) *Faith and Political Philosophy: The Correspondence between Leo Strauss and Eric Voegelin, 1934–1964*, Columbia: University of Missouri Press.

Emmet, D. (1994) *The Role of the Unrealisable: A Study in Regulative Ideals*, New York: St Martin's Press.

Feuerbach, L. (1986) *Principles of the Philosophy of the Future*, Indianapolis: Hackett.

Fine, R. (2001) *Political Investigations: Hegel, Marx, Arendt*, London: Routledge.

(2002) *Democracy and the Rule of Law*, Caldwell, NJ: Blackburn Press.

(2003) 'Kant's theory of cosmopolitanism and Hegel's critique', *Philosophy and Social Criticism* 29(6): 609–30.

(2011) 'Cosmopolitanism and natural law: Rethinking Kant', in Rovisco, M. and Nowicka, M. (eds.) *The Ashgate Research Companion to Cosmopolitanism*, Farnham: Ashgate.

(2012) 'Contra Leviathan: Hegel's contribution to cosmopolitan critique', in Buchwalter, A. (ed.) *Hegel and Global Justice*, New York: Springer.
(2013) 'Natural right and critical theory: Dialectical affinities', *Journal of Classical Sociology* 13(2): in press.
Fine, R. and Smith, W. (2003) 'Jürgen Habermas's theory of cosmopolitanism', *Constellations* 10(4): 469–87.
Finnis, J. (1980) *Natural Law and Natural Rights*, Oxford: Clarendon Press.
Foucault, M. (2001) *The Order of Things: An Archaeology of the Human Sciences*, London: Routledge.
Frisby, D. (2002) *Georg Simmel*, London: Routledge.
Frisby, D. and Sayer, D. (1986) *Society*, London: Ellis Horwood and Tavistock.
Fulda, H. (2004) 'The rights of philosophy', in Pippin, R. and Höffe, O. (eds.) *Hegel on Ethics and Politics*, Cambridge University Press.
Gadamer, H. G. (1985) *Philosophical Apprenticeships*, MIT Press.
Gane, M. (1988) *On Durkheim's Rules of Sociological Method*, London: Routledge.
Gangas, S. (2004) 'Axiological and normative dimensions in Georg Simmel's philosophy and sociology: A dialectical interpretation', *History of the Human Sciences* 17(4): 17–44.
Gay, P. (1970) *The Enlightenment: An Interpretation. The Rise of Modern Paganism*, London: Weidenfeld and Nicolson.
(1977) *The Enlightenment: An Interpretation. The Science of Freedom*, New York: W. W. Norton.
Giddens, A. (1978) *Durkheim*, London: Fontana.
(1993) *New Rules of Sociological Method*, Cambridge: Polity Press.
(2003) *Capitalism and Modern Social Theory*, Cambridge: Polity Press.
Goudsblom, J. (1977) *Sociology in the Balance: A Critical Essay*, New York: Columbia University Press.
Gouldner, A. (1959) 'Introduction', in Durkheim, E. *Socialism and Saint-Simon*, London: Routledge and Kegan Paul.
(1965) *Enter Plato: Classical Greece and the Origins of Social Theory*, London: Routledge and Kegan Paul.
(1970) *The Coming Crisis of Western Sociology*, London: Heinemann.
(1975) *For Sociology: Renewal and Critique in Sociology Today*, Middlesex, Penguin.
Gregor, M. (1993) 'Kant on "natural rights"', in Beiner, R. and Booth, W. (eds.) *Kant and Political Philosophy: The Contemporary Legacy*, New Haven: Yale University Press.
Haakonssen, K. (1996) *Natural Law and Moral Philosophy*, Cambridge University Press.
Habermas, J. (1972) *Knowledge and Human Interest*, London: Heinemann.
(1974) *Theory and Practice*, London: Heinemann.
(1978) *Theorie und Praxis*, Frankfurt: Suhrkamp.
(1984a) *The Theory of Communicative Action*. Vol. I: *Reason and the Rationalization of Society*, London: Heinemann.
(1984b) *Communication and the Evolution of Society*, Cambridge: Polity Press.
(1987) *The Theory of Communicative Action*. Vol. II: *Lifeworld and System: A Critique of Functionalist Reason*, Boston: Beacon Press.

(1988) *On the Logic of the Social Sciences*, MIT Press.
(1989) *The Structural Transformation of the Public Sphere*, Cambridge: Polity Press.
(1990a) *Moral Consciousness and Communicative Action*, Cambridge: Polity Press.
(1990b) *The Philosophical Discourse of Modernity*, Cambridge: Polity Press.
(1992a) *Postmetaphysical Thinking*, Cambridge: Polity Press.
(1992b) 'Further reflections on the public Sphere', in Calhoun, C. (ed.) *Habermas and the Public Sphere*, MIT Press.
(1996) *Between Facts and Norms*, MIT Press.
(1998) *The Inclusion of the Other*, MIT Press.
(1999) 'Bestiality and humanity: A war on the border between legality and morality', *Constellations* 6(3): 263–72.
(2001a) *The Postnational Constellation*, Cambridge: Polity Press.
(2001b) 'Why Europe needs a constitution', *New Left Review* 11: 5–26.
(2001c) *On the Pragmatics of Social Interaction*, Cambridge: Polity Press.
(2002) *On the Pragmatics of Communication*, Cambridge: Polity Press.
(2003a) 'Interpreting the fall of a monument', *Constellations* 10(3): 364–70.
(2003b) *Truth and Justification*, MIT Press.
(2003c) *The Future of Human Nature*, Cambridge: Polity Press.
(2006) *The Divided West*, Cambridge: Polity Press.
(2008) *Between Naturalism and Religion*, Cambridge: Polity Press.
(2010) 'The concept of human dignity and the realistic utopia of human rights', *Metaphilosophy* 41(4): 464–80.
Habermas, J. and Luhmann, N. (1971) *Theorie der Gesellschaft oder Sozialtechnologie*, Frankfurt: Suhrkamp.
Harrington, A. (2004) 'Introduction to Georg Simmel's essay "Europe and America in world history"', *European Journal of Social Theory* 8(1): 63–72.
(2008) 'Theological history and the legitimacy of the modern social sciences: considerations on the work of Hans Blumenberg', *Thesis Eleven* 94: 6–28.
Harris, J. (2001) 'General introduction', in Tönnies, F. *Community and Civil Society*, Cambridge University Press.
Hawthorn, G. (1976) *Enlightenment and Despair: A History of Social Theory*, Cambridge University Press.
Hegel, G. (1975) *Natural Law*, Philadelphia: University of Pennsylvania Press.
(1977) *The Phenomenology of Spirit*, New York: Oxford University Press.
(1989) *Lectures on the Philosophy of World History*, Cambridge University Press.
(1991) *The Philosophy of Right*, Cambridge University Press.
Heilbron, J. (1995) *The Rise of Social Theory*, Minneapolis: University of Minnesota Press.
Hobbes, T. (1996) *Leviathan*, Cambridge University Press.
(1999) *Human Nature and de Corpore Politico*, Oxford University Press.
Hochstrasser, T. (2000) *Natural Law Theories in the Early Enlightenment*, Cambridge University Press.
Höffe, O. (2002) *Categorical Imperatives of Law: A Counterpoint to Modernity*, Philadelphia: Pennsylvania State University Press.

Honnefelder, L. (1995) 'Rationalization and natural law: Max Weber's and Ernst Troeltsch's interpretation of the Medieval doctrine of natural law', *Review of Metaphysics* 49(2): 275–94.

Honneth, A. (2004) 'Organized self-realization: Some paradoxes of individualization', *European Journal of Social Theory* 7(4): 463–78.

Honneth, A. and Joas, H. (1988) *Social Action and Human Nature*, Cambridge University Press.

Horstmann, R.-P. (2004) 'The role of civil society in Hegel's political philosophy', in Pippin, R. and Höffe, O. (eds.) *Hegel on Ethics and Politics*, Cambridge University Press.

Hughes, H. S. (1974) *Consciousness and Society: The Reorientation of European Social Thought 1890–1930*, Suffolk: Paladin.

Husserl, E. (1970) *The Crisis of European Sciences and Transcendental Phenomenology*, Evanston: Northwestern University Press.

Inglis, D. (2009) 'Cosmopolitan sociology and the classical canon: Ferdinand Tönnies and the emergence of global *Gesellschaft*', *British Journal of Sociology* 60(4): 813–32.

Inglis, D. and Robertson, R. (2004) 'Beyond the gates of the *polis*: reconfiguring sociology's ancient inheritance', *Journal of Classical Sociology* 4(2): 165–89.

(2008) 'The elementary forms of globality: Durkheim and the emergence and nature of global life', *Journal of Classical Sociology* 8(2): 5–25.

Jaspers, K. (1989) *On Max Weber*, New York: Paragon House.

(2011) *The Origin and Goal of History*, Routledge: New York.

Joas, H. (2004) 'Foreword' in Durkheim, E., *Notes from the Lycee de Sens Course, 1883–1884*, Cambridge University Press.

Joas, H. and Knöbl, W. (2009) *Social Theory: Twenty Introductory Lectures*, Cambridge University Press.

Jones, S. (2001) *Durkheim Reconsidered*, Cambridge: Polity Press.

Kant, I. (1973) *Critique of Pure Reason*, London: Macmillan.

(1996) *The Metaphysics of Morals*, Cambridge University Press.

(1997) *Groundwork of the Metaphysics of Morals*, Cambridge University Press.

(1999) *Political Writings*, Cambridge University Press.

Kelsen, H. (1949) 'The natural-law doctrine before the tribunal of science', *The Western Political Quarterly* 2(4): 481–513.

Kielmansegg, P., Mewes, H. and Glaser-Schmidt, E. (eds.) (1997) *Hannah Arendt and Leo Strauss: German Émigrés and American Political Thought after World War II*, Cambridge University Press.

Kiliminster, R. (1998) *The Sociological Revolution: From the Enlightenment to the Global Age*, London: Routledge.

Koselleck, R. (2004) *Futures Past: On the Semantics of Historical Time*, New York: Columbia University Press.

LaCapra, D. (2001) *Emile Durkheim: Sociologist and Philosopher*, Aurora, Colorado: The Davies Group.

Laslett, P. (1988) 'Introduction', in Locke, J. *Two Treatises of Government*, Cambridge University Press.

Lassman, P., Velody, I. and Martins, H. (eds.) (1989) *Max Weber's 'Science as a Vocation'*, London: Unwin Hyman.

la Torre, M. (2006) 'On two distinct and opposing versions of natural law: "exclusive" versus "inclusive"', *Ratio Juris* 19(2): 197–216.
Latour, B. (1993) *We Have Never been Moderns*, Cambridge, MA: Harvard University Press.
Layder, D. (1994) *Understanding Social Theory*, London: Sage.
Layne, N. (1973) 'Durkheim as pacifist', *Sociological Inquiry* 43(2): 99–103.
Lepenies, W. (1988) *Between Literature and Science: The Rise of Sociology*, Cambridge University Press.
Levine, D. (1980) *Simmel and Parsons: Two Approaches to the Study of Society*, New York: Arno Press.
(1991) 'Simmel and Parsons reconsidered', in Robertson, R. and Turner, B. (eds.) *Talcott Parsons: Theorist of Modernity*, London: Sage.
(1995) *Visions of the Sociological Tradition*, University of Chicago Press.
Löwith, K. (1964) *Meaning in History*, University of Chicago Press.
(1966) *Nature, History and Existentialism*, Evanston: Northwestern University Press.
(1967) *From Hegel to Nietzsche*, London: Anchor.
(1993) *Max Weber and Karl Marx*, London: Routledge.
(1995) *Martin Heidegger and European Nihilism*, New York: Columbia University Press.
(1998) *El Hombre en el Centro de la Historia. Balance Filosófico del Siglo XX*, Barcelona: Herder.
Luhmann, N. (1995) *Social Systems*, Stanford University Press.
Lukes, S. (1973) *Emile Durkheim: His Life and Work*, London: Penguin.
Manent, P. (1998) *The City of Man*, Princeton University Press.
Mann, M. (1986) *The Sources of Social Power*. Vol. I: *A History of Power from the Beginning to AD 1760*, Cambridge University Press.
(1993) *The Sources of Social Power*. Vol. II: *The Rise of Classes and Nation-States, 1760–1914*, Cambridge University Press.
Marcuse, H. (1973) *Reason and Revolution*, London: Routledge and Kegan Paul.
Marx, K. (1973) *Grundrisse*, London: Penguin.
(1975) *Early Writings*, London: Penguin.
(1976) *Capital*. Vol. I, London: Penguin.
Marx, K. and Engels, F. (1974) *The German Ideology*, London: Lawrence and Wishart.
McCarthy, G. (2003) *Classical Horizons: The Origins of Sociology in Ancient Greece*, Albany: State University of New York.
McCarthy, T. (1993) *Ideals and Illusions: On Reconstrcuction and Deconstruction in Contemporary Critical Theory*, MIT Press.
McMahon, D. (2001) *Enemies of the Enlightenment: The French Counter-enlightenment and the Making of Modernity*, Oxford University Press.
Messner, J. (1964) *Sociología moderna y derecho natural*, Barcelona: Herder.
Mestrovic, S. (1992) *Durkheim and Postmodern Culture*, New York: Aldine de Gruyter.
Milbank, J. (2006) *Theology and Social Theory: Beyond Secular Reason*, Oxford: Blackwell.

Montesquieu, C. (1989) *The Spirit of the Laws*, Cambridge University Press.
Moore, B. (1967) *Social Origins of Dictatorship and Democracy: Lord and Peasant in the Making of the Modern World*, London: Penguin.
Mouzelis, N. (1995) *Sociological Theory: What Went Wrong?*, London: Routledge.
(2008) *Modern and Postmodern Social Theorizing: Bridging the Divide*, Cambridge University Press.
Muthu, S. (2003) *Enlightenment against Empire*, Princeton University Press.
Neuhouser, F. (2000) *Foundations of Hegel's Social Theory: Actualizing Freedom*, Cambridge, MA: Harvard University Press.
Nisbet, R. (1967) *The Sociological Tradition*, London: Heinemann.
(1976) *The Social Philosophers*, Frogmore: Paladin.
(1977) *Sociology as an Art Form*, Oxford University Press.
Norton, A. (2004) *Leo Strauss and the Politics of American Empire*, New Haven: Yale University Press.
Oakley, F. (2005) *Natural Law, Laws of Nature, Natural Rights: Continuity and Discontinuity in the History of Ideas*, New York and London: Continuum.
Outhwaite, W. (1975) *Understanding Social Life: The Method Called Verstehen*, Sussex: George Allen and Unwin.
(1994) *Habermas: A Critical Introduction*, Cambridge: Polity Press.
(2006) *The Future of Society*, Oxford: Blackwell.
Outram, D. (1995) *The Enlightenment*, Cambridge University Press.
Pagden, A. (1987) 'Introduction', in Pagden, A. *The Languages of Political Theory in Early-Modern Europe*, Cambridge University Press.
Parsons, T. (1968) *The Structure of Social Action*, 2 Vols, New York: The Free Press.
Pippin, R. (1992) 'The modern world of Leo Strauss', *Political Theory* 20(3): 448–72.
(1999) *Modernity as a Philosophical Problem*, Oxford: Blackwell.
(2004) 'Introduction', in Pippin, R. and Höffe, O. (eds.) *Hegel on Ethics and Politics*, Cambridge University Press.
Porter, C. (2002) 'Eric Voegelin on Nazi political extremism', *Journal of the History of Ideas* 63(1): 151–71.
Purcell, B. (1999) 'The philosophical context of the "Hitler and the Germans" lectures', in *The Collected Works of Eric Voegelin*, Vol. XXXI, Columbia: University of Missouri Press.
Quante, M. (2004) '"The personality of the will" as the principle of abstract right: an analysis of §§34–40 of Hegel's *Philosophy of Right* in terms of the logical stricture of the concept', in Pippin, R. and Höffe, O. (eds.) *Hegel on Ethics and Politics*, Cambridge University Press.
Radkau, J. (2009) *Max Weber: A Biography*, Cambridge: Polity Press
Rawls, J. (1999) *A Theory of Justice*, Oxford University Press.
(2000) *Lectures on the History of Moral Philosophy*, Cambridge, MA: Harvard University Press.
Riesterer, B. (1969) *Karl Löwith's View of History: A Critical Appraisal of Historicism*, The Hague: Martinus Nijhoff.
Ritzer, G. (2001) *Explorations in Social Theory: From Metatheorizing to Rationalization*, London: Sage.

Rommen, H. (1998) *The Natural Law: A Study in Legal and Social History and Philosophy*, Indianapolis: The Liberty Fund.

Rorty, R. (1989) *Contingency, Irony, and Solidarity*. Cambridge University Press.

Roth, G. (1965) 'Political critiques of Max Weber: Some implications for political sociology', *American Sociological Review* 30(2): 213–23.

Rose, G. (1984) *Dialectic of Nihilism: Post-structuralism and the Law*, Oxford: Blackwell.

(2009) *Hegel contra Sociology*, London: Verso.

Rosen, S. (2009) 'Leo Strauss and the problem of the modern', in Smith, S. (ed.) *The Cambridge Companion to Leo Strauss*, Cambridge University Press.

Rousseau, J. (1993a) 'Has the restoration of the arts and sciences had a purifying effects upon morals?', in *The Social Contract and Discourses*, London: Everyman.

(1993b) 'What is the origin of inequality among men, and is it authorized by natural law?', in *The Social Contract and Discourses*, London: Everyman.

(1993c) 'The Social Contract', in *The Social Contract and Discourses*, London: Everyman.

(1993d) 'The general society of the human race', in *The Social Contract and Discourses*, London: Everyman.

Rundell, J. (1987) *Origins of Modernity: The Origins of Modern Social Theory from Kant to Hegel to Marx*, University of Wisconsin Press.

Schlecker, M. (2011) 'Universalist rationality and Simmel's sacrifice model of value', *Anthropological Theory* 11(3): 309–25.

Schluchter, W. (1996) *Paradoxes of Modernity: Culture and Conduct in the Theory of Max Weber*, Stanford University Press.

Schnädelbach, H. (1980) *La Filosofía de la Historia después de Hegel*, Barcelona: Alfa.

Schneewind, J. B. (1993) 'Kant and natural law ethics', *Ethics* 104(1): 53–74.

(1998) *The Invention of Autonomy: A History of Modern Moral Philosophy*, Cambridge University Press.

Schrader-Klebert, K. (1968) 'Der Begriff der Gesellschaft als regulative Idee', *Soziale Welt* 19: 97–118.

Scott, J. (1995) *Sociological Theory: Contemporary Debates*, Cheltenham: Edward Elgar.

Seidman, S. (1983) *Liberalism and the Origins of European Social Theory*, Oxford: Basil Blackwell.

(1998) *Contested Knowledge: Social Theory in the Postmodern Era*, Oxford: Blackwell.

Selznick, P. (1961) 'Sociology and natural law', *Natural Law Forum* 6: 84–108.

Sheppard, E. (2006) *Leo Strauss and the Politics of Exile: The Making of a Political Philosopher*, Waltham, MA: Brandeis University Press.

Shijun, T. (2009) 'Varieties of universalism', *European Journal of Social Theory* 12(4): 449–63.

Shils, E. (1980) *The Calling of Sociology and Other Essays on the Pursuit of Learning*, The University of Chicago Press.

Simmel, G. (1896a) 'Superiority and subordination as subject-matter of sociology', *American Journal of Sociology* 2(2): 167–89.

(1896b) 'Superiority and subordination as subject-matter of sociology II', *American Journal of Sociology* 2(3): 392–415.

(1902a) 'The number of members as determining the sociological form of the group. I', *American Journal of Sociology* 8(1): 1–46.

(1902b) 'The number of members as determining the sociological form of the group. II', *American Journal of Sociology* 8(2): 158–96.

(1906) 'The sociology of secrecy and of secret societies', *American Journal of Sociology* 11(4): 441–98.

(1909) 'The problem of sociology', *American Journal of Sociology* 15(3): 289–320.

(1949) 'The sociology of sociability', *American Journal of Sociology* 55(3): 254–61.

(1950) 'Fundamental problems of sociology (individual and society)', in Wolf, K. (ed.), *The Sociology of Georg Simmel*, Glencoe, IL: The Free Press.

(1971) 'Freedom and the individual', in Levine, D. (ed.) *Georg Simmel on Individuality and Social Forms*, University of Chicago Press.

(1977) *The Problems of the Philosophy of History: An Epistemological Essay*, New York: The Free Press.

(1994) 'The problem of sociology', in Frisby, D. (ed.) *George Simmel: Critical Assessments*, Vol. I, London: Routledge.

(2005) *The Philosophy of Money*, London: Routledge.

Skinner, Q. (2008) *Hobbes and Republican Liberty*, Cambridge University Press.

Smith, A. (1985) *The Wealth of Nations*. Books I–III, London: Penguin.

Specter, M. (2010) *Habermas: An Intellectual Biography*, Cambridge University Press.

Stark, W. (1963) *The Fundamental Forms of Social Thought*, New York: Fordham University Press.

Strasser, H. (1976) *The Normative Structure of Sociology: Conservative and Emancipatory Themes in Social Thought*, London: Routledge and Kegan Paul.

Strauss, L. (1952) 'The idea of natural right', *Social Research* 19: 23–60.

(1974) *Natural Right and History*, University of Chicago Press.

(1988a) 'What is political philosophy?', in Strauss, L. *What is Political Philosophy?*, University of Chicago Press.

(1988b) 'On the basis of Hobbes's political philosophy', in Strauss, L. *What is Political Philosophy?*, University of Chicago Press.

(1989) 'Three waves of modernity', in Strauss, L. *An Introduction to Political Philosophy: Ten Essays*, Detroit: Wayne State University Press.

(1997a) 'Progress or return?', in Strauss, L. *Jewish Philosophy and the Crisis of Philosophy*, Albany: State University of New York Press.

(1997b) 'Introduction to *Persecution and the art of writing*', in Strauss, L. *Jewish Philosophy and the Crisis of Philosophy*, Albany: State University of New York Press.

(2004a) 'Restatement on Xenophon's Hiero', in Emberley, P. and Cooper, B. (eds.) *Faith and Political Philosophy: The Correspondence between Leo Strauss and Eric Voegelin, 1934–1964*, Columbia: University of Missouri Press.

(2004b) 'Letter to Eric Voegelin (10.4.1950)', in Emberley, P. and Cooper, B. (eds.) *Faith and Political Philosophy: The Correspondence between Leo Strauss and Eric Voegelin, 1934–1964*, Columbia: University of Missouri Press.
Strydom, P. (2000) *Discourse and Knowledge: The Making of Enlightenment Sociology*, Liverpool University Press.
Suganami, H. (1989) *The Domestic Analogy and World Order Proposals*, Cambridge University Press.
Swedberg, R. (2003) 'The changing picture of Max Weber's sociology', *Annual Review of Sociology* 29: 283–306.
Syse, H. (2000) 'Karl Löwith and Eric Voegelin on Christianity and history', *Modern Age*, summer: 253–62.
Tanguay, D. (2007) *Leo Strauss: An Intellectual Biography*, New Haven: Yale University Press.
Taylor, C. (2004) *Modern Social Imaginaries*, Durham and London: Duke University Press.
Thornhill, C. (2007) *German Political Philosophy*, London: Routledge.
(2013) 'Natural law, state formation and the foundations of social theory', *Journal of Classical Sociology* 13(2): in press.
Tönnies, F. (1932) *Hobbes. Vida y Doctrina*, Madrid: Revista de Occidente.
(1974) *Marx: His Life and Teachings*, Michigan State University Press.
(2001) *Community and Civil Society*, Cambridge University Press.
(2005) 'Ways and goals of sociology', in Adair-Toteff, C. *Sociological Beginnings: The First Conference of the German Society for Sociology*, Liverpool University Press.
Toulmin, S. (1990) *Cosmopolis: The Hidden Agenda of Modernity*, University of Chicago Press.
Troeltsch, E. (1958) 'The ideas of natural law and humanity', in Gierke, O. *Natural Law and the Theory of Society: 1500 to 1800*, Cambridge University Press.
(2005) 'Stoic-Christian natural law and modern profane natural law', in Adair-Toteff, C. *Sociological Beginnings: The First Conference of the German Society for Sociology*, Liverpool University Press.
Tuck, R. (1999) *The Rights of War and Peace: Political Thought and the International Order from Grotius to Kant*, Oxford University Press.
Turner, B. S. (2013) 'Alasdair MacIntyre on morality, community and natural law', *Journal of Classical Sociology* 13(2): in press.
Voegelin, E. (1962) 'World-empire and the unity of mankind', *International Affairs* 38(2): 170–88.
(1999) 'Hitler and the Germans', in *The Collected Works of Eric Voegelin*, Vol. XXXI, Columbia: University of Missouri Press.
(2000a) 'The new science of politics', in *The Collected Works of Eric Voegelin*, Vol. V, Columbia: University of Missouri Press.
(2000b) *Order and history*, Vol. IV: *The Ecumenic Age*, in *The Collected Works of Eric Voegelin*, Vol. XVII, Columbia: University of Missouri Press.
Wagner, P. (1994) *A Sociology of Modernity: Liberty and Discipline*, London and New York: Routledge.
(2001) *A History and Theory of the Social Sciences*, London: Sage.

(2006) 'Social theory and political philosophy', in Delanty, G. (ed.) *Handbook of European Social Theory*, London: Routledge.

(2008) *Modernity as Experience and Interpretation: A New Sociology of Modernity*, London: Sage.

Wallace, R. (1981) 'Progress, secularization and modernity: the Löwith–Blumenberg debate', *New German Critique* 22: 63–80.

(1983) 'Translator's introduction', in Blumenberg, H. *The Legitimacy of the Modern Age*, MIT Press.

Weber, M. (1949) *The Methodology of the Social Sciences*, New York: The Free Press.

(1968a) *Economy and Society*, Vol. I, New York: Bedminster.

(1968b) *Economy and Society*, Vol. II, New York: Bedminster.

(1970a) 'Science as a vocation' in Gerth, H. and Mills, C. W. (eds.) *From Max Weber: Essays in Sociology*, London: Routledge and Kegan Paul.

(1970b) 'The social psychology of the world religions' in Gerth, H. and Mills, C. W. (eds.) *From Max Weber: Essays in Sociology*, London: Routledge and Kegan Paul.

(1970c) 'Religious rejections of the world and their directions' in Gerth, H. and Mills, C. W. (eds.) *From Max Weber: Essays in Sociology*, London: Routledge and Kegan Paul.

(1971) *The Interpretation of Social Reality*, London: Michael Joseph.

(1975) *Roscher and Knies: The Logical Problems of Historical Economics*, New York: The Free Press.

(1994) *Political Writings*, Cambridge University Press.

(2001) *The Protestant Ethic and the Spirit of Capitalism*, London: Routledge.

Weber, M. S. (1975) *Max Weber: A Biography*, New York: John Wiley and Sons.

Wellmer, A. (1998) *Endgames*, MIT Press.

Wolin, R. (1995) 'Karl Löwith and Martin Heidegger – contexts and controversies: an introduction', in Löwith, K., *Martin Heidegger and European Nihilism*, New York: Columbia University Press.

(2001) *Heidegger's Children: Hannah Arendt, Karl Löwith, Hans Jonas and Herbert Marcuse*, Princeton University Press.

Yack, B. (1997) *The Fetishism of Modernities*, Indiana: University of Notre Dame Press.

(2006) 'Naming and reclaiming the Enlightenment', *European Journal of Political Theory* 5(3): 343–54.

Zeitlin, I. (1968) *Ideology and the Development of Sociological Theory*, New Jersey: Prentice-Hall.

Index